# The Bioarchaeology of Violence

*Bioarchaeological Interpretations of the Human Past: Local, Regional, and Global Perspectives*

UNIVERSITY PRESS OF FLORIDA

Florida A&M University, Tallahassee
Florida Atlantic University, Boca Raton
Florida Gulf Coast University, Ft. Myers
Florida International University, Miami
Florida State University, Tallahassee
New College of Florida, Sarasota
University of Central Florida, Orlando
University of Florida, Gainesville
University of North Florida, Jacksonville
University of South Florida, Tampa
University of West Florida, Pensacola

# The Bioarchaeology of Violence

Edited by Debra L. Martin, Ryan P. Harrod,
and Ventura R. Pérez

Foreword by Clark Spencer Larsen

University Press of Florida

Gainesville · Tallahassee · Tampa · Boca Raton

Pensacola · Orlando · Miami · Jacksonville · Ft. Myers · Sarasota

The publication of this book was funded in part by a grant from
the University of Nevada, Las Vegas.

This book may be available in an electronic edition.

First cloth printing, 2012
First paperback printing, 2013

A copy of cataloging-in-publication data is available from the Library of Congress.

ISBN 978-0-8130-4150-6 (cloth)
ISBN 978-0-8130-4950-2 (pbk.)

The University Press of Florida is the scholarly publishing agency for the State University
System of Florida, comprising Florida A&M University, Florida Atlantic University,
Florida Gulf Coast University, Florida International University, Florida State University,
New College of Florida, University of Central Florida, University of Florida, University
of North Florida, University of South Florida, and University of West Florida.

University Press of Florida
15 Northwest 15th Street
Gainesville, FL 32611-2079
http://www.upf.com

# Contents

# Figures

# Tables

# Foreword

Violence is at the top of any list of central discussions in social science. One has only to look at leading professional periodicals in sociology, political science, and psychology to see the strong presence of academic considerations of conflict in these literatures. Today, reporting of violence permeates the popular press and at all levels, from accounts of personal attacks to gang violence to full-blown warfare involving conflicts between nations. This important book underscores the point that violence and most of its motivations have been with humans since the beginning of written history and well back into the remote past, including in ancient hominids living hundreds of thousands of years ago. Simply put, violence is part of the fabric of humanness.

Violence is a topic that is ripe for exploration and study by anthropologists. Yet, as Phillip Walker pointed out a decade ago, anthropologists have had a remarkably minimal presence in discussions of this topic. This is surprising because anthropologists have a range of theoretical and methodological tools that provide both the means to create the record of violence and to develop an informed understanding of its causes and consequences. As the chapters in this book demonstrate, bioarchaeology is well situated to provide important insights into developing a history of violence, the social identities of victims and perpetrators, and the causes and outcomes of aggression of a person or persons toward another person or persons. This is the case because skeletons are the only direct record of violence. The skeletal record is not subject to the interpretative nuances characteristic of at least some written records, especially those written by a dominant power or authority. Moreover, bioarchaeology views this record in a highly contextualized setting, drawing from a range of sources—archaeology, mortuary behavior, ecology, climate history, ethnohistory, ethnography, and economics.

This volume speaks to the growing interest in and importance of human remains from archaeological contexts. It addresses issues that affected past societies and that have implications for understanding the human condition and for addressing fundamental questions about the history of human aggression. I am especially impressed with the point raised time and again in the book that bioarchaeology is not just about the skeletons. Rather, the skeletons are viewed through an integrative lens, focusing on the centrality of context in interpreting the bioarchaeological record.

The various contributions to the book build on the fact that violence is a socially informed act. It is motivated by society and values placed on certain social, political, and economic interests. As is demonstrated by the authors of these chapters, the book explores social context, addressing key questions such as Who are the victims? Who are the perpetrators? What are the relationships between victims and perpetrators? What are the cultural, social, political, and ecological landscapes of the time and place that provide the conditions in which violent acts occur?

The book makes especially clear that violence should be viewed from the perspective of both victim and perpetrator and is not limited to the bumps, bruises, and contusions (and far worse!) displayed by the victim. For example, violence is structural: Social structures impair the ability of groups of individuals to access key resources, rendering them unable to meet their needs. A number of the contributors show how this structured violence means that some individuals—as defined by their age, sex, ethnicity, or rank—have worse health and a decreased ability to maintain homeostasis and survive. Moreover, these victims are not victims once in their lifetimes. Rather, as documented ethnographically and in skeletons, victimization is recidivistic, occurring over and over again in the lifetime of the person.

Violence is a record of social relationships, sometimes involving related individuals. This volume provides new avenues of inquiry, making the case that skeletons provide a repository of genetic data that presents clues to origins and relationships of the victims. This approach shows the importance of older methods (such as biodistance based on dental traits) and the application of new developments in genetics and ancient DNA analysis in defining kin or non-kin relationships.

Understanding the causes of violence gets at central concerns of the discipline of anthropology, namely explaining human behavior viewed in all times and all places. The power of anthropology is that it strives to shed the racial constructions that even today shackle social and biomedical sciences and develop approaches to the study of violence that go beyond simple statistics of violent acts. The public rightly requires reports of violence, but they also deserve to be informed about its larger causes. This book is a step in that direction in part because it underscores the remarkable variation of violence, develops methods and theories for explaining this variation, and provides contextualized discussion of its causes, outcomes, and circumstances. Other disciplines would be well advised to adopt the kind of integrative, contextualized, and comprehensive approaches to documenting and interpreting violence that bioarchaeology offers.

*Clark Spencer Larsen*
*Series Editor*

## Reference Cited

Walker, P. L.
2001    A Bioarchaeological Perspective on the History of Violence. *Annual Review of Anthropology* 30:573–596.

# Introduction

## Bioarchaeology and the Study of Violence

DEBRA L. MARTIN, RYAN P. HARROD, AND VENTURA R. PÉREZ

Ancient human remains and the mortuary contexts in which they are located represent a uniquely rich data set for a wide range of investigations. Yet criticisms have been rightly made of earlier analysis that disconnected burials from their larger mortuary contexts and from their connection to living descendants (Martin 1998, 171). An additional problem that has limited the full interpretive power that may be gained from burial data is that researchers rarely used strong theoretical models or frameworks to pose hypotheses or questions that could be addressed with data derived from the skeletal remains. Left as largely descriptive studies focused on paleodemography and paleopathology, earlier studies failed to play much of a role in explaining the origin and evolution of human behavior and social relations.

In an attempt to rectify this, bioarchaeology emerged as a way to integrate human remains into research programs that are responsive to the concerns of descendant populations and as a field that seeks to solve human problems. Bioarchaeology took shape in the early 1980s as processual archaeology began to provide a set of scientific principles and a focus on ecological explanations (Buikstra 1977). Concurrently, the concept of human adaptability developed within biological anthropology as a means of combining interests in evolutionary change with concern for the various adaptive problems humans face today, especially those living in limited and ecologically marginal environments (Buikstra and Cook 1980; Goodman et al. 1988; Larsen 1987). With questions that focus on how humans manage to survive and adapt (behaviorally, physiologically, developmentally, or genetically) to environmental constraints and stressors, human adaptability clearly shared an ecological perspective with processual archaeology and bioarchaeology.

The fact that bioarchaeology is interdisciplinary ensures that data collection and, more important, data interpretation will be scrutinized and challenged by people from a number of backgrounds with a variety of viewpoints on the appropriate use and meaning of data derived from human skeletal remains (Armelagos 2003). Bioarchaeological practice facilitates and provides an integrative methodology to bring together a number of previously decoupled aspects of burial analysis:

1. Bioarchaeology considers the connections between past and living groups.
2. Bioarchaeology's raison d'être is to consider simultaneously the burial in its many contexts—for example, mortuary and funerary treatments, placement within particular areas, and the larger archaeological site and regional context.
3. Bioarchaeology considers the taphonomic (natural and cultural) aspects of human remains.
4. Finally, bioarchaeology as a disciplinary practice can be infused with theory related to known and hypothesized social dimensions, linking social and political processes with biological consequences. The chapters in Agarwal and Glencross (2011) provide excellent examples of this methodology, which is becoming known as "social bioarchaeology."

## Signatures of Violence and New Methodologies in Bioarchaeology

Bioarchaeology offers empirical data that help unravel large and important questions about humans and their long relationship with violence. Scheper-Hughes and Locke (1987, 31) presented a compelling metaphorical and theoretical framework for considering the embodiment of pain and suffering. They wrote that "the individual body should be seen as the most immediate terrain where social truths and social contradictions are played out . . . as well as the locus of personal and social resistance and struggle." This notion provides a perfect metaphor for what bioarchaeological studies aim to do—reconstruct the ways that bodies are implicated in ideological, political, economic, and social processes (Sofaer 2006).

Only bioarchaeology bridges the gap between the dead and living with such a robust and grounded data set. While archaeologists can provide the physical and cultural contexts of conflict and warfare with analysis of grave goods, iconography, architecture, and site layout, these studies often cannot infer anything about the once-living humans who prepared the grave goods or who made the murals or who built the structures. The human remains provide the most direct evidence of violence (both lethal and nonlethal forms) and can be used in conjunction with other data to infer patterns. The value of analyzing human remains is that it provides direct evidence about the ways ideology, violence, and power are used to maintain social control.

By creating empirical links between trauma, pathology, and culture, this collection of studies provides insights into the human propensity for constructing and legitimizing violent cultural scripts that play out in the life and death of individuals.

## The Chapters

The chapters in this volume are presented by scholars interested in understanding problems today related to the topic of violence. Although the case studies are from cultures long ago, the authors are grappling with big questions: What is the origin and evolution of human violence? What role does violence play in shaping human behavior? What are the implications of institutionalized forms of violence on everyday life? How do ritual acts and cultural sanctions make violence acceptable? Will there ever be an end to violence?

The first three chapters of the volume lay the groundwork for new approaches in method and theory in the bioarchaeology of violence, and the rest of the chapters provide a range of spatially and temporally distinctive cultures that experienced violence in a number of ways, including interpersonal, intergroup, and intercommunity violence. Collectively these case studies examine three distinctive contexts for which violence is used: small-scale conflict, warfare, and ritualized violence. The divisions represent a heuristic device for parsing the most obvious features of different aspects of violent behavior.

Ventura R. Pérez (chapter 1) presents a complex cultural model for thinking about violence that moves beyond viewing it as an abhorrent act with little or no meaning. The chapter makes a strong argument for studying violence in a way that includes not just how it affects the physical body but also how it shapes psychological, political, economic, and socio-cultural dynamics as well. The chapter explores the concept of the "politicization of the dead," the notion that human remains become a medium through which the living can manipulate cultural practices and behaviors of their own group or of the "other." The treatment of individuals who die as a result of violent encounters (both at the time of death and after) become a crucial indicator of the cultural realities of the group. The value of this approach is that it does not consider violence to be an isolated act but sees it as a collective practice of a group that has meaning that continues long after death.

Haagen D. Klaus (chapter 2) provides another useful approach to bioarchaeological analysis of violence. Like Perez, he argues that bioarchaeologists need to take more factors into consideration when studying violence than a simple focus on the presence or absence of skeletal trauma. This chapter provides a somewhat different approach, however; it builds a case that focusing on structural violence is possible and productive in bioarchaeology. Klaus demonstrates this by providing a case study that shows how structural violence, which essentially normalizes everyday violence, promotes social inequalities in such things as health, nutrition, and general access to resources. These more insidious and invisible forms of violence as deduced from the human remains (e.g., disease, malnutrition, trauma, growth disruption) are created and kept in place by cultural ideologies about political-economic processes. According to Klaus, structural violence does not exist in all societies. It is most likely present only in cultures with established hierarchical systems where one group has coercive control over another group's well-being.

This kind of violence is often not even considered to be violence per se because it is culturally normalized and culturally sanctioned within the society. It is part of everyday life in ways that reproduce and maintain it so that it persists over many generations. For bioarchaeologists, the value of understanding structural violence is that it provides an interpretive framework for analyzing and understanding the empirical data (that is, the skeletal signatures) derived from the archaeological context.

A third and quite different approach to expanding the approaches to the bioarchaeology of violence is offered by Ryan P. Harrod, Pierre Liénard, and Debra L. Martin (chapter 3). They challenge bioarchaeologists to think about studies conducted in cooperation with contemporary populations that can shed light on how to interpret violence in the past. They argue that the bones alone cannot provide insight into the motivations for and functions of violent social interactions that occur today or in the past. Building on the work by Walker and Hewlett (1990), the study provides an ethnobioarchaeological approach to understanding violence in the deep past. This approach is similar to ethnoarchaeology and focuses on using information from living people to infer behaviors in the past. By analyzing and interpreting patterns of trauma in a group of Turkana pastoralists who experience a wide range of daily, seasonally, and yearly acts of violence, the authors were able to link specific nonlethal traumatic injuries with the actions that caused them.

Just as researchers attempt to interpret the violence-related trauma found on past human remains by studying modern cases of forensic and clinical trauma, bioarchaeologists can also study violent social interactions among extant or living populations to determine why it may have existed and persisted in the past. The research agenda of this approach also includes nonlethal violence. Nonlethal violence (and the survivors of violent interaction) can provide a much better indicator of day-to-day violence within a population than lethal injuries, which typically represent the most extreme manifestations of social conflict.

Robert T. Montgomery and Megan Perry (chapter 4) provide a case study of six individuals from a seventh–eighth century Early Period Islamic site in Jordan called Qasr Hallabat. Their research sought to provide insight into the social interactions between groups living in the region at this time. Early Period Islamic Jordan during this period was in a state of upheaval because there was a shift in political power from one ruling group (Umayyad) to another (Abbasids), the climatic conditions were becoming increasingly arid, and a major earthquake occurred that was significant enough to destroy some of the buildings in Qasr Hallabat. Although historical accounts have described this as a period of relative peace, through the analysis of patterns of trauma and pathology as indicators of the sociopolitical relations, the authors provide a more accurate understanding of how people reacted in these uncertain times.

In chapter 5, Ann M. Palkovich provides another case study of community-centered violence, this time in a fourteenth-century Ancestral Pueblo site in the American Southwest, Arroyo Hondo. The study examines the skeletal remains of adults and children who suffered traumatic injury or were subject to bodily manipulation around the time of death. Palkovich asks questions about who these individuals were and what conditions put them at increased risk of victimization. Palkovich argues that the presence of violence does not necessarily indicate conflict and that given the ideology of the culture, it is possible that people were victimized because they were perceived as the "other" or their deaths were necessary for the survival of the society.

Kristin A. Kuckelman's study (chapter 6) provides a good transition from the small-scale conflicts discussed in chapters 1 through 5 to the emergence of warfare in the general San Juan region of the American Southwest. At the end of the thirteenth century, the Southwest was experiencing a series of repeated and severe droughts that eventually resulted in the depopulation of the region as people and whole communities migrated to areas that were less resource deficient. Prior to migration however, the combination of declining environmental conditions and increasing sociopolitical stress increased hostile relations in the region. The result of this hostility was conflict that escalated to the point that violent encounters occurred between multiple communities, not just between individuals or groups within a single community.

Heather Worne, Charles R. Cobb, Giovanna Vidoli, and Dawnie Wolfe Steadman (chapter 7) discuss the evidence of violence in ancient Tennessee from skeletal remains and explore how violent encounters affect how societies organize themselves spatially. They explore the theory that although some geophysical locations are optimal for gaining and maintaining access to resources (e.g., river valleys), societies must also ensure that they are less vulnerable to attack. Because of this, villages were not always located in the most optimal places.

This study provides an excellent example of early forms of warfare. While the violent encounters in the Middle Cumberland Region of Tennessee during the eleventh century are similar to the conflict that began to develop in the Southwest during the thirteenth century, they are different in several ways. Hostilities in the region did not increase as a result of environmental stress, as they did in the Southwest; this region is fairly rich in terms of natural resources. While the increasing conflict did lead to an increase in site fortification and the selection of more remote site locations, the people in this region did not abandon the region.

Continuing in this vein, Vera Tiesler and Andrea Cucina (chapter 8) examine the patterns of violence among the Mayan culture during the Classic to Postclassic periods. They analyze the individuals who are most targeted and the reasons for violent altercations. Tiesler and Cucina discuss how to identify the bioarchaeological correlates of violence through the analysis of weaponry and the patterns they leave on the skeleton. They identified a shift in who is involved in violent encounters over time; in the earlier period of their study, there was less violence than in the later time periods, and in the later period, males were more likely to be involved in the violence. Although this suggests the emergence of a warrior class, Tiesler and Cucina did not find evidence to suggest the presence of a standing army among the Mayan culture.

Tiffiny A. Tung (chapter 9) presents a good example of early standing armies among the Wari culture. She examines violent encounters among the Wari groups in the Peruvian Andes, where archaeological research has demonstrated the creation and maintenance of a warrior class so highly defined that it can accurately be called a military complex. Tung examines the functions of this military class, which was active in raiding and in abducting individuals from local and distant locations as a way to reaffirm ideological notions of the Wari power. Abductees were often used as slaves and in ritual activities. Tung's innovative theoretical framework involves the archaeological reconstruction of how warfare affected the people living under the influence of this system of violence. While much has been written about the males and children who were captured, little is known about the fate of the females. Developing an understanding of how females were treated is important because it offers one more perspective that could help uncover the motivations and functions of this particular aspect of warfare.

The remainder of the studies in the volume focus on the cultural means by which violence becomes normalized. Understanding how violence can become ritualized offers a way to explain why and how certain forms of violence emerge. In reference to understanding what occurs when violence becomes a part of ritual belief, Riches (1991, 294) states, "The key point is perhaps that, in such instances, normal notions of intentionality are absent: sealed off from the flow of everyday affairs, participants conceive of one another as if objects, their social strategy directed to the watching audience and not to whomever it is who would be the 'victim.'" The consequence of removing the notion of a victim is that the act is no longer considered violent (violence requires a victim, a perpetrator, and a witness) (Krohn-Hansen 1994).

Mallorie A. Hatch (chapter 10) expands this theoretical approach with empirical data on ritualized violence in the form of cannibalism. Her study, which analyzes a commingled burial pit at the Mississippian Larsen site in Illinois that contains elements from at least 10 individuals, makes clear the challenges and difficulties of differentiating between warfare, cannibalism, and secondary mortuary processing in the interpretation of commingled remains. Hatch offers methodological innovations in sorting out various hypotheses concerning ritualized violence.

In a similar approach to ritual violence, Kathryn M. Koziol (chapter 11) discusses the challenges of interpreting variation in trauma within sites. Koziol uses the treatment of captives and slaves as an example of the ways that trauma can vary significantly among individuals within the same society. Her research discusses the cultural, historical, and ideological factors responsible for these differences through the analysis of human remains from Cahokia. Understanding violence instead involves recognition that violence is often an important part of the cosmology and it is used in performative rituals that solidify particular kinds of social relationships.

William N. Duncan's study (chapter 12) on ritual violence is methodologically unique from the others in that it focuses less on qualitative analysis of the presence or absence of trauma but attempts to understand the nature of ritual violence through the quantitative analysis of biodistance (the relatedness of different groups) among a collection of crania from Postclassic Petén of Guatemala. Sacrificial victims were identified with the population, but there was no clear understanding of whether these victims were locals or foreigners. Duncan analyzed both metric and nonmetric dental traits to assess kinship and thus identify something about the relatedness (or nonrelatedness) of the sacrificial victims to the others. The results of his research suggests that some of the individuals who were sacrificed were related, meaning they were likely part of a lineage or other corporate group that may have been selected for sacrifice as a result of being captured in battle or by a raiding party.

## Themes in the Volume

This volume focuses on the long legacy of violence in a number of cultures that represent different temporal periods and cross a variety of cultures. Individuals at risk can be identified as the victims, but new methods in bioarchaeology have begun to reveal how the perpetrators can also be viewed in the archaeological record. This is a large and worthy problem to tackle in light of humankind's continued engagement with warfare and violence.

What sets apart the chapters in this volume is the fact that the authors interpret the robust empirical database within a variety of theoretical frameworks that facilitate doing what anthropologists and most scientists want to do—to *explain human behavior*. Without a strong theoretical orientation, bioarchaeological data is descriptive but not explanatory. Using practice theory, evolutionary theory, violence theory, or political-economic theory, these studies provide a way to filter out what is likely less important and to highlight and contextualize the data that have explanatory power. In the absence of theory, all data are of equal weight. Theory helps situate descriptive data in a rich matrix of possibilities and trajectories.

The authors provide a wide array of ways to think about and define violence. In almost every manifestation, violence is related to ideology, inequality, and power. It is shorthand for dominance, a proxy for hatred, and a symbol of power and control. By its very nature it is embedded with meanings that are biological (it does damage to corporeal bodies and neurological processes) and cultural (it produces individual, household, community, and intercommunity reactions). It is a flashpoint for pain that can be physical, mental, and collective. It is prismatic in that its meaning is different when viewed from the perspective of the perpetrator, the victim, or the bystander (i.e., a witness) (Krohn-Hansen 1994). It is also difficult to define precisely because definitions are filtered through lived experience, history, and ideology. What looks like violence to one may not be labeled as such by others. Without theory that includes pathways to understanding various ways that violence takes on meaning within cultural contexts, all is lost. With theory, there is movement toward explanation.

The authors of these chapters each integrate the archaeological data from skeletal remains with theory to build a series of interpretations that take the reader one step closer to understanding the role of violence in human societies.

## References Cited

Agarwal, S. C., and B. A. Glencross (editors)
2011    *Social Bioarchaeology*. Wiley-Blackwell, Malden.

Armelagos, G. J.
2003    Bioarchaeology as Anthropology. In *Archaeology Is Anthropology,* edited by S. D. Gillespie and D. L. Nichols, pp. 27–41. Archaeological Papers of the American Anthropological Association no. 13. American Anthropological Association, Washington, D.C.

Buikstra, J. E.
1977    Biocultural Dimensions of Archaeological Study: A Regional Perspective. In *Biocultural Adaptation in Prehistoric America,* edited by R. L. Blakey, pp. 67–84. University of Georgia Press, Athens.

Buikstra, J. E., and D. C. Cook
1980    Palaeopathology: An American Account. *Annual Review of Anthropology* 9: 433–470.

Goodman, A. H., R. B. Thomas, A. C. Swedlund, and G. J. Armelagos
1988    Biocultural Perspectives on Stress in Prehistoric, Historical, and Contemporary Population Research. *American Journal of Physical Anthropology* 31(S9): 169–202.

Krohn-Hansen, C.
1994    The Anthropology of Violent Interaction. *Journal of Archaeological Research* 50(4): 367–381.

Larsen, C. S.
1987    Bioarchaeological Interpretations of Subsistence Economy and Behavior from Human Skeletal Remains. In *Advances in Archaeological Method and Theory,* vol. 10, edited by M. B. Schiffer, pp. 339–445. Academic Press, San Diego.

Martin, D. L.
1998    Owning the Sins of the Past: Historical Trends in the Study of Southwest Human Remains. In *Building a New Biocultural Synthesis: Political-Economic Perspectives on Human Biology,* edited by A. H. Goodman and T. L. Leatherman, pp. 171–190. University of Michigan Press, Ann Arbor.

Riches, D.
1991    Aggression, War, Violence: Space/Time and Paradigm. *Man,* n.s. 26(2): 281–297.

Scheper-Hughes, N., and M. M. Lock
1987    The Mindful Body: A Prolegomenon to Future Work in Medical Anthropology. *Medical Anthropology Quarterly,* n.s. 1(1): 6–41.

Sofaer, J. R.
2006    *The Body as Material Culture: A Theoretical Osteoarchaeology.* Cambridge University Press, Cambridge.

Walker, P. L., and B. S. Hewlett
1990    Dental Health Diet and Social Status among Central African Foragers and Farmers. *American Anthropologist* 92(2): 383–398.

# PART I

# METHOD AND THEORY

# 1

## The Politicization of the Dead

### Violence as Performance, Politics as Usual

VENTURA R. PÉREZ

## Introduction

Violence has played an essential role in human social relations. Explanatory models that use a single disciplinary lens are not sufficient to provide the temporal and spatial expanse or the cross-cultural analysis that an interdisciplinary approach to the study of violence offers (Pérez 2010). The literature on violence and warfare has become so large that a truly comprehensive overview is no longer feasible. Some of it is theory driven, but most of it is written to address social problems rather than build general models and research paradigms. Perspectives on violence have been too narrowly conceived, and it is time for theoretical paradigms to be broadened.

This is why it is essential that anthropologists try to understand and explain the cultural mediation of real-world conditions that foster the use of violence. Arguably the most influential current definition of violence is from Riches's *The Anthropology of Violence,* which classifies violence as "an act of physical hurt deemed legitimate by the performer and illegitimate by (some) witness" (Riches 1986, 8). Although not everyone who studies violence agrees with this definition, most believe it to be a good starting point. Most contemporary violence researchers (e.g., Aijmer and Abbink 2000; Scheper-Hughes and Bourgois 2004; Schröder and Schmidt 2001; Whitehead 2004), myself included, agree that "violence is pervasive, ancient, infinitely various, and a central fact of human life, but also that it is poorly understood in general" (Whitehead 2004, 55).

The study of violence has often been conducted with little or no consideration for the specific and often unique cultural meanings associated with it. Warfare and violence are not merely reactions to a set of external variables but are encoded with intricate cultural meaning. To ignore these cultural expressions or, worse yet, suggest they do not exist minimizes our understanding of violence as a complex expression of cultural performance. Violence should never be reduced to its physicality when trying to understand its use (Scheper-Hughes and Bourgois 2004). This is because violent acts often exemplify intricate social and cultural dimensions and are frequently themselves defined by these same social contexts.

The symbolic aspects of violence have the potential to create order and disorder. depending on the specific social context within which the violence is expressed (Galtung 1990; Sluka 1992). This is the apparent paradox of violence studies. Most cultures feel that their safety lies in their ability to control violence with violence. While people fear and abhor violent acts they see as senseless, they are more than willing to condone the "legitimate" use of violence to promote social control and economic stability (Turpin and Kurtz 1997). Sluka (1992, 28) refers to this apparent paradox as the dual nature of conflict. Violence and conflict often have the ability to unite, create stability, and be progressive and at the same time generate the antithesis of these positive forces.

This is why Whitehead (2005, 23) argues that acts of violence and warfare should be viewed as cultural performances that may be unfamiliar to Western cultural experience. The consequence of not doing so is that violence may come to be seen as a "natural" component of human behavior rather than as contingent upon historical actions (Ember and Ember 1997; Ferguson 1997; Knauft 1991; Sluka 1992).

Most of the violence practiced in human societies is not considered deviant behavior. In fact, it is often seen as honorable when it is committed in the service of conventional social, economic, and political norms. These social and cultural contexts are what give violence its power and meaning. Seeing violence as an aberrant behavior committed only by deviants blinds us to the role violence has and continues to play in the foundation of many human societies (Kurtz and Turpin 1997, 207). Violence must be seen as more than just abhorrent behavior if we hope to do justice to the survivors and victims of violent events. Anthropologists have a responsibility to attempt to (re)construct the past without reducing the events to some simplistic notion of deviant behavior that is simply labeled (e.g., cannibalism, raiding, warfare) but is not explained.

## Politicization of the Dead

One theoretical framework that is useful for analyzing violence uses the concept of the "politicization of the dead." This is based on the idea that the corpse is a transitional object for the victors and the vanquished that centers on the passage from life to death (Robben 2000, 85). As Strathern (1996, 25) illustrates, the body becomes a depository of sociocultural symbolism. There is a duality in this body politic, as Connerton (1989, 104) points out. The body is not only socially constructed as an object of knowledge but also "culturally shaped" by the actual practices and behaviors of the group. This means that the manipulation of the corpse holds significance for both those committing violence to the corpse and the community to which the corpse belongs. Dead bodies have unique properties that make them powerful symbols. We humans can very easily identify with any manipulation of a corpse because of our ability for self-identification through our own bodies (Verdery 1999, 33).

This type of violence happens in complex sociocultural contexts that interlink the psychological, political, economic, and sociocultural dimensions. This is why Suárez-Orozco and Robben (2000, 194) argue that collective violence should not be limited to a single analytical unit; violence targets the body, the psyche, and the social fabric of the society in which it takes place. A form of physical and psychological violence is waged through both political and sociocultural violence. Political violence is manifested in the "annihilation" of the dead. Complete destruction of human remains symbolizes the undisputed success of the victors and serves as a transition from war to victory. The disarticulation and mutilation of bodies symbolizes the political dismemberment of the vanquished and emphasizes their total subjugation and reinforces the power and dominant ideology of the victors. The absence/annihilation of a corpse makes it impossible to perform burial rights, and this can produce anxiety and impair the mourning process.

The politicization of the dead through the use of political and sociocultural violence is designed to create a spectacle or statement. Through the display of the remains, the victors can demonstrate the power and

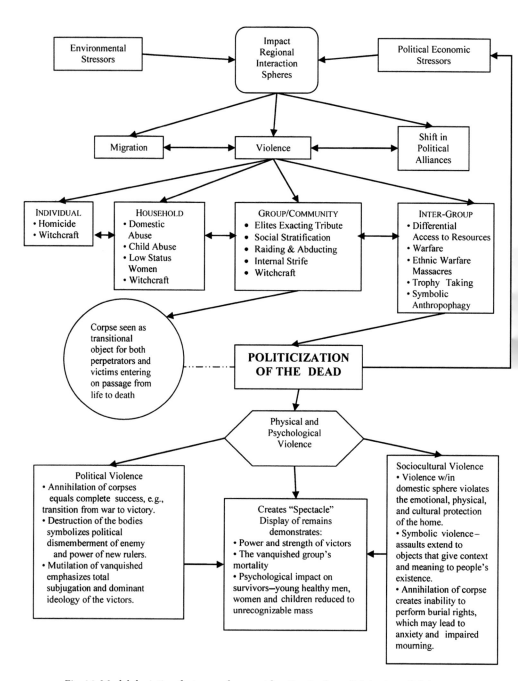

Fig. 1.1. Model depicting factors under consideration in the politicization of violence.

strength of their military while signifying the vanquished group's mortality. By killing young and old alike and reducing them to an unrecognizable mass, the aggressors create a substantial psychological impact on the regional interaction sphere in which they are operating. Figure 1.1 integrates the multiple variables that can impact regional interaction spheres, including environmental, political, and economic stressors that tend to create the propensity for migration, violence, and a shift in political alliances or a combination of the three. If violence is used, it will manifest in one of four categories: individual, household, intercommunity, or intergroup.

Recent history has provided numerous examples of cultural performances embedded in local sociocultural relationships. These include the use of rape and killing with mallets and hammers during Bosnia's "ethnic cleansing," the taking of hands and feet of prisoners during civil war in Sierra Leone, kneecapping in Northern Ireland, and dismembering and anal impalements during the Rwandan genocide (Whitehead 2004, 74).

These types of atrocities become formulaic in their production. During the lead-up to the Rwandan genocide, political cartoons such as those published in *Umurangi,* a Rwandan political journal, used powerful symbolic imagery to create an "in-group" (those doing the killing) and a "less than human group" (those to be killed). These types of images help create the "othering" effect necessary to carry out extreme violence and genocide (Arnold 2002; Chretien et al. 1995; Eriksen 1993; Maybury-Lewis 2002; Schafft 2002).

During the 1994 genocide in Rwanda, pregnant Tutsi women were eviscerated, incest was forced upon families before they were executed, individuals were impaled, and individuals were forced to cannibalize members of their own family (Taylor 1999, 105). The bodies of these victims became the stage upon which "the anatomists of pain" (Foucault 1979, 11) acted out their ancient drama of power and dominance. In order to comprehend the violence used, it is essential that the expression of biological death be understood in the larger social, political, economic, and ecological environment. Recognizing the symbolism expressed on the bodies of the tortured provides insight into the agenda of the torturer (Suárez-Orozco 1987). The signs and symbols associated with violence can easily be lost if all we concentrate on are site fortifications and skeletal material that provides evidence of trauma.

It would be a mistake to reduce the Rwandan genocide to a pragmatic analysis that focuses on the maximum number of enemy combatants killed while creating the most potent psychological damage possible. This type of analysis, although accurate, misses the profundity of the vehement hatred the participants of this atrocity had for their victims. The practical necessity of killing your enemy does not mean that you must exclude the possibility of sending a powerful symbolic message about yourself and how you feel about them (Taylor 1999, 144). Taussig references both Casement and Timerman in his book *Shamanism, Colonialism, and the Wild Man*:

> From the accounts of Casement and Timerman it is also obvious that torture and terror are ritualized art forms and that, far from being spontaneous, sui generis, and an abandonment of what are often called the values of civilization, such rites of terror have a deep history deriving power and meaning from those values. (Taussig 1987, 133)

Violence is truly understandable only in terms of local symbolism. In 100 days between April 6, 1994, and mid-July of that same year, an estimated 800,000 Rwandans were killed. The brutality of this genocidal war was carried out primarily with machetes. The bodies were often dismembered and the bones were crushed or broken and burned in houses, churches, or mass graves. In this instance, as for violence in the Ancestral Pueblo, in situ ethnic strife is a viable working hypothesis.

Anthropologists have long used the human body as a lens through which to examine cultural processes. How dead bodies are processed, hidden, and displayed can be used as a point of departure for examining the forms of violence that produced the deaths. We can observe how the deaths are perceived and further used as people try to make sense of violent acts. Dead bodies are far more than just decaying matter. As Mary Douglas (1966, 115) has said, "The body is a model which can stand for any kind of bound system." Doing even minimal justice to the symbolic complexity of the human body requires us to consider its political symbolism and cultural death rituals and analyze the type of corpse manipulation within the wider regional cultural dynamics and how the manipulation of the corpse will impact local histories and create spatial memory (Verdery 1999, 3).

The body is often seen as a "natural symbol" through which the social world can be ordered (Douglas 1973). When the body is viewed in this way, the beliefs, phobias, fears, and obsessions of a society are revealed. Meaning flows from the body to the cosmos or through the body and society. When this flow is interrupted, the consequence can be profoundly damaging for the grieving family and its community (Martin and Pérez 2001). This is because the mourners' transition from grief to the affirmation of their own lives, their own certain deaths, and their own journey to the afterlife is echoed in the fate of that corpse.

## Modeling Ancestral Pueblo Violence through the Politicization of the Dead

There is no doubt that violence and small-scale warfare played a role in Ancestral Pueblo life (see also chapters 5 and 6 in this volume). Isolated hilltop villages, stockades, and *trincheras* (dry-laid rock walls) date to AD 1000 (Wilcox 1979, 1989; Wilcox and Haas 1994). LeBlanc (1999) has documented a long history of apparent defensive settlement behavior in at least some regions of the Southwest. However, some researchers have challenged his evidence (see Fish and Fish 1989; Haas 1999).

At the core of the debates about the kinds of violence used by Ancestral Pueblo people are disarticulated, processed, and culturally modified bone assemblages and the archaeological data on defensive structures and the likelihood of warfare. Margolis (2000) presents a detailed description of the methodology and data Turner and Turner (1999) presented in support of their cannibalism hypothesis and LeBlanc presented (1999) in support of his hypothesis of increasing intimidation and widespread warfare. He suggests that a third hypothesis about witchcraft accusations and the executions of accused witches (Darling 1998; Walker 1996) better fits the data. LeBlanc bases his warfare theory primarily on archaeological data, but he incorporates osteological data from Turner and Turner as part of his overall model. LeBlanc's interpretation of violence in the Southwest is based on the claim that warfare and aggressive behavior is a universal trait practiced by the majority of human groups. Borrowing from Keeley (1996), LeBlanc provides several lines of evidence to support the notion that violence is the norm in most human groups and that the absence of violence happens only when extraneous constraints are in place.

Collectively, the archaeological data on fortification and strategic location and the osteological data on victims and mass graves suggest that violence in the form of ambushes, raids, skirmishes, witch executions, and attacks by a group of aggressors may have been the status quo in many parts of the Southwest before contact (Haas 1990; Lambert 2002; chapter 5 and chapter 6 in this volume; LeBlanc 1999). Haas and Creamer (1993) suggest that these patterns of "chronic warfare" pushed previously egalitarian and loosely connected groups into larger, politically centralized units from AC 1100 to 1300. The socioeconomic, political, and environmental stress caused by this transition would impact regional interaction spheres (see Fig. 1.1).

Community and intergroup violence has the potential to exploit the politicization of the dead. Because the corpse is seen as a transitional object between life and death for both the perpetrators and victims, ritually destroying or mutilating it sends a powerful message. The physical and psychological impact of this type of cultural performance is staggering. This type of violence creates a spectacle in which the display of the remains demonstrates the power and strength of the victors and the mortality of the vanquished group and creates massive psychological trauma for the survivors. This is accomplished through the transformation of young healthy men, women, and children into an unrecognizable mass of body parts.

Political violence centers on the complete annihilation of corpses to demonstrate complete success; that is, the transition from war to victory. The destruction of the bodies symbolizes the political dismemberment of the enemy and the power of the new rulers. Mutilation of the vanquished also emphasizes total subjugation and the dominant ideology of the victors. Sociocultural violence manifests itself in several ways, including violence within the domestic sphere that violates the notion of the home as a place of emotional, physical, and cultural protection. Symbolic violence is created with assaults against objects that give context and meaning to people's existence.

The challenge for bioarchaeologists who wish to model violent behavior lies in finding data sets that support a scenario for violence that explains the variability within structural, cultural, and direct violence. Linking osteological information to the archaeological context of the site provides a more precise analysis of the spectrum of violent behavior. The diversity of the osteological evidence—showing individuals with nonlethal injuries, recidivistic individuals, and individuals with health problems—suggests that violence could play out in different ways. The range of variability in the disarticulated and culturally modified human remains makes it extremely unlikely that such modifications are a result of a single cultural practice or violent event. A single activity, such as mini-armies carrying out public executions, could not account for the differences in placement, type of modification, degree of breakage, pattern of cutting, and types of individuals in the group. This is why macroscopic and microscopic analysis of cut marks to determine their morphology, direction, depth, and placement on the processed remains is so important. This information makes it possible to identify the types of lithic tools used and infer behavioral and cultural practices (Pérez 2002, 2003; Pérez, Nelson, and Martin 2008). It allows the researcher to understand the cultural logic that underlies the modification of the human remains and its relationship to violence or veneration.

The mass grave in Polacca Wash resulting from the Awatovi executions is an example of an assemblage of disarticulated human remains that some researchers have analyzed as showing evidence of cannibalism (Turner and Morris 1970; Turner and Turner 1999). In this example, the claim of cannibalism not only clashes with the ethnographic data but dates to a period outside the realm of the Chacoan phenomenon. There is no data to suggest that warrior-cultists from Mexico or a standing mini-army of the dominant elite were responsible for the dismemberment at Polacca Wash. Instead, the processed human remains, based on the evidence cited above, are most likely the result of a long-standing Puebloan belief in witchcraft and the execution of nonconformists.

Across cultures, witches have been punished to restore order. This can take several different broad forms such as exile, ostracization, monetary penalties, torture, or murder (see Sanders 2003; Darling 1998; Walker 1998). Ritual violence against witches (both antemortem and postmortem) is universal (Walker 1998). People killed witches, often violently; they would club or stone them, and some were then dismembered. Dismembering witches was a way to neutralize evil power, not to mention humiliating the person and serving as a warning to other witches (Walker 1998, 271). In some instances people also pounded the witch's corpse or burned it. Bodies were left to rot or were buried in shallow graves (Darling 1998). Witches were not accorded the same burial "rite of passage" as nonwitches.

Both Malotki (1993) and Voth (1905) present accounts of the destruction of Hopi villages by other Hopi. Of all of the villages that were destroyed, the best-known account is the demise of Awatovi. The general theme of the destruction of Awatovi and the other villages is that the inhabitants of the villages strayed from traditional practices and beliefs, an extremely serious issue for the Hopi. In the story, the initial reaction to the suggestion that Awatovi be destroyed was rejected because the Awatovi were fellow Hopi (Malotki 1993, 393). The Hopi have ties not just within their village but also to the other Hopi villages that make up their cluster. However, Awatovi and the other pueblos in similar stories were destroyed because they strayed from Hopi ideals. Thus, for the Hopi, this could only mean that the entire community had been consumed by witchcraft. Such violence, of course, broke Puebloan customs of nonaggression within their own communities. This disjuncture was remedied by using accusations of witchcraft as justification for the aggression. The inhabitants of Awatovi were slain as witches for breaking Puebloan norms (Malotki 1993, 275–295). Therefore, the villages of the accused were ritually destroyed along with the deviating individuals, families, and clans.

There is truly a remarkable range in the types of violence found through the occupation of the Colorado Plateau by the Ancestral Pueblo. Disarticulated human remains do not provide the only important osteological data sets on violence. Untold thousands of Ancestral Pueblo burials with a number of mortuary styles exist (Akins 2001; Martin and Akins 2001; Neitzel 2000; Stodder 1987), and some of these burial collections have been analyzed for pathologies and causes of death that reveal violence-related injuries. For example, healed and unhealed fractures, dislocations and traumatic injuries, contusions and concussions, bones broken at the time of death, bodies flung or thrown into structures, bones with spear points embedded, spear points found near burials, and mass burials all need to be considered simultaneously with the disarticulated assemblages and archaeological evidence of violence. Additional complexity is created by the fact that at any given site there may be traditional articulated burials, unusual unprepared burials, and disarticulated assemblages, such as at Chaco Canyon (Akins 1986), Aztec Ruins (Morris 1924), La Plata (Martin et al. 2001; Morris 1939), and the greater Mesa Verde Region (Billman, Lambert, and Leonard 2000; Kuckelman, Lightfoot, and Martin 2000, 2002; chapter 6 in this volume).

Alternative explanations for these massive trauma events do exist among historic Puebloan people, including the persecution and killing of witches. Regardless of whether the disarticulated remains from Ancestral

Pueblos present on the Colorado Plateau were the result of anthropophagy, witchcraft persecution, violence, or ancestor veneration, bioarchaeologists must move beyond the abstract notions of their hypotheses and
consider the practical realities of such behaviors.

## Conclusion

The politicization of the dead is one way that violence due to stress placed
on the regional spheres of interaction can become manifest. Robben
(2000) discussed this idea with regard to the Argentine war that raged
from 1976 to 1983. Many of his ideas may be useful in helping to explain
the intercommunity and intergroup violence present in the Southwest
after AD 900 (Fig. 1.1). The politicization of the dead model helps to integrate the bioarchaeological and ethnohistorical data that is accumulat-
ing from the study of Ancestral Pueblo violence. Violence reconfigures
its victims and the social environment in which it occurs (Daniel 1996;
Feldman 1991; Green 1999; Nordstrom and Martin 1998). It must never be
viewed as a transitory punctuating event that leaves only a memory with
no lasting effects. This is because violence becomes the determining factor
that shapes future realities for both individuals and cultures. According
to Kluckhohn and Strodtbeck (1961, 298), "Pueblo culture and society are
integrated to an unusual degree, all sectors being bound together by a
consistent, harmonious set of values, which pervade and homogenize the
categories of world view, ritual art, social organization, economic activity,
and social control."

Thus, we must look at cultural realities as they are brought into existence by daily practice and not as some static entity. Many cultural systems
exist, and these systems will continue to change as the situations around
the community change. It should be the goal of the violence researcher
(or any anthropologist, for that matter) to avoid searching for a single
event that delineates and homogenizes a systematic function of a group
(warfare or violence) but instead try to reach an analysis of how people
are bound by events and processes that allows for a fluidity of responses to
multiple stimuli. The disarticulated assemblages of human remains found
in the Southwest provide direct evidence of this type of complex sociocultural response.

# References Cited

Aijmer, G., and J. Abbink (editors)
2000    *The Meaning of Violence: A Cross-Cultural Perspective.* Berg Publishers, New York.

Akins, N. J.
1986    *A Biocultural Approach to Human Burials from Chaco Canyon, New Mexico.* Reports of the Chaco Center no. 9. National Park Service, Santa Fe, N.M.
2001    Chaco Canyon Mortuary Practices: Archaeological Correlates of Complexity. In *Ancient Burial Practices in the American Southwest: Archaeology, Physical Anthropology, and Native American Perspectives,* edited by D. R. Mitchell and J. L. Brunson-Hadley, pp. 167–190. University of New Mexico Press, Albuquerque.

Arnold, B.
2002    Justifying Genocide: Archaeology and the Construction of Difference. In *Annihilating Difference: The Anthropology of Genocide,* edited by A. L. Hinton, pp. 95–116. University of California Press, Berkeley.

Billman, B. R., P. M. Lambert, and B. L. Leonard
2000    Cannibalism, Warfare, and Drought in the Mesa Verde Region in the Twelfth Century AD. *American Antiquity* 65: 1–34.

Chretien, J. P., J. F. Dupaquier, M. Kabanda, and J. Ngarambe
1995    *Rwanda: Les Medias du Genocide.* Karthala, Paris.

Connerton, P.
1989    *How Societies Remember.* Cambridge University Press, Cambridge.

Daniel, E. V.
1996    *Charred Lullabies: Chapters in an Anthropography of Violence.* Princeton University Press, Princeton, N.J.

Darling, A. J.
1998    Mass Inhumation and the Execution of Witches in the American Southwest. *American Anthropologist,* n.s. 100(3): 732–752.

Douglas, M.
1966    *Purity and Danger: An Analysis of the Concepts of Pollution and Taboo.* Routledge and Keegan Paul, London.
1973    *Natural Symbols: Exploration in Cosmology.* Vintage Books, New York.

Ember, C. R., and M. Ember
1997    Violence in the Ethnographic Record: Results of Cross-Cultural Research on War and Aggression. In *Troubled Times: Violence and Warfare in the Past,* edited by D. L. Martin and D. W. Frayer, pp. 1–20. Gordon and Breach, Amsterdam.

Eriksen, T. H.
1993    *Ethnicity and Nationalism: Anthropological Perspectives.* Pluto Press, London.

Feldman, A.
1991    *Formations of Violence: The Narrative of the Body and Political Terror in Northern Ireland.* University of Chicago Press, Chicago.

Ferguson, R. B.
1997    Violence and War in Prehistory. In *Troubled Times: Violence and Warfare in the*

*Past,* edited by D. L. Martin and D. W. Frayer, pp. 321–355. Gordon and Breach, Amsterdam.

Fish, P. R., and S. K. Fish

1989    Hohokam Warfare from a Regional Perspective. In *The Marana Community in the Hohokam World,* edited by S. K. Fish, P. R. Fish, and J. H. Madsen, pp. 97–105. University of Arizona, Tucson.

Foucault, M.

1979    *Discipline and Punish: The Birth of the Prison.* Translated by A. Sheridan. Vintage Books, New York.

Galtung, J.

1990    Cultural Violence. *Journal of Peace Research* 27(3): 291–305.

Green, L.

1999    *Fear as a Way of Life: Mayan Widows in Rural Guatemala.* Columbia University Press, New York.

Haas, J.

1990    *The Anthropology of War.* Cambridge University Press,. Cambridge.

1999    The Origins of War and Ethnic Violence. In *Ancient Warfare: Archaeological Perspectives,* edited by J. Carman and A. Harding, pp. 11–24. Sutton Publishing, Stroud, Gloucestershire.

Haas, J., and W. Creamer

1993    *Stress and Warfare among the Kayenta Anasazi of the Thirteenth Century A.D.* Fieldiana, Anthropology, New Series no. 21. Field Museum of Natural History, Chicago.

Keeley, L. H.

1996    *War before Civilization.* Oxford University Press, New York.

Kluckhohn, F. R., and F. L. Strodtbeck

1961    *Variations in Value Orientations.* Greenwood Press, Westport.

Knauft, B. M.

1991    Violence and Sociality in Human Evolution. *Current Anthropology* 32: 391–428.

Kuckelman, K. A., R. R. Lightfoot, and D. L. Martin

2000    Changing Patterns of Violence in the Northern San Juan Region. *Kiva* 66(1): 147–165.

2002    The Bioarchaeology and Taphonomy of Violence at Castle Rock and Sand Canyon Pueblos, Southwestern Colorado. *American Antiquity* 67: 486–513.

Kurtz, L. R., and J. Turpin

1997    Conclusion: Untangling the Web of Violence. In *The Web of Violence: From Interpersonal to Global,* edited by J. Turpin and L. R. Kurst, pp. 207–232. University of Illinois Press, Urbana.

Lambert, P. M.

2002    The Archaeology of War: A North American Perspective. *Journal of Archaeological Research* 10(3): 207–241.

LeBlanc, S. A.

1999    *Prehistoric Warfare in the American Southwest.* University of Utah Press, Salt Lake City.

Malotki, E. (editor)

1993    *Hopi Ruin Legends. Narrated by M. Lomatuway'ma, L. Lomatuway'ma and S. Namingha.* University of Nebraska Press, Lincoln.

Margolis, M. M.

2000    Warriors, Witches, and Cannibals: Violence in the Prehistoric American Southwest. *Southwestern Lore* 66(2): 3–21.

Martin, D. L., and N. J. Akins

2001    Unequal Treatment in Life as in Death: Trauma and Mortuary Behavior at La Plata (AD 1000–1300). In *Ancient Burial Practices in the American Southwest,* edited by D. R. Mitchell and J. L. Brunson-Hadley, pp. 223–248. University of New Mexico Press, Albuquerque.

Martin, D. L., N. J. Akins, A. H. Goodman, and A. C. Swedlund

2001    *Totah: Time and the Rivers Flowing Excavations in the La Plata Valley.* Vol. 5 of *Harmony and Discord: Bioarchaeology of the La Plata Valley.* Office of Archaeological Studies, Museum of New Mexico, Santa Fe, N.M.

Martin, D. L., and V. R. Pérez

2001    Commentary: Dead Bodies and Violent Acts. *Anthropology News* 42(7): 8–9.

Maybury-Lewis, D.

2002    Genocide against Indigenous Peoples. In *Annihilating Difference: The Anthropology of Genocide,* edited by A. L. Hinton, pp. 43–53. University of California Press, Berkeley.

Morris, E. H.

1924    *Burials in the Aztec Ruin.* The Archer M. Huntington Survey of the Southwest. American Museum Press, New York.

1939    *Archaeological Studies in the La Plata District, Southwestern Colorado and Northwestern New Mexico.* Carnegie Institution of Washington Publication 519. Carnegie Institution of Washington, Washington, D.C.

Neitzel, J. E.

2000    Gender Hierarchies: A Comparative Analysis of Mortuary Data. In *Women and Men in the Prehispanic Southwest: Labor, Power, and Prestige,* edited by P. L. Crown, pp. 137–168. School of American Research Press, Santa Fe.

Nordstrom, C., and J. Martin

1998    Deadly Myths of Aggression. *Journal of Aggressive Behavior* 24(2): 147–159.

Pérez, V. R.

2002    La Quemada Tool Induced Bone Alterations: Cutmark Differences between Human and Animal Bone. *Archaeology Southwest* 16(1): 10.

2003    Nahualli Tlamatini/Tlahueliloc Nahualli: The Power of Anthropological Discourse. In *Indigenous People and Archaeology,* edited by T. Peck and E. Siegfried, pp. 135–153. Archaeological Association of the University of Calgary, Calgary.

2010    From the Editor: An Introduction to Landscapes of Violence. *Landscapes of Violence* 1(1): Article 1. Available at http: //scholarworks.umass.edu/lov/vol1/iss1/1/.

Pérez, V. R., B. A. Nelson, and D. L. Martin

2008    Veneration of Violence? A Study of Variations in Patterns of Human Bone Modification at La Quemada. In *Social Violence in the Prehispanic American*

*Southwest,* edited by D. L. Nichols and P. L. Crown, pp. 123–142. University of Arizona Press, Tucson.

Riches, D. (editor)
1986    *The Anthropology of Violence.* Blackwell, New York.

Robben, A. C. G. M.
2000    The Assault of Basic Trust: Disappearances, Protest, and Reburial in Argentina. In *Cultures under Siege: Collective Violence and Trauma,* edited by A. C. G. M. Robben and M. M. Suárez-Orozco, pp. 70–101. Cambridge University Press, Cambridge.

Sanders, T.
2003    Reconsidering Witchcraft: Postcolonial Africa and Analytic (Un)Certainties. *American Anthropologist* 105: 338–352.

Schafft, G. E.
2002    Scientific Racism in the Service of the Reich: German Anthropologists in the Nazi Era. In *Annihilating Difference: The Anthropology of Genocide,* edited by A. L. Hinton, pp. 117–134. University of California Press, Berkeley.

Scheper-Hughes, N., and P. Bourgois
2004    Introduction: Making Sense of Violence. In *Violence in War and Peace: An Anthology,* edited by N. Scheper-Hughes and P. Bourgois, pp. 1–32. Blackwell Publishing, Malden.

Schröder, I. W., and B. E. Schmidt
2001    Introduction: Violent Imaginaries and Violent Practices. In *Anthropology of Violence and Conflict,* edited by B. E. Schmidt and I. W. Schröder, pp. 1–24. Routledge, London.

Sluka, J. A.
1992    The Anthropology of Conflict. In *The Paths to Domination, Resistance, and Terror,* edited by C. Nordstrom and J. Martin, pp. 18–36. University of California Press, Berkeley.

Stodder, A. L. W.
1987    The Physical Anthropology and Mortuary Practice of the Dolores Anasazi: An Early Pueblo Population in Local and Regional Context. In *Dolores Archaeological Program: Supporting Studies: Settlement and Environment,* edited by K. L. Petersen and J. D. Orcutt, pp. 336–504. Bureau of Reclamation, Engineering and Research Center, Denver.

Strathern, A. J.
1996    *Body Thoughts.* University of Michigan Press, Ann Arbor.

Suárez-Orozco, M. M.
1987    The Treatment of Children in the "Dirty War": Ideology, State Terrorism and the Abuse of Children in Argentina. In *Child Survival: Anthropological Perspectives on the Treatment and Maltreatment of Children,* edited by N. Scheper-Hughes, pp. 227–256. D. Reidel Publishing Company, Dordrecht.

Suárez-Orozco, M. M., and A. C. G. M. Robben
2000    Interdisciplinary Perspectives on Violence and Trauma. In *Cultures under*

*Siege: Collective Violence and Trauma,* edited by A. C. G. M. Robben and M. M. Suárez-Orozco, pp. 194–226. Cambridge University Press, Cambridge.

Taussig, M.

1987    *Shamanism, Colonialism, and the Wildman: A Study in Terror and Healing.* University of Chicago Press, Chicago.

Taylor, C. C.

1999    *Sacrifice as Terror: The Rwandan Genocide of 1994.* Berg Press, Oxford.

Turner, C. G., II, and N. T. Morris

1970    A Massacre at Hopi. *American Antiquity* 35: 320–331.

Turner, C. G., II, and J. A. Turner

1999    *Man Corn: Cannibalism and Violence in the Prehistoric American Southwest.* University of Utah Press, Salt Lake City.

Turpin, J., and L. R. Kurtz (editors)

1997    *The Web of Violence: From Interpersonal to Global.* University of Illinois Press, Urbana.

Verdery, K.

1999    *The Political Lives of Dead Bodies: Reburial and Postsocialist Change.* Columbia University Press, New York.

Voth, H. R.

1905    *The Traditions of the Hopi.* Anthropological Series no. 96. Field Columbia Museum, Chicago.

Walker, W. H.

1996    Ritual Deposits: Another Perspective. In *River of Change: Prehistory of the Middle Little Colorado River Valley, Arizona,* edited by E. C. Adams, pp. 75–91. Arizona State Museum, University of Arizona, Tucson.

1998    Where Are the Witches of Prehistory? *Journal of Archaeological Method and Theory* 5(3): 245–308.

Whitehead, N. L.

2004    On the Poetics of Violence. In *Violence,* edited by N. L. Whitehead, pp. 55–77. School of American Research Press, Santa Fe, N.M.

2005    War and Violence as Cultural Expression. *Anthropology News* 46: 23–26.

Wilcox, D. R.

1979    The Warfare Implications of Dry-Laid Masonry Walls. *Kiva* 45: 15–38.

1989    Hohokam Warfare. In *Cultures in Conflict: Current Archaeological Perspectives,* edited by D. C. Tkaczuk and B. C. Vivian, pp. 163–172. Proceedings of the 20th Annual Chacmool Conference. University of Calgary, Calgary.

Wilcox, D. R., and J. Haas

1994    The Scream of the Butterfly: Competition and Conflict in the Prehistoric Southwest. In *Themes in Southwest Prehistory,* edited by G. J. Gumerman, pp. 211–238. School of American Research, Santa Fe, N.M.

# 2

## The Bioarchaeology of Structural Violence

### A Theoretical Model and a Case Study

HAAGEN D. KLAUS

## Introduction

Bioarchaeologists are uniquely positioned to explore the origins, nature, and variations in the expressions of human violence and nonviolence because of the cross-cultural, empirical, and diachronic perspectives that human skeletons can provide (Walker 2001, 574). The bioarchaeology of violence has advanced significantly over the past 30 years. Key methodological advances involved a long-needed standardization of descriptive protocols (Buikstra and Ubelaker 1994; Lovell 1997) and the identification and differential diagnosis of traumatic injury within a biomechanical framework (Galloway 1999; Ortner 2003). These developments helped stimulate the other leading edge: thematic and theoretical advances focused on population-based and contextual studies of lifestyle, intergroup conflict, technology, ritual and symbolic systems, gender, ideology, human-environment interplay, cannibalism, and statecraft (e.g., Chacon and Dye 2007; Chacon and Mendoza 2007a, b; Eisenberg and Hutchinson 1996; Fiorato, Boylston, and Knüsel 2000; Klaus, Centurión, and Curo 2010; Larsen 1997; Martin 1997; Martin and Frayer 1997; Melbye and Fairgrieve 1994; Verano 2008; Walker 2001; chapters in this volume) along with forensic applications (Kimmerle and Baraybar 2008). Emerging from a synthesis of these developments is a history of human violence extending back into the Pleistocene that emphasize links between envi-

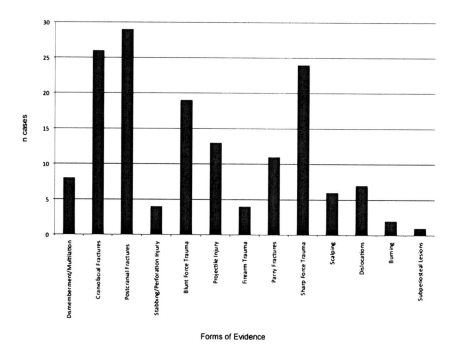

Fig. 2.1. Diagram showing the count data for the most frequently described skeletal evidence of violence.

ronmental deterioration, population size, and (perhaps most centrally) diminished access to resources (Larsen and Walker 2010, 387).

The intrinsic and operational epistemology of violence in bioarchaeology is worthy of introspection, however. Since the pioneering work of Aleš Hrdlička and Earnest Hooton, physical anthropology's engagement with violence has been intertwined with the study of skeletal trauma, and today it includes Walker's (2001, 575–576) conservative term "violent injury" to describe skeletal damage where there is relatively clear evidence of malevolent intent. Moreover, the search keywords "violence" and "trauma" yielded 65 papers from 1997 to 2010 in the *American Journal of Physical Anthropology* and the *International Journal of Osteoarchaeology*. In the simple count data of skeletal evidence of violence in these papers, the most frequently injuries are postcranial bone fractures, followed in decreasing frequency by reports of craniofacial fractures, sharp force trauma, blunt force trauma, projectile injuries, parry fractures, dismemberment/decapitations, dislocations, scalpings, firearm injuries, stabbing/

perforation injuries, burns, and subperiosteal lesions (Fig. 2.1). And let there be no doubt—these forms of evidence are appropriate, productive, and insightful bases for bioarchaeological studies of violence. However, are broken bones and cut marks the only reflection of violence in human skeletons? Is this the only way to perceive and interpret violent human interactions in bioarchaeology?

In this chapter, I propose a broadening of the concept of violence in bioarchaeology. I consider the applicability and extension of concepts of structural violence from social theory and medical anthropology, and I suggest that empirical studies of health outcomes, properly interpreted in their contextual frameworks, can serve as evidence of violence that is invisible or is not represented in the skeletal trauma record. The study of structural violence naturally complements data on interpersonal trauma. Through a case study of health in colonial Peru, I aim to illustrate that such trauma may often ultimately stem from acts more harmful, wide-spread, and enduring than those that produce broken bones and weapons injuries.

## Bioarchaeology and Structural Violence

Violence represents just one component of a complex continuum of human interpersonal and intergroup behaviors. Sociologist Johan Galtung (1969) first coined the term "structural violence" more than four decades ago to describe social structures that suppress agency and prevent individuals, groups, and societies from reaching their social, economic, and biological potential. In other words, structural violence promotes the "avoidable impairment of fundamental human needs or . . . the impairment of human life, which lowers the actual degree to which someone is able to meet their needs below that which would otherwise be possible" (Galtung 1993, 106). The phenomenon is *structural* because its mechanisms are within the political and economic constructions of a social world, and it is *violent* because it causes direct injury or death to human beings (Farmer et al. 2006). Structural violence is often considered an invisible or subtle form of violence because it is embedded in long-standing and multigenerational social structures. Social institutions and the habitus of daily life actively normalize the suffering that such violence produces. Its expression is exerted systematically but indirectly by everyone who is part of a structurally violent social order simply by the fact of their participation in and reproduction of that order (Farmer 2004). Structural violence involves an attempt to understand the mechanisms and effects of what transpires when superordinate social entities marginalize and manipulate subordinate social entities.

Cultural anthropologists such as Paul Farmer, Philippe Bourgois, and Nancy Scheper-Hughes have most notably engaged with the issue of structural violence through analysis of the contemporary cultural issues of poverty, health, commodified medicine, elitism, colonialism, classism, racism, sexism, heterosexism, drug abuse, and homelessness (Bourgois 1995, 2010; Bourgois and Schonberg 2009; Farmer 1999, 2003, 2004; Farmer, Connors, and Simmons 1996; Farmer et al. 2006; Scheper-Hughes 1992). But just how applicable is structural violence in bioarchaeology? Some bioarchaeologists might balk at using the concept of structural violence in their analysis because of its focus on living populations: its perspectives are achieved because the study population is alive and has not gone through the myriad filters of time and taphonomy. The concept of structural violence is deeply intertwined with a clarion call for social justice and is entangled with many elements of social theory. Thus, there is a possible mismatch with the empirical, hypothetico-deductive, and evolutionary paradigms of bioarchaeological science. However, I argue that structural violence as an interpretive framework is an opportunity to (1) bridge the science/culture divide in anthropology (Goodman and Leatherman 1998); (2) further develop the promising bioarchaeology of political economy; and (3) recursively inform anthropological understandings of modern violence. Its use can promote balanced integration of empirical studies of ancient skeletons and social theories used to interpret skeletal data. The concept of structural violence in bioarchaeological analysis can also be used productively in conjunction with Walker's (2001, 575) definition of violence: "All injuries resulting from the marginalization of one group by another through territorial expansion, social dominance, or economic exploitation meet the definition of violence if the dominant group shows callous disregard for the safety and physical well-being of the people they have marginalized." Promising initial perspectives along these lines have emerged in bioarchaeology (Klaus 2008; Perez this volume; Steadman 2008) and forensic anthropology (Steadman 2009).

## Theoretical Model

Cross-disciplinary integration of structural violence theory into bioarchaeology requires critical deliberation to identify specific and appropriate applications in interpretation, synthesis, and theory. The following is an attempt to provide a very basic model of structural violence in bioarchaeology. It is not intended to be comprehensive or law-like; rather, it is best thought of as the outline of a starting point that seeks to stimulate debate and generate new questions, hypotheses, agendas, and styles of research.

A fundamental cultural link between anthropology and bioarchaeology involves how structural violence promotes disparities in health outcomes. This is observed in the prevalence of patterns of disease such as HIV and tuberculosis and in childhood mortality rates (e.g., Farmer 2006; Farmer et al. 2006). Structural violence makes a great deal of bioarchaeological sense when placed into the current materialist-processual paradigm of skeletal health and biological stress (Goodman and Martin 2002; Goodman et al. 1984). This is further correlated with a wealth of global evidence that finds that skeletal morbidity correlated with lower social status (Cohen n.d.; Danforth 1999; Larsen 1997).

The lynchpin of a bioarchaeology of structural violence involves how social inequality is often produced and exercised in a hierarchical society: one social entity's influence, control, or appropriation of resources excludes similar control by other social entities. Under such conditions of inequality, culture acts less as a buffer and more as a stressor (Schell 1997) for members of subordinate social groups (Fig. 2.2). Thus, culturally induced stressors appear to be the primary locus of structural violence, as these elements can physically constrain a subordinate social entity's access to the nutritional resources, adequate living conditions, and uncontaminated drinking water required to maintain biological homeostasis. The effects of unequal access to resources propagate powerfully throughout the chain of biological causality, affecting the expression of genes, developmental pathways, and epigenetic inputs during a person's ontogeny. One effect is compromised immunocompetence, which leads to more frequent disruptions of biological homeostasis and produces observable patterns of increased morbidity, such as disease, disruption of growth, and pathological processes among populations.

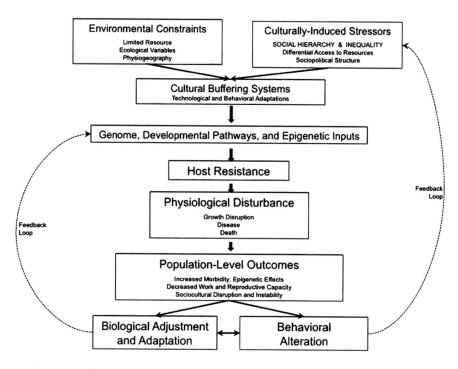

Fig. 2.2. Model showing biocultural relationships with feedback loops.

Thus, one group's active denial of resources to another can inflict physiological disturbance. In bioarchaeological terms, structural violence can be the cause of suffering and morbidity associated with the relatively well understood pathogenesis of conditions such as enamel hypoplasias, anemia, stunted growth, and infection. Direct causation of osseous fractures often embody just a moment or two of direct physical violence; structural violence potentially produces lifelong functional injuries experienced throughout an individual's life history: proponents of the biological damage hypothesis (Clark et al. 1986; Goodman and Armelagos 1988) argue that childhood stress is strongly associated with elevated adult morbidity and early mortality. Research in human biology has demonstrated that yet earlier stress that begins in fetal life (Barker 1994; Kuzawa 2008; Langley-Evans 2004; McDade and Kuzawa 2004; Wintour and Owen 2006) can result in canalized biological damage or pre-programming of negative adult health outcomes, including immunological deficiencies.

The basic theoretical premise of structural violence in bioarchaeology is relatively simple. Socially constructed restriction of resources can and does cause harm and death, evidence of which can manifest in skeletal and dental tissue. Under such conditions, disparities in health reflect a form of violence. Furthermore, modern ethnography is replete with examples of structural violence boiling over and leading directly to group conflict, war, racial violence, and genocide (e.g., Farmer 2004); such events put structural violence in a causal relationship with physical violence in the continuum of violent interaction (Fig. 2.3).

However, I urge careful and critical use of structural violence in bioarchaeological analysis. It is not a label to be attached to just any case of differing health outcomes between distinct social entities. First, structural violence, especially in its modern expressions, is a historically contingent element of the specific trajectories of Western European and Euroamerican societies (sensu Wolf 1982). It is probably most applicable to Western contexts and capitalist-style political economies. Extending the concept to non-Western premodern settings may seriously problematize a bioarchaeology of structural violence. My work over the last decade as part of the Sicán Archaeological Project on Peru's north coast has found unambiguous evidence of higher morbidity among commoners living in the highly stratified Middle Sicán theocratic state (AD 900–1100) (Klaus, Shimada, Shinoda, and Muno n.d.). But within this society, attempts to compensate for gross power differences took the form of reciprocal social organizations that created socioeconomic obligations (albeit asymmetrical and somewhat symbolic) between rulers and the ruled (Ramírez 1996). The Middle Sicán culture may represent a case of an elite class intensely manipulating a political economy to the detriment of the health of the non-elite. But if this is structural violence, it may be a very different structural violence: the setting, history, organization, and evolution of these relationships followed very different historical and cultural trajectories in the complex societies of Peru and Europe.

Second, structural violence may likely be a feature that only a rigidly hierarchical society can achieve; bioarchaeological application to bands or tribes in the past deserves serious deliberation, but the lack of requisite complexity may prevent the emergence of structurally violent relationships. Ranked chiefdoms may also generally lack the kinds of stark political-economic disjunctions and health disparities associated with structural violence (cf. Powell 1988; Powell 1991; though see Steadman

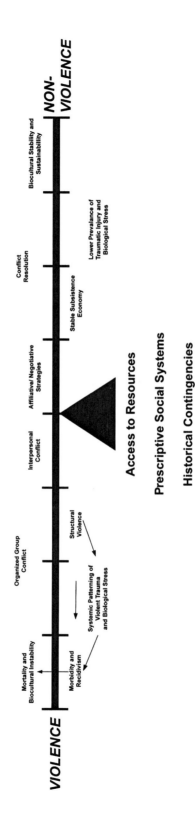

Fig. 2.3. Model showing the bioarchaeology of structural violence as a function of access to resources, prescriptive social systems, and historical contingencies.

2008, 62, for a thought-provoking counterexample). Third, as Bourgois and Scheper-Hughes (2004) note, structural violence is not just a crucial concept for understanding human life experiences; its relationship to other forms of violence and power must be examined in tandem to prevent analysis from becoming too linear, deterministic, or reductionist. Fourth, we must be on guard against portraying recipients of structural violence as passive victims. While the agency of subordinate groups is often constrained, marginalized people should be expected to exercise as much agency as possible. Fifth, and most important, the key to a bioarchaeology of structural violence is a thoroughly and deeply embedded engagement with archaeological and historic contexts (Buikstra 2006; Palkovich 1996). This point requires no elaboration. Without this, the bioarchaeology of structural violence has neither interpretive power nor a point.

## Case Study: Structural Violence and Health in Colonial Peru

Historic Peru and the Lambayeque Valley

A basic case study of structural violence can be developed from the ongoing research on the effects of European conquest and colonization of the north coast of Peru. Colonial Peru is a society and time period for which detailed contextual information exists in ethnohistory (e.g., Pillsbury 2008) and in an archaeological corpus that has recently begun to develop (Klaus 2008; Quilter 2007; Wernke 2007). Colonial Peru emerged as a center of the Spanish imperial state, first as a transplanted European feudal society and later as a precarious pre-capitalist state. The colonial Spanish had two basic agendas: (1) extraction of the maximum amount of natural and human resources and (2) converting indigenous peoples into Catholic, tax-paying, and economically productive members of the Spanish state—goals that were often implemented with the aggressive public policies and techniques of the Inquisition. What emerged over some 350 years was a hybrid colonial society (Klaus 2012a; Wernke 2007) that was often on the verge of collapse and that was constantly evolving from interplays between internal political competition, an emerging global economy, intense social strife, and demographic instability.

The viceroyalty of Peru was characterized by a rigid, hierarchical, and patriarchal structure that was intimately intertwined with the economy. The threat of violent repression was omnipresent and sometimes involved physical violence (Murphy, Gaither, Goycochea, Verano, and Cock 2010). Colonial Peru was characterized by immense disparities in the distribution of wealth and sociopolitical capital. Inequality was widely justified on the grounds of biologically deterministic views of race. Occupying the top social tier was a small, homogeneous, and urban white European elite that was supported by tribute income and was composed of bureaucrats, powerful clergy, and businessmen and merchants who secured power through monopoly. Mestizo peoples occupied the middle tier of colonial Peruvian culture, but the majority of the society was composed of a multiplicity of Andean ethnic and linguistic groups whom the Spanish amalgamated into a single category: *indio,* or Indian. Native peoples were journeyman, market people, peddlers, miners, farmers, servants, and unskilled and other low-wage laborers (Burkholder and Johnson 1998, 179). The colonizers envisioned their subjects living in a fictive *república de indios* that had different rights, laws, and economic obligations. Indigenous labor was a commodity to be bought, sold, and often abused. Denial of access to sociopolitical capital and vulnerability to fluctuating labor markets often led to a destitute, hand-to-mouth existence (Stern 1982). Although Africans came to Peru as slaves, they eventually experienced less marginalization and somewhat greater freedom than native Andeans (Bowser 1974).

The local outcomes of colonization in Peru appear highly variable (Murphy, Goyochea, and Cock 2010; Quilter 2010; Wernke 2010), but one region about which very little empirical information exists is the Lambayeque Valley Complex on the northern north coast of Peru (Fig. 2.4). Some 700 kilometers north of Lima, Lambayeque was the nexus of major pre-Hispanic developments, including the florescent Moche (Alva and Donnan 1993; Shimada 1994) and Middle Sicán cultures (Shimada 2000, 2012). However, most of the population from at least AD 100 to the modern era can be identified as ethnically Muchik (or Mochica) (Klaus 2012b). The early Spanish colonists recognized the economic potential of this region, which had a relatively sunny and mild year-round climate, potential seaports, and high-volume rivers that flowed through large and fertile alluvial plains (Ramírez 1986). Although colonization of Lambayeque began in 1534, the region lacked a dedicated chronicler. Careful study of

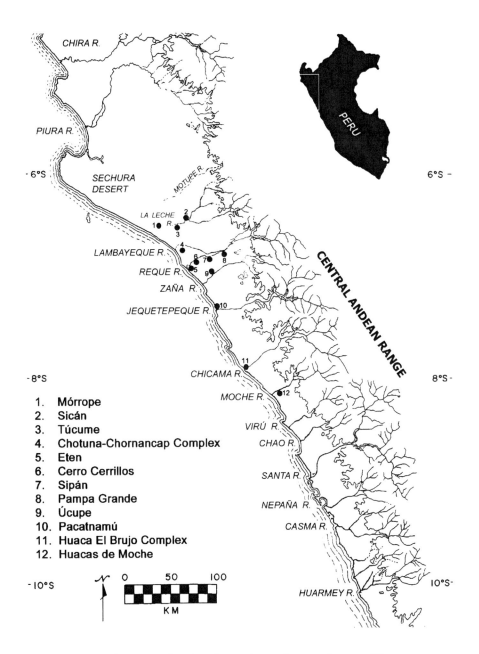

Fig. 2.4. The Lambayeque Valley Complex on the northern north coast of Peru.

scattered legal documents, census data, wills, and other nonsystematic accounts help provide a portrait of life in the colonial Lambayeque region (Ramírez-Horton 1974; Ramírez 1986, 1996). While the initial impacts of conquest were limited, the people of Lambayeque experienced a full socioeconomic rupture within 50 years of contact, including major alterations of the political landscape, drastic economic restructuring, forced resettlement, religious persecution, anthropogenic transformations of the environment, and the dismantling of social systems that promoted community well-being and relative economic self-sufficiency (Klaus 2008, 281–347; Ramírez 1996; also see below).

## Methods and Materials

In part drawing from Schaedel's (1992) call for the development of a historic Peruvian archaeology, the Lambayeque Valley Biohistory Project launched a multidecade, regional, and holistic study of the colonial era. The first site selected for excavation was the Chapel of San Pedro de Mórrope, chosen for its large and intact colonial Muchik cemetery and its relatively detailed ethnohistory (Rubiños y Andrade 1936 [1782]). Mórrope was at the frontier of the Lambayeque Valley Complex on the edge of the Sechura Desert. Mórrope was one of the first forced resettlements, or *reducciónes*, of perhaps as many as 20 local communities in June 1536 (Rubiños y Andrade 1936 [1782], 298) into a microenvironment that featured highly saline soils and chronic water shortages, though a community-level specialization involves ceramic production (Cleland and Shimada 1998). But for the Europeans, this ecologically stressful locale was strategic; it was located at one end of the route by which goods, information, and people traversed the vast desert between Lambayeque and Piura.

With Peruvian co-director Manuel Tam, excavation at the Chapel of San Pedro de Mórrope from 2004 to 2005 recovered a socially and demographically representative sample of 322 burials containing the remains of at least 870 individuals who lived between AD 1536 and 1750 (Klaus 2008) (Fig. 2.5). Multiple lines of skeletal data were examined to reconstruct the health, diet, and lifestyle of the Muchik in the colonial era. These data were compared to a socially representative pre-Hispanic sample of 212 Muchik skeletons spanning AD 900–1532 (Klaus 2008, Table 8.1). The quantitative techniques, differential diagnoses, and comparative subsample sizes used in this study are discussed in extensive detail below. Four

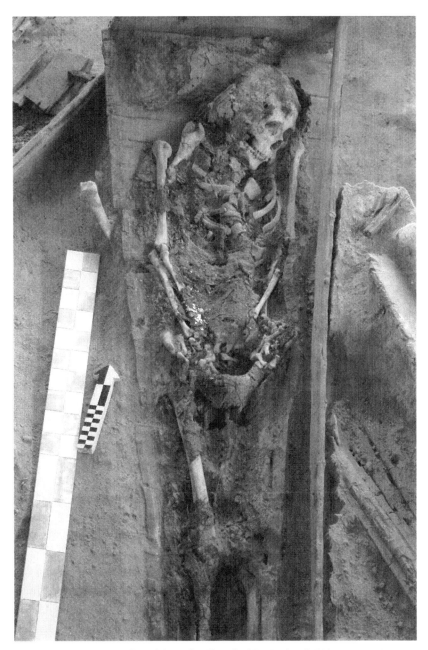

Fig. 2.5. A representative burial from the Chapel of San Pedro de Mórrope.

independent and complementary categories of skeletal phenomenon are examined here.

First, subadult and adult systemic biological stress (Klaus and Tam 2009) were examined in six ways:

1. Linear enamel hypoplasias resulting from acute childhood metabolic stress that results in bands of decreased enamel thickness on teeth associated with infection, inadequate nutrition, and weanling diarrhea (Goodman and Rose 1991)
2. Porotic hyperostosis lesions in the cranial vault indicative of a range of chronic childhood stress including hemolytic and megaloblastic anemia often rooted in vitamin B12 deficiency (Walker et al. 2009)
3. Subadult growth velocity as estimated from the comparative length of the femur among cohorts of children at 2, 5, 10, and 12 years of age (Lovejoy, Russell, and Harrison 1990)
4. Terminal adult stature, as the final culmination of subadult growth, an overall measure of the relationship between economic status, environment, and growth (Bogin and Keep 1999)
5. Nonspecific periostosis, or chronic nonfatal bilateral infection of the tibiae that provides a useful baseline of immune status and community health (Larsen 1997)
6. Female fertility, a paleodemographic function related to female health and energetic status. The D30+/D5+ ratio estimates fertility as the relative proportion of skeletal individuals older than 30 years over the number of individuals older than 5 years (Buikstra, Konigsberg, and Bullington 1986).

Second, diet was reconstructed (Klaus and Tam 2010) through the study of linked pathological conditions of dental caries and antemortem tooth loss (AMTL) (Hillson 1996, 2008), the prevalence of which are linked to the consumption of carbohydrates. Third, inferences about physical activity (Klaus, Larsen, and Tam 2009) were derived from the prevalence of degenerative joint disease (DJD) in the principal load-bearing joint systems. This shed light on habitual movements of bodies (Hemphill 1999; Liverse et al. 2007). Fourth, documentation of traumatic injury included all forms of perimortem and antemortem bone fractures, sharp force, and projectile-related injury (Klaus 2008).

Skeletal ages were calculated using the summary age procedure (Lovejoy et al. 1985) and sex was estimated using the standard morphological variations of the os coxae and skull (Buikstra and Ubelaker 1994). Using SAS 9.1 software (SAS Institute Inc. 2003), age class–stratified prevalence differences were calculated between the comparative late pre-Hispanic sample and the Mórrope population using odds ratios, which Waldron (2007) argues avoids many of the mathematical pitfalls of crude prevalence comparisons. G-tests were best suited for analysis of oral health data (Sokal and Rohlf 1995).

## Results

### Overall Prevalence Changes

The comparison between late pre-Hispanic Lambayeque Valley Muchik skeletons and the colonial-era Muchik series from Mórrope reveals a number of statistically significant increases in systemic stress among the Muchik during the colonial era (Klaus and Tam 2009, Tables 3, 6, 7, 8, 9). The prevalence of porotic hyperostosis rose over 154 percent. Femoral growth velocity at ages 5, 10, and 12 fell significantly below the pre-Hispanic means. However, no statistically discernable changes to adult male and adult female stature were observed. Linear enamel hypoplasia prevalence decreased some 1.84 times, a finding intriguingly inconsistent with the other lines of health data. Among colonial adults, periosteal infection skyrocketed by 471 percent.

A statistically significant elevation of DJD in the joint systems of the upper limb is observed (Klaus, Larsen, and Tam 2009, Table 4): the shoulder joint in postcontact skeletons was affected by a 220 percent increase in DJD, prevalence in the elbow increased 277 percent, and prevalence in the wrist increased 560 percent. The only other significant change is found in the knee joint, where postcontact prevalence of DJD was elevated 360 percent. Colonial-era traumatic injury included examples of broken bones attributable to accidental rather than interpersonal causes. One exception is a colonial Muchik man who displays a well-healed left maxillary bone fracture consistent with a direct blow to the face. Quantitatively, crude prevalence of any kind of trauma in Mórrope is low (6/213 [or 6.19 percent] of the skeletons ≤ 50 percent complete) and does not significantly differ from the precontact population rate (Klaus 2008, Table 10.9).

G-tests reveal a broadly increased prevalence of dental caries and AMTL in the colonial era (Klaus and Tam 2010, Tables 3, 4, 5, 6), especially in the posterior teeth of older Muchik individuals.


## Discussion

There are two ways to measure effects of structural violence in bioarchae-ology. The best way may be through examination of prevalence differ-ences between members of archaeologically defined supra- and subor-dinate social formations. Yet there are no samples of Spaniard skeletons from Peru generally or the Lambayeque Valley Complex in particular. So a second approach can be used: analysis of a contextualized diachronic sequence of health outcomes. It is well established that in colonial Peru, native populations such as the Muchik were at the bottom of the social hierarchy and suffered the greatest effects of well-documented margin-alization, racism, ethnocentrism, religious intolerance, forced labor, and multiple forms of physical, psychosocial, and sexual violence (Andrien 2001; Guaman Poma de Ayala 1980 [1615]; Ramírez 1996; Saignes 1999; Silverblatt 1987) promoted by the implantation of a Western European colonial socioeconomic system. Mórrope appears to have been a place that was ripe for structural violence. The priest Rubiños y Andrade (1936 [1782]) depicts Mórrope as a marginalized Muchik community that was partially rooted in a pre-Hispanic past and was experiencing very stressful and mostly unsuccessful political and economic conflicts with neighbor-ing native communities, the Church, and secular authorities over sparse water, land, and mining rights. The priest, in his unfinished but somewhat detailed eighteenth-century manuscript, expresses very negative views of the Muchik, referring to them as "savages," "animals," and "ignorant brutes" that lacked dignity or humanity. He vaguely alludes to or describes isolated acts of physical violence against the Muchik in this document. Oral histories from nearby Túcume included descriptions of purported immolation of natives who did not convert to Christianity (Heyerdahl, Sandweiss, and Narváez 1995).

### Structural Violence, Labor, and Political Economy

Manipulation of native labor was a hallmark of the colonial program; slave labor and exploitation were embedded components of the political economy. Stern (1982, 138–139) argues that the insidious secret of exploitation in the Andes involved not so much physical force but the effect of a subtle, structurally violent coercion of dependence. Invented "pressures of necessity" drove people to volunteer themselves for exploitation; the colonial reality meant that the exploited needed their exploiters for subsistence and survival. Social organization, the legal system, and religion were thus used by colonial elites to coerce tribute and labor from the indigenous peasantry (Stern 1982). For example, the promise of wages for seasonal laborers (even though such wages were low) was enough for local workers to be attracted to work in rural landed estates so they could earn cash and supposedly buy their way out of the iniquitous and dreaded *mita,* or tribute labor tax system. Natives on the central coast in the 1620s were recruited by estate owners, offered a cash advance, a small plot of land, and shelter from *mita* service. However, excessive duties were exacted from their low pay, and many indigenous peoples fell into debt and became legally bound to their employers (Andrien 2001, 87): a poverty trap was set, and the colonizers made escape as difficult as possible.

Perhaps the most direct evidence of the presence and effects of structural violence in Mórrope is embodied by DJD patterning. While DJD is complex and highly multifactorial, intrinsic causes other than the "stress hypothesis" can be ruled out in this setting (Klaus, Larsen, and Tam 2009). The strenuous lifestyle of the Muchik in the colonial period involved elevated biomechanical loading, wear and tear, and injury to joint systems. Such evidence is consistent with local and regional sources that describe significant economic intensification. While it is unwise to infer specific habitual behaviors from patterns of DJD, a great deal of labor tax in Mórrope appears to have been extracted in the form of mining. Mórrope priests in particular exacted extensive tribute and ecclesiastical rents through mining of gypsum for nearly two centuries (Rubiños y Andrade 1936 [1782]). Its modern practice is associated with strenuous habitual use of the upper limbs, repetitive bending involving flexion of the torso and knees, and manual lifting of heavy loads. Such actions are not incompatible with the movements and motions inferred from DJD patterns (Klaus, Larsen, and Tam 2009). The prevalence of DJD in the colonial era highlights how indigenous bodies were employed in resource extraction and production for the benefit of a hegemonic proto-capitalist state. Qualitative analysis of DJD lesion severity in Mórrope suggests that for some individuals, labor continued to be extracted well after joints were physically destroyed. Such activity was quite unlikely to have been voluntary under these degenerative conditions.

### Structural Violence and Health within the Reducción

Worsened childhood and adult health among the Muchik may also be understood as a function of structural violence related to the physicality of the town itself. After Mórrope was established as a *reducción,* it experienced perhaps a 400 percent increase in population density. A central element of Spanish policy involved the creation of a nucleated, taxable indigenous population that could be controlled as a workforce, an illustration of the Foucauldian notion of the creation of docile physical bodies (Foucault 1979). By 1548, the population of the small village of Mórrope was 2,000 people or more. Sudden and sustained aggregation would have formed a novel microenvironment and new sets of biological stressors. In essence, a socioeconomic policy created a so-called disease reactor. A poor and resource-restricted indigenous labor pool was forced into a settlement pattern that featured substantially elevated risks of exposure to biological stress and disease, all exacerbated by the marginal ecology of the northwest Lambayeque region. Unsurprisingly, at least one early Lambayeque account describes an unnamed resettlement in "sickly" terrain where 200 native people rapidly perished (Ramírez 1996, 31).

In Mórrope, skeletal data conform well to the contextual signals of unhealthy living circumstances. Nonspecific periosteal inflammation among adults responded in a textbook fashion: its prevalence skyrocketed under conditions of elevated population density and social stress. A variety of ecological and social factors are now recognized as key to the etiologies of porotic hyperostosis, especially population nucleation. Aggregation increases exposure to a wide variety of vectors such as flies, rodents, dogs, bacteria (e.g., E. coli, Shigella, Salmonella); viruses (e.g., parvoviruses and rotaviruses); and parasites (e.g., helminths and protozoal or amoebic infections). All of these biological stressors lead to chronic gastrointestinal infection and less bioavailable iron, which elicits an anemic response in children (Kent 1986, 623). Gastrointestinal infection is also a well-established cause of disrupted long bone growth (Martorell et al. 1975), and the appearance of slower femoral growth velocity after age 2 may be linked to the introduction of a contaminated solid food diet following cessation of breastfeeding but was likely not enough to alter terminal adult stature.

Observed disruption followed the end of the critical period of 0–2 years when future adult stature is permanently stunted (Klaus and Tam 2009).

A decrease in LEH prevalence during the colonial era was puzzling especially in light of other sweeping declines in health. After eliminating various possibilities, the working hypothesis holds that acute childhood stress shifted from survivable metabolic insults during the pre-Hispanic era (hence producing a preponderance of stress survivors with LEH) to a pattern of high-mortality infection that killed Muchik children in Mórrope far more swiftly (Klaus and Tam 2009). That is, involuntary residence inside a disease reactor created ideal conditions for the transmission of acute infections. A larger proportion of children likely did not survive infections such as smallpox, mumps, rubella, scarlet fever, and influenza to form enamel defects. Decreased LEH prevalence in Mórrope in the postcontact period may represent a special case that underestimates morbidity (Cohen and Crane-Kramer 2007, 346).

*Dietary Change and Muchik Agency*

The creative adaptive strategies that had served this population and its ancestors for several millennia (Shimada 1994, 35–60) were overridden by the new political economy. Once the indigenous communities were moved out, Iberian colonists established industrial-scale sugar cane plantations in the fertile alluvium of the valley that was once used for food production (Ramírez-Horton 1974). Disease and the widespread slaughter of vast coastal llama and alpaca herds transpired such that by 1600 European livestock bred for the production of soap and leather no longer had to compete with coastal camelids for grazing land. Sugar cane and other cash crops consumed so much water that many Muchik, who by that point were living near the termini of irrigation networks, had little or no water for farming or drinking (Ramírez 1996). Livestock roamed freely into unfenced indigenous farms to graze. Swine had become notorious for uprooting and eating subsistence crops by the 1540s. Grazing animals also destroyed canals, filling them with so much silt and debris that many were abandoned (Netherly 1984), and the desert reclaimed fields. Food, especially meat, became more than a commoditized item as a cash-based economy emerged on the colonial north coast; it also emerged as an active expression of social status and power. In colonial Peru, people of higher status clearly enjoyed diets that included ample quantities of protein, carbohydrates, and other nutrients, while poorer native diets were a stark contrast (Burkholder and Johnson 1998, 219–223). As another element of the aforementioned poverty trap, indigenous Andeans including the Muchik found that expensive, higher quality, and nutritious foods were often out of their reach.

The increases in dental caries and AMTL prevalence among the people of Mórrope is most consistent with intensified exploitation of starchy cultigens in response to dietary shortfalls, lack of regular access to traditional food sources, and resettlement into resource-poor areas (Klaus and Tam 2010). Because of a neglectful laissez-faire attitude among the authorities in Mórrope, the local people appear to have been largely responsible for meeting their own subsistence needs. It is likely that the Muchik in Mórrope made the decision to rely on lower-quality but economical fallback foods. Rubiños y Andrade (1936 [1782]) described modest harvests of mostly starchy corn and beans produced by the people. This may have been part of a more pervasive and persistent strategy: German ethnologist H. H. Brüning portrayed late nineteenth-century Lambayeque Muchik foodways as dominated by starchy foods that were relatively cheap to produce, including maize, yucca, camote, and *cancha*. Brüning noted the centrality of *söd* and *chococha*—varieties of toasted, mashed, and cooked maize (Schaedel 1988, 115). This diet was a great contrast from the diversity of Prehispanic diets (Klaus 2008) and spelled doom for oral health.

In colonial Mórrope, increased exploitation of carbohydrates would have provided a less nutritious and diverse diet, but evidently it contributed enough supplementary bulk and energy to maintain the functional population depicted in ethnohistorical accounts. The skeletal markers of nutritional status discussed earlier are fully consistent with such a shift (Klaus and Tam 2009). A higher-carbohydrate diet would have been a synergistic contribution to the observed elevation of the prevalence of porotic hyperostosis, and the presence of phosphates and oxalates in many starchy foods would have inhibited bioabsorption of heme iron. Poorer nutrition is consistent with a depressed velocity of subadult growth among Mórrope children, and among Mórrope adults another well-documented factor driving chronic periosteal infection is nutritional stress that compromises immunocompetence (Larsen 1997). Fallback foods involved a distinct trade-off in Mórrope. Patterns of oral health help open a window on an effort to buffer against gross malnutrition, starvation, and extinction; such patterns seem closely linked to the combination of insufficient nutrition and the effects of living in a highly dense and unhealthy *reducción*.

## Health Changes among Women and Children

The worst health outcomes and the greatest magnitudes of change were concentrated among women and children in Mórrope. The magnitude of the increase of the prevalence of nonspecific chronic infection among colonial women was 2.31 times greater than that for men (Klaus 2008, 491). A calculation of differences in prevalence between pre-Hispanic and colonial women revealed that the women in Mórrope had elevated prevalence in all of the joint systems but one (the hip), and several of the increases were statistically significant (Klaus, Larsen, and Tam 2009, Table 7). The female fertility rate declined in Mórrope from a pre-Hispanic maximum of 0.4397 to 0.6028 during the colonial era (Klaus and Tam 2009, Table 9).

Native women occupied the lowest possible social strata in colonial Peru. The legal status of an adult indigenous woman was equivalent to that of a child, and many sources indicate that this created a maximum degree of social, economic, and sexual exploitation of these women (Graubart 2000; Silverblatt 1987). Conquest also altered native expressions of sex and gender roles in the Andes. Colonial systems eradicated widespread institutions of mutual labor obligations and gender complementarity. "Male" became associated with heavy labor and "female" became linked to food preparation, the domestic sphere, and childcare (Graubart 2000). Colonial Andean women did not have the labor mobility of their male counterparts and became a kind of captive labor force that was managed by authorities (Graubart 2000). Men often went outside the community to fulfill *mita* labor taxes, but women were often confined to a rigid domestic domain. Such sedentism was likely a factor in the greater prevalence of chronic infection for this group. Native Lambayeque women were also associated with the tasks of food production and cooking and probably spent many isolated hours processing cariogenic foods (including some in their mouths), which increased the risk of poor oral health (Walker, Sugiyama, and Chacon 1998).

Thus, as native women became producers in the Western sense, they may have become predisposed to worse oral health than native males, who may have consumed a less cariogenic or a more mixed diet when they were at home and when they were laboring away from home to meet tribute quotas. However, the indications of elevated female physical activity, the infection burden, and a lower quality diet all converge on one variable: fertility. Increased physiological stress along these three independent lines are known to place the female body in an energetic state below the level required to become pregnant or maintain pregnancy (Bogin 2001; Ellison 1994), which is consistent with the drop in relative fertility observed in Mórrope. Epidemic disease is often considered to be the "prime mover" behind historical depopulation, but structural violence experienced by women that resulted in a depressed birthrate must also be considered as a factor in colonial Peru's demographic instability (Cook 1981).

Children are probably the most revealing category of person in terms of the biological status of a population because of their ongoing ontogeny and developmental plasticity. Children may also be the most biologically sensitive to the presence and effects of structural violence. Subadult bioarchaeology can occupy a special role in studies of structural violence. As already discussed, political economy, social policy, and settlement patterns put Mórrope children at risk and contributed strongly to experiences of acute and chronic stress that included anemia and growth disruption. The stressful existence of Mórrope women probably affected the health of their fetuses in a way that predisposed them to diminished well-being later in life (Kuzawa 2008), but this is nearly impossible to observe in skeletal tissue. Children in colonial Peru were also laborers (Stern 1982). Examination of DJD prevalence by age cohort shows that younger Mórropanos had the greatest increases of DJD. Jurmain (1999) suggests that the earlier age of DJD onset is likely related to activity-induced joint injury in youth. Muchik children and adolescents in the colonial period may have engaged in more frequent and strenuous activities that began earlier in life than did their counterparts in the pre-Hispanic era.

## Conclusion

This chapter offers a basic outline of a theory of structural violence in bioarchaeology as a way to conceptualize how violence may manifest in human skeletons beyond broken bones and weapon wounds. In this case study, I examined three broad categories of skeletal evidence—about systemic biological stress, physical activity, and diet—in a diachronic sequence spanning the late pre-Hispanic to the late colonial eras in series of

Muchik individuals from the north coast of Peru. I embedded these data in local historical contexts and in an interpretive framework of structural violence. Native health appeared to have widely suffered as a result of the actions of a superordinate social entity, in this case the Spanish, whose policies created (1) highly unhealthy living conditions in an attempt to purge the autonomy of native peoples who were seen as racially or otherwise inferior; (2) a monopoly over all means of production that restricted access to nutritional resources and extracted the maximum amount of labor from native people by placing them in a structural poverty trap, and; (3) a political economy that usurped virtually all arable land for the production of noncomestible cash crops, which meant that the people were unable to feed themselves adequately. In essence, one group of people created a fundamentally exploitative and marginalizing socioeconomic order that harmed another group. The results were anemia, depression of growth, chronic infection, fertility decline, destruction of joints, dental decay, and loss of teeth. Women and children in Mórrope appear to have been particularly impacted by these changes. If the evidence and setting were modern, there would be no debate: this is a *sensu stricto* portrait of structural violence. It meets Walker's (2001) bioarchaeological criteria of intent, externality, and disregard for the safety and physical well-being of a client population.

This work contributes to growing theoretization of bioarchaeology (e.g., Knudson and Stojanowski 2008). If we are to further develop structural violence as a theme in bioarchaeological interpretation, caution is required. I wish to reiterate that the most appropriate use of structural violence theory is in bioarchaeological interpretation of the biological effects of inequality resulting from hierarchical social relationships. It is probably most applicable to historical and modern Western societies. Structural violence can be a useful model for work in historic bioarchaeology in the Americas (e.g., Blakey 2001; Grauer 1995; Larsen and Milner 1994; Sledzik and Sandberg 2002). Extension of structural violence theory to other social and temporal contexts is possible, but it is incumbent upon future researchers to make notions of cross-cultural and situational variations of the development, expressions, and effects of structural violence a major focus of attention. I also caution against simplistic portrayals of victims of structural violence as passive; the example of how the people of Mórrope creatively relied on fallback foods is a good example of indigenous agency, just as are multiple expressions of pre-Hispanic culture that were encoded in mortuary rituals at Mórrope (Klaus and Tam 2009, in press).

This chapter also aimed to broaden the definition of violence in bioarchaeology. The low prevalence of trauma in Mórrope might seem to lack information about violence or even suggest a fairly peaceful colonial setting. Upon closer examination, however, the bioarchaeological evidence tells a different story. In their efforts to integrate indigenous people into the colonial regime, the Spaniards did not often use violence that was forceful enough to break bones. Instead, they relied on more subtle and coercive means that resulted in physical suffering that can be measured in the health status of indigenous people. When properly contextualized, the prevalence of LEH, anemia, DJD, and infection reveal forms of violence that may have been far more destructive and harmful over the long term than a broken bone. Evidence of structural violence should help us reconsider how we think about the causes of violence (cf. Krieger 2001). We may look at how structural violence reveals sources of the uprisings, resistance, and millenarian movements that started in Peru beginning in the sixteenth century, such as the Taki Onqoy insurrection that unfolded during the 1560s (Stern 1982) and perhaps even more so with the later rebellions of Tomás Katari, Tupac Amaru II, and Tupac Katari into the eighteenth century (Andrien 2001). Skeletal trauma may represent the expression of forms of violence that were far more deeply situated and historically embedded than those we typically consider. Related to this last point, bioarchaeologists can and should address violence from the opposite perspective as well: what can skeletons reveal about the causes and conditions of the absence of violence? Our current epistemology of violence has led to powerful and compelling understandings, but trauma and structural violence represent but one end of a more complex spectrum of human behavior that includes conscious strategies that succeed in avoiding violence (e.g., Fry 2005) and may well involve empirically healthier societies. Ortner (1984) and Liebmann and Murphy (2011) observe that over recent decades something of a disciplinary myopia has set in, such that anthropological attention on conflict and violence has drawn our focus away from collaboration, nonviolence, and peace-making strategies. This is the larger context for the bioarchaeology of violence, and as we strive to attain a better balance between these dimensions of human behavior, bioarchaeology will attain an even more complete accounting of the origins, nature, and variations of violence in the past and in the present.

## Acknowledgments

The field research was generously supported by grants from the Wenner-Gren Foundation for Anthropological Research (Dissertation Field Research Grant No. 7302) and the Office of International Affairs, the Center for Latin American Studies, and the Department of Anthropology at The Ohio State University. I thank Deb Martin and Ryan Harrod for the invitation to participate in the 2010 AAPA symposium in Albuquerque. Ang DeMarco ably quantified the results of the review of violence literature in the pages of the *American Journal of Physical Anthropology* and the *International Journal of Osteoarchaeology*. I gratefully acknowledge the many contributions of Rosabella Alvarez-Calderón, Brian Burch, Steven Clark, Victor Curay, Carlos Elera, Gabriela Jakubowska, Cesar Maguiña, Emily Middleton, Raul Saavedra, Juan Carlos Santoyo, Paul Sciulli, Manuel Tam, Carlos Wester, and David Yells. Clark Larsen, Daniel Temple, and Rhonda Coolidge, and the editors of this volume kindly provided insightful critiques.

## References Cited

Alva, W., and C. B. Donnan
1993    *Royal Tombs of Sipán*. Fowler Museum of Cultural History, University of California, Los Angeles.
Andrien, K. J.
2001    *Andean Worlds: Indigenous History, Culture, and Consciousness under Spanish Rule, 1523–1825*. University of New Mexico Press, Albuquerque.
Barker, D. J. P.
1994    *Mothers, Babies, and Disease in Later Life*. BMJ Publishing, London.
Blakey, M. L.
2001    Bioarchaeology of the African Diaspora in the Americas: Its Origin and Scope. *Annual Review of Anthropology* 30: 387–422.
Bogin, B.
2001    *The Growth of Humanity*. Wiley-Liss, New York.
Bogin, B., and R. Keep
1999    Eight Thousand Years of Economic and Political History in Latin America Revealed by Anthropometry. *Annals of Human Biology* 26: 333–351.

Bourgois, P.

1995    *In Search of Respect: Selling Crack in El Barrio.* Cambridge University Press, Cambridge.

2010    Recognizing Invisible Violence: A Thirty-Year Ethnographic Retrospective. In *Global Health in Times of Violence,* edited by B. Rylko-Bauer, L. Whiteford, and P. Farmer. School for Advanced Research Press, Santa Fe, N.M.

Bourgois, P., and N. Scheper-Hughes

2004    Comment on "An Anthropology of Structural Violence." *Current Anthropology* 45: 317–318.

Bourgois, P., and J. Schonberg

2009    *Righteous Dopefiend.* University of California Press, Berkeley.

Bowser, F. P.

1974    *The African Slave in Colonial Peru.* Stanford University Press, Stanford, Calif.

Buikstra, J. E.

2006    A Historical Introduction. In *Bioarchaeology: The Contextual Analysis of Human Remains,* edited by J. E. Buikstra and L. A. Beck, pp. 7–25. Academic Press, Burlington.

Buikstra, J. E., J. W. Konigsberg, and J. Bullington

1986    Fertility and the Development of Agriculture in the Prehistoric Midwest. *American Antiquity* 51: 528–546.

Buikstra, J. E., and D. H. Ubelaker

1994    *Standards for Data Collection from Human Skeletal Remains.* Arkansas Archaeological Research Series no. 44. Arkansas Archaeological Survey, Fayetteville.

Burkholder, M. A., and L. Johnson

1998    *Colonial Latin America.*3rd ed. Oxford University Press, Oxford.

Chacon, R. J., and D. H. Dye (editors)

2007    *The Taking and Displaying of Human Body Parts as Trophies by Amerindians.* Springer Science and Business Media, New York.

Chacon, R. J., and R. G. Mendoza (editors)

2007a   *Latin American Indigenous Warfare and Ritual Violence.* University of Arizona Press, Tucson.

2007b   *North American Indigenous Warfare and Ritual Violence.* University of Arizona Press, Tucson.

Clark, G. A., N. R. Hall, G. J. Armelagos, G. A. Borkan, M. M. Panjabi, and F. T. Wetzel

1986    Poor Growth Prior to Early Childhood: Decreased Health and Life-Span in the Adult. *American Journal of Physical Anthropology* 70: 145–160.

Cleland, K. M., and I. Shimada

1998    Paleteade Potters: Technology, Production Sphere, and Sub-Culture in Ancient Peru. In *Andean Ceramics: Technology, Organization, and Approaches,* edited by I. Shimada, pp. 111–150. Museum Applied Science Center for Archaeology, University of Pennsylvania Museum of Archaeology and Anthropology, Philadelphia.

Cohen, M. N. (editor)
n.d.      *The Bioarchaeology of Hierarchy.*
Cohen, M. N., and G. M. M. Crane-Kramer
2007      Appendix. In *Ancient Health: Skeletal Indicators of Agricultural and Economic Intensification,* edited by M. N. Cohen and G. M. M. Crane-Kramer, pp. 345–347. University Press of Florida, Gainesville.
Cook, N. D.
1981      *Demographic Collapse, Indian Peru, 1520–1620.* Cambridge University Press, Cambridge.
Danforth, M. E.
1999      Nutrition and Politics in Prehistory. *Annual Review of Anthropology* 28: 1–25.
Eisenberg, L. E., and D. L. Hutchinson (editors)
1996      Special Issue on Violence. *International Journal of Osteoarchaeology* 6: 1–118.
Ellison, P. T.
1994      Advances in Human Reproductive Ecology. *Annual Review of Anthropology* 23: 255–275.
Farmer, P.
1999      Pathologies of Power: Rethinking Health and Human Rights. *American Journal of Public Health* 89(10): 1486–1496.
2003      *Pathologies of Power: Health, Human Rights, and the New War on the Poor.* University of California Press, Berkeley.
2004      An Anthropology of Structural Violence. *Current Anthropology* 45(3): 305–325.
2006      *AIDS and Accusation: Haiti and the Geography of Blame.* 2nd ed. University of California Press, Berkeley.
Farmer, P., M. Connors, and J. Simmons (editors)
1996      *Women, Poverty, and AIDS: Sex, Drugs, and Structural Violence.* Common Courage Press, Monroe.
Farmer, P., B. Nizeye, S. Stulac, and S. Ksehavjee
2006      Structural Violence and Clinical Medicine. *PLoS Medicine* 3: 1686–1691.
Fiorato, V., A. Boylston, and C. Knüsel
2000      *Blood Red Roses.* Oxbow Book Publishers, Oxford.
Foucault, M.
1979      *Discipline and Punish: The Birth of the Prison.* Translated by A. Sheridan. Vintage Books, New York.
Fry, D. P. (editor)
2005      *The Human Potential for Peace: An Anthropological Challenge to Assumptions about War and Violence.* Oxford University Press, New York.
Galloway, A. (editor)
1999      *Broken Bones: Anthropological Analysis of Blunt Force Trauma.* Charles C. Thomas, Springfield.
Galtung, J.
1969      Violence, Peace and Peace Research. *Journal of Peace Research* 6: 167–191.

1993    Kultuerlle Gewalt. *Der Burger im Staat* 43: 106–112.

Goodman, A. H., and G. J. Armelagos

1988    Childhood Stress and Decreased Longevity in a Prehistoric Population. *American Anthropologist* 90: 936–944.

Goodman, A. H., and T. L. Leatherman (editors)

1998    *Building a New Biocultural Synthesis: Political-Economic Perspectives on Human Biology.* University of Michigan Press, Ann Arbor.

Goodman, A. H., and D. L. Martin

2002    Reconstructing Health Profiles from Skeletal Remains. In *Backbone of History: Health and Nutrition in the Western Hemisphere,* edited by R. H. Steckel and J. C. Rose, pp. 11–60. Cambridge University Press, Cambridge.

Goodman, A. H., D. L. Martin, G. J. Armelagos, and G. Clark

1984    Indications of Stress from Bone and Teeth. In *Paleopathology at the Origins of Agriculture,* edited by M. N. Cohen and G. J. Armelagos, pp. 13–39. Academic Press, New York.

Goodman, A. H., and J. C. Rose

1991    Dental Enamel Hypoplasias as Indicators of Nutritional Status. In *Advances in Dental Anthropology,* edited by M. A. Kelley and C. S. Larsen. Wiley-Liss, New York.

Graubart, K. B.

2000    Weaving and the Construction of a Gender Division of Labor in Early Colonial Peru. *American Indian Quarterly* 24: 537–561.

Grauer, A. L. (editor)

1995    *Bodies of Evidence: Reconstructing History through Skeletal Analysis.* Wiley-Liss, New York.

Guaman Poma de Ayala, F.

1980 [1615]    *El Primer Nueva Corónica y Buen Gobierno.* Edited by J. V. Murra and R. Adorno. Translated by J. I. Urioste. Siglo Veintiuno, México, D.F.

Hemphill, B. E.

1999    Wear and Tear: Osteoarthritis as an Indicator of Mobility among Great Basin Hunter-Gatherers. In *Prehistoric Lifeways in the Great Basin Wetlands: Bioarchaeological Reconstruction and Interpretation,* edited by B. E. Hemphill and C. S. Larsen, pp. 241–289. University of Utah Press, Salt Lake City.

Heyerdahl, T., D. Sandweiss, and A. Narváez

1995    *Pyramids of Tucume: The Quest for Peru's Forgotten City.* Thames and Hudson, London.

Hillson, S. W.

1996    *Dental Anthropology.* Cambridge University Press, Cambridge.

2008    The Current State of Dental Decay. In *Technique and Application in Dental Anthropology,* edited by J. D. Irish and G. C. Nelson, pp. 111–135. Cambridge University Press, Cambridge.

Jurmain, R.

1999    *Stories from the Skeleton: Behavioral Reconstruction in Osteoarchaeology.* Gordon and Breach Publishers, Amsterdam.

Kent, S.
1986    The Influence of Sedentism and Aggregation on Porotic Hyperostosis and Anaemia: A Case Study. *Man,* n.s. 21: 605–636.

Kimmerle, E. H., and J. P. Baraybar (editors)
2008    *Skeletal Trauma: Identification of Injuries Resulting from Human Remains Abuse and Armed Conflict.* CRC Press, Boca Raton.

Klaus, H. D.
2008    Out of Light Came Darkness: Bioarchaeology of Mortuary Ritual, Health, and Ethnogenesis in the Lambayeque Valley Complex, North Coast Peru, A.D. 900–1750. Ph.D. dissertation, Ohio State University.

2012a    Hybrid Cultures . . . and Hybrid Peoples: Bioarchaeology of Genetic Change, Religious Architecture, and Burial Ritual in the Colonial Andes. In *Hybrid Material Culture: The Archaeology of Syncretism and Ethnogenesis,* edited by J. Card. Center for Archaeological Investigations, Southern Illinois University Carbondale.

2012b    La Persistencia de Identidad: Una Aproximación Inicial del Fenómeno Muchik el Lambayeque Prehispanico Tardio. In *Atras la Mascara de Oro: La Cultura Sicán,* edited by I. Shimada. Editorial del Congreso del Peru, Lima.

Klaus, H. D., C. Centurión, and M. Curo
2010    Bioarchaeology of Human Sacrifice: Violence, Identity, and the Evolution of Ritual Killing at Cerro Cerrillos, Peru. *Antiquity* 84(326): 1102–1122.

Klaus, H. D., C. S. Larsen, and M. E. Tam
2009    Economic Intensification and Degenerative Joint Disease: Life and Labor on the Postcontact North Coast of Peru. *American Journal of Physical Anthropology* 139: 204–221.

Klaus, H. D., and M. E. Tam
2009    Contact in the Andes: Bioarchaeology of Systemic Stress in Colonial Mórrope, Peru. *American Journal of Physical Anthropology* 138: 356–368.

2010    Oral Health and the Postcontact Adaptive Transition: A Contextual Reconstruction of Diet in Mórrope, Peru. *American Journal of Physical Anthropology* 141: 594–609.

In press  Requiem Aeternum? Archaeothanatology of Mortuary Ritual in Colonial Mórrope, North Coast of Peru. In *Between the Living and the Dead in the Andes,* edited by I. Shimada and J. Fitzsimmons. University of Arizona Press, Tucson.

Klaus, Haagen D., I. Shimada, K.-I. Shinoda, and S. Muno
n.d.    Middle Sicán Mortuary Archaeology, Skeletal Biology, and Genetic Structure: Human Biocultural Variation in an Ancient South American Complex Society. In *The Bioarchaeology of Hierarchy,* edited by M. N. Cohen.

Knudson, K. J., and C. M. Stojanowski
2008    New Directions in Bioarchaeology: Recent Contributions to the Study of Human Social Identities. *Journal of Archaeological Research* 16: 397–432.

Krieger, N.
2001    Theories for Social Epidemiology in the 21st Century. *International Journal of Epidemiology* 30: 668–677.

Kuzawa, C. W.

2008    The Developmental Origins of Adult Health: Intergenerational Inertia in Adaptation and Disease. In *Evolutionary Medicine and Health: New Perspectives,* edited by W. R. Trevathan, E. O. Smith and J. J. McKenna, pp. 325–349. Oxford University Press, Oxford.

Langley-Evans, S. C. (editor)

2004    *Fetal Nutrition and Adult Disease: Programming of Chronic Disease through Fetal Exposure to Undernutrition.* CABI Publishing, Oxfordshire.

Larsen, C. S.

1997    *Bioarchaeology: Interpreting Behavior from the Human Skeleton.* Cambridge University Press, Cambridge.

Larsen, C. S., and G. R. Milner (editors)

1994    *In the Wake of Contact: Biological Responses to Conquest.* Wiley-Liss, New York.

Larsen, C. S., and P. L. Walker

2010    Bioarchaeology: Health, Lifestyle, and Society in Recent Human Evolution. In *A Companion to Biological Anthropology,* edited by C. S. Larsen, pp. 379–394. Wiley-Blackwell, Chichister.

Liebman, Matthew, and Melissa S. Murphy

2011. Rethinking the Archaeology of "Rebels, Backsliders, and Idolaters." In *Enduring Conquests: Rethinking the Archaeology of Resistance to Spanish Colonialism in the Americas,* edited by Matthew Liebman and Melissa S. Murphy, pp. 3–18. School for Advanced Research Press, Santa Fe, N.M.

Liverse, A. R., A. W. Weber, V. I. Bazaliiski, O. I. Goriunova, and N. A. Savel'ev

2007    Osteoarthritis in Siberia's Cis-Baikal: Skeletal Indicators of Hunter-Gatherer Adaptation and Cultural Change. *American Journal of Physical Anthropology* 132: 1–16.

Lovejoy, C. O., R. S. Meindl, R. P. Mensforth, and T. J. Barton

1985    Multifactorial Determination of Skeletal Age at Death: A Method and Blind Tests of Its Accuracy. *American Journal of Physical Anthropology* 68: 1–14.

Lovejoy, C. O., K. F. Russell, and M. L. Harrison

1990    Long Bone Growth Velocity in the Libben Population. *American Journal of Human Biology* 2: 533–541.

Lovell, N. C.

1997    Trauma Analysis in Paleopathology. *Yearbook of Physical Anthropology* 40: 139–170.

Martin, D. L.

1997    Violence against Women in the La Plata River Valley (A.D. 1000–1300). In *Troubled Times: Violence and Warfare in the Past,* edited by D. L. Martin and D. W. Frayer, pp. 45–75. Gordon and Breach, Amsterdam.

Martin, D. L., and D. W. Frayer (editors)

1997    *Troubled Times: Violence and Warfare in the Past.* Gordon and Breach, Amsterdam.

Martorell, R., C. Yarborough, A. Lechtig, J. Habicht, and R. E. Klein
1975    Diarrheal Diseases and Growth Retardation in Preschool Guatemalan Children. *American Journal of Physical Anthropology* 43: 341–352.

McDade, T. W., and C. W. Kuzawa
2004    Fetal Programming of Immune Function. In *Fetal Nutrition and Adult Disease: Programming of Chronic Disease through Fetal Exposure to Undernutrition,* edited by S. C. Langley-Evans, pp. 311–332. CABI Publishing, Oxfordshire.

Melbye, J., and S. I. Fairgrieve
1994    A Massacre and Possible Cannibalism in the Canadian Arctic: New Evidence from the Saunaktuk Site (NgTn-1). *Arctic Anthropology* 31(2): 57–77.

Murphy, M. S., C. Gaither, E. Goycochea, J. W. Verano, and G. Cock
2010    Violence and Weapon-Related Trauma at Puruchuco-Huaquerones, Peru. *American Journal of Physical Anthropology* 142: 636–649.

Murphy M. S., E. Goyochea, and G. Cock
2010    Resistance, Persistence and Accommodation at Puruchucho-Huaquerones. In *Enduring Conquests: Rethinking the Archaeology of Resistance to Spanish Colonialism in the Americas,* edited by M. Liebmann and M. S. Murphy, pp. 57–76. School for Advanced Research Press, Santa Fe, N.M.

Netherly, P. J.
1984    The Management of Late Andean Irrigation Systems on the North Coast of Peru. *American Antiquity* 49: 227–254.

Ortner, D. J.
2003    *Identification of Pathological Conditions in Human Skeletal Remains.* Academic Press, London.

Ortner, S. B.
1984    Theory in Anthropology since the Sixties. *Comparative Studies in Society and History* 26: 126–166.

Palkovich, A. M.
1996    Historic Depopulation in the American Southwest: Issues of Interpretation and Context-Embedded Analyses. In *Bioarchaeology of Native American Adaptation in the Spanish Borderlands,* edited by B. J. Baker and L. Kealhofer, pp. 179–197. University Press of Florida, Gainesville.

Pillsbury, J.
2008    *Guide to Documentary Sources for Andean Studies, 1530–1900.* 3 vols. University of Oklahoma Press, Norman.

Powell, M. L.
1988    *Status and Health in Prehistory: A Case Study of the Moundville Chiefdom.* Smithsonian Institution Press, Washington, D.C.

1991    Ranked Status and Health in the Mississippian Chiefdom at Moundville. In *What Mean These Bones? Studies in Southeastern Bioarchaeology,* edited by M. L. Powell, P. S. Bridges, and A. M. W. Mires, pp. 22–51. University of Alabama Press, Tuscaloosa.

Quilter, J.
2007    El Brujo a Inicios de La Colonia/El Brujo at the Beginning of the Colonial Pe-
        riod. In *El Brujo: Huaca Cao, Centro Ceremonial Moche en el Valle de Chicama/
        Huaca Cao, a Moche Ceremonial Center in the Chicama Valley,* edited by E.
        Mujica, pp. 287–308. Fundación Wiese, Lima.
2010    Cultural Encounters at Magdalena de Cao Viejo in the Early Colonial Period. In
        *Enduring Conquests: Rethinking the Archaeology of Resistance to Spanish Colo-
        nialism in the Americas,* edited by M. Liebmann and M. S. Murphy, pp. 103–125.
        School for Advanced Research Press, Santa Fe, N.M.

Ramírez, S. E.
1986    *Provincial Patriarchs: Land Tenure and the Economies of Power in Colonial Peru.*
        University of New Mexico Press, Albuquerque.
1996    *The World Upside Down: Cross-Cultural Contact and Conflict in Sixteenth-Cen-
        tury Peru.* Stanford University Press, Stanford.

Ramírez-Horton, S. E.
1974    *The Sugar Estates of the Lambayeque Valley, 1670–1800: A Contribution to Peru-
        vian Agricultural History.* Land Tenure Center, Madison, Wis.

Rubiños y Andrade, J. M.
1936 [1782]    Noticia Previa por el Liz. D. Rubiños, y Andrade, Cura de Mórrope Año
        de 1782. *Revista Historica* 10: 291–363.

Saignes, T.
1999    The Colonial Condition in the Quechua-Ayamara Heartland (1570–1780). In
        *South America,* edited by F. Salomon and S. Schwartz, pp. 59–137. Vol. 3, Part
        2 of *The Cambridge History of the Native Peoples of the Americas.* Cambridge
        University Press, Cambridge.

SAS Institute Inc.
2003    SAS 9.1. SAS Institute Inc., Cary, N.C.

Schaedel, R. P.
1988    *La Ethnografia Muchik en las Fotografias de H. Brüning 1886–1925.* COFIDE,
        Lima.
1992    The Archaeology of the Spanish Colonial Experience in South America. *Antiq-
        uity* 66: 214–242.

Schell, L. M.
1997    Culture as a Stressor: A Revised Model of Biocultural Interaction. *American
        Journal of Physical Anthropology* 102: 67–77.

Scheper-Hughes, N.
1992    *Death without Weeping: The Violence of Everyday Life in Brazil.* University of
        California Press, Berkeley.

Shimada, I.
1994    *Pampa Grande and the Mochica Culture.* University of Texas Press, Austin.
2000    The Late Prehispanic Coastal Societies. In *The Inca World: The Development
        of Pre-Columbian Peru, A.D. 1000–1534,* edited by L. Laurencich Minelli, pp.
        49–110. University of Oklahoma Press, Norman.

2012    *Atras la Mascara de Oro: La Cultura Sicán.* Editorial del Congreso del Peru, Lima.

Silverblatt, I.

1987    *Moon, Sun, and Witches: Gender Ideologies and Class in Colonial Peru.* Princeton University Press, Princeton.

Sledzik, P. S., and L. G. Sandberg

2002    The Effects of Nineteenth-Century Military Service on Health. In *The Backbone of History: Health and Nutrition in the Western Hemisphere,* edited by R. H. Steckel and J. C. Rose, pp. 185–207. Cambridge University Press, Cambridge.

Sokal, R. R., and F. J. Rohlf

1995    *The Principles and Practice of Statistics in Biological Research.* 3rd ed. Freeman and Company, New York.

Steadman, D. W.

2008    Warfare Related Trauma at Orendorf, a Middle Mississippian Site in West-Central Illinois. *American Journal of Physical Anthropology* 136(1): 51–64.

2009    *Hard Evidence: Case Studies in Forensic Anthropology.* 2nd ed. Pearson Education, Inc., Upper Saddle River.

Stern, S. J.

1982    *Peru's Indian Peoples and the Challenge of Spanish Conquest: Huamanga to 1640.* University of Wisconsin Press, Madison.

Verano, J. W.

2008    Trophy Head-Taking and Human Sacrifice in Andean South America. In *The Handbook of South American Archaeology,* edited by H. Silverman and W. H. Isabell, pp. 1047–1060. Springer, New York.

Waldron, T.

2007    *Paleoepidemiology: The Measure of Disease in the Human Past.* Left Coast Press, Walnut Creek.

Walker, P. L.

2001    A Bioarchaeological Perspective on the History of Violence. *Annual Review of Anthropology* 30: 573–596.

Walker, P. L., R. R. Bathurst, R. Richman, T. Gjerdrum, and V. A. Andrushko

2009    The Causes of Porotic Hyperstosis and Cribra Orbitalia: A Reappraisal of the Iron-Deficiency-Anemia Hypothesis. *American Journal of Physical Anthropology* 139: 109–125.

Walker, P. L., L. S. Sugiyama, and R. J. Chacon

1998    Diet, Dental Health, and Cultural Change among Recently Contacted South American Indian Hunter-Horticulturists. In *Human Dental Development, Morphology, and Pathology: A Tribute to Albert A. Dahlberg,* edited by J. R. Lukacs, pp. 355–386. University of Oregon Anthropological Papers no. 54. Department of Anthropology, University of Oregon, Eugene.

Wernke, S. A.

2007    Analogy or Erasure? Dialectics of Religious Transformation in the Early Doctrinas of the Colca Valley, Peru. *International Journal of Historical Archaeology* 11: 152–182.

2010     Convergences: Producing Early Colonial Hybridity at a *Doctrina* in Highland Peru. In *Enduring Conquests: Rethinking the Archaeology of Resistance to Spanish Colonialism in the Americas*, edited by Matthew Liebmann and Melissa S. Murphy, pp. 77–101. School for Advanced Research Press, Santa Fe, N.M.

Wintour, E. M., and J. A. Owen (editors)
2006     *Early Life Origins of Health and Disease.* Springer, New York.

Wolf, E. R.
1982     *Europe and the People without History.* University of California Press, Berkeley.

# 3

# Deciphering Violence in Past Societies

## Ethnography and the Interpretation of Archaeological Populations

RYAN P. HARROD, PIERRE LIÉNARD, AND DEBRA L. MARTIN

## Introduction

Research on violence and warfare has typically focused on modern populations and on ancient civilizations for which there are written records.
However, a growing body of research focuses on interpersonal, collective,
and organized violence among prestate and precontact societies. Research
on violence in the past includes ethnographic work (Chagnon 1974; Evans-
Pritchard 1968; Schmidt and Schröder 2001), historic and ethnohistorical
accounts (Chacon and Mendoza 2007a, 2007b; Ferguson and Whitehead
1992; Gat 2006; Whitehead 2004), archaeological reconstructions (Arkush
and Allen 2006; Haas 1990; Kelly 2000), and bioarchaeological analysis of
skeletal remains (Bridges, Jacobi, and Powell 2000; Jurmain 1991; Lambert
1994, 2007; Lambert and Walker 1991; Liston and Baker 1996; Martin and
Frayer 1997; Milner 1999; Milner, Anderson, and Smith 1991; Owsley and
Jantz 1994; Walker 1989; Walker 2001).

Violence has been documented from earliest times into the present,
and there is no question that it has been a fundamental part of human
existence. However, the lack of records for many prestate populations and
the reliance on material culture in reconstructing such groups makes it
challenging to investigate the motivation and cultural reasons behind violent interactions. Furthermore, the range of variability across cultures and

through time suggests that there is a lot yet to be learned about the role violence plays in human groups.

## Bioarchaeological Approaches to Violence

Bioarchaeology is especially suited to understanding violent encounters because it often employs a biocultural approach and violence is a biological and cultural phenomenon (Walker 2001). Unlike archaeology that relies on indirect evidence of violence (e.g., defensive architecture and weapon-like artifacts), human remains provide direct evidence about the causes and consequences of violence for individuals through temporal and spatial variability in mortality and morbidity. Thus, analysis of human remains in conjunction with archaeological site data is a better method of identifying the presence of violence in the past.

The presence of trauma by itself provides no insight into why and how violence occurs. For example, it is possible that some of the trauma on human remains may be the result of an accident or an occupational hazard. Violent encounters, accidents, and occupational hazards may result in similar injuries that are hard difficult to distinguish osteologically (Cybulski 1992; Grauer and Roberts 1996; Judd 2002; Judd and Roberts 1999; Kilgore, Jurmain, and Van Gerven 1997; Novak, Allen, and Bench 2007).

In intragroup conflict, nonlethal violence is similar to lethal violence in that the desired outcome of confrontations is to gain status or resources through the submission of the other individual(s). However, small-scale conflict is typically nonlethal and can be repetitive. Victims often fall prey to numerous violent encounters over the course of a lifetime. This pattern of domination and exploitation is a successful strategy for the assailing party; they are able to secure and, more importantly, maintain access to resources (Maschner and Reedy-Maschner 1998).

The challenge of analyzing nonlethal trauma in bioarchaeology is that although the methodology for identifying healed trauma in archaeological populations is well established, the interpretation of the evidence is complicated by many factors. Nonlethal trauma can be an indicator of intragroup conflict (e.g., one-on-one combat or domestic abuse). It can also provide insight into a reoccurring exposure to violence over an individual's lifespan (i.e., recidivistic injuries).

Bioarchaeologists seek to use multiple lines of evidence that help confirm or reject various hypotheses about the causes and consequences of violence. These lines of evidence come largely from the remains them-selves, but they also come from a wide array of contextual information obtained from the archaeological site. One underdeveloped approach that could be extremely useful in bioarchaeological interpretations is the use of ethnographic analogy.

## Ethnography and Bioarchaeology

Ethnography is an important potential source of information for bioar-chaeologists. Ethnography uses real-time observations and can obtain a large body of information about things such as ideology, political struc-ture, economic base, subsistence, kinship, and health. Thus, ethnography provides a set of models to be used to reverse-engineer the osteological and forensic evidence and to refine as well as test the claims made about systemic, structural, or random causes of that evidence (Halbmayer 2001).

Gould and Watson (1982), who promote the incorporation of ethnog-raphers' work in archaeological interpretation (i.e., ethnoarchaeology), suggest two approaches: (1) the direct historical approach, which favors the transfer of interpretive models between historically linked extant and past cultures that are set in the same ecological niche and share a com-parable technology; and (2) the comparative approach, which promotes the observation of specific behavioral, symbolic, and political patterns observable in extant cultures in order to orient the scientific inferences made about past societies without the qualification that they be related temporally or spatially. In this research we selected the comparative ap-proach because our intent is to provide a new method for interpreting violence in the past across many groups rather than to understand violent interactions in one particular group.

Ethnographic analogy is useful for research in bioarchaeology because it allows researchers to move beyond understanding the mechanisms of injury and attempts to identify behavior, ideology, and motivations for vi-olent encounters. Walker and colleagues (1998, 381) have coined the term "ethnobioarchaeology," which they define as "studies in which ethno-graphic and physical anthropological data are collected as part of collab-orative efforts to answer ethnographic and bioarchaeological questions."

Ethnobioarchaeology provides information that typically is unavail-able to bioarchaeologists, who must rely primarily on the archaeo-logical context and human remains. They generally do not have direct documentation of daily patterns of conflict. The primary focus of this study was to provide a new way to identify and interpret the causes and underlying factors that contribute to violence among existing populations as a model for interpreting signatures of interpersonal and intergroup violence found on skeletal remains. Of particular interest are the signatures of nonlethal violence. Our research was designed to provide data on (1) who is at risk for repeated violent interactions, (2) how individuals accrue trauma and wounds throughout the course of their lifetime, and (3) the relationship between injuries and other variables such as age, sex, status, and health problems.

## Case Study: Turkana

We used the ethnobioarchaeological approach in a research project involving the documenting of cases of healed trauma among a population sample from a Turkana herding community in northwest Kenya. The research protocol was designed to provide data on subgroups at risk for being subjected to repeated violence. Special attention was given to the accumulation of traumatic markers and other wounds throughout the course of the individual's lifetime and to the relationship between types of injuries and common health problems. In this sense, the study provides information that is typically unavailable to bioarchaeologists. The overall objective of the study was to uncover the systemic causes of nonlethal violence among the Turkana.

Our data on nonlethal violence and accidental trauma was collected from 38 individuals: 8 pre-adult teenagers (up to the age of 18) and 30 adults (aged 20 to 70). A questionnaire and a body diagram for mapping wounds and other evidence of trauma were used. The questionnaire included sixty queries about the participant's life and reproductive history, general health, self-reported stress levels (occupational or otherwise), nutrition and diet, and traumatic event history. The participants were asked to indicate on the body diagram the location of all their healed wounds, broken bones, and traces of other injuries. Particular attention was paid to wounds and injuries to the head. Scars and soft tissue damage were documented as well.

## Turkana

The polygynous and pastoralist Turkana society of Eastern Africa (Gulliver 1951; Lamphear 1988) is a good model for investigating the specific patterns of violence associated with particular environmental, social, and economic conditions. Among pastoralists, the violence associated with frequent interethnic raiding and cattle rustling and with domestic life has been extensively documented (Belay, Beyene, and Manig 2005; Evans-Pritchard 1940; Fleisher 2000; Gray et al. 2003; Gunasekaran 2007; Heald 2000; Hendrickson, Mearns, and Armon 1996; Leslie and Little 1999; Lindner 1981; McCabe 2004; Mulder 1999; Tornay 1993, 2001). Adapting to the significant variations in access to resources and the security concerns of the areas where they dwell, the herding Turkana populations are extremely mobile. That lifestyle results in an increased risk of specific occupational stress and hazards. It also has an important health cost (Odegi-Awuondo 1990; Pike 2004).

The male ethos among the Turkana is extremely competitive (Koji 1990; Liénard and Anselmo 2004). In societies where intensive male competition is promoted there are higher rates of violence within families (e.g., domestic abuse) and within the larger kin groups (Wilson and Daly 1995). Indeed, Turkana child-rearing practices are harsh, and interpersonal violence between husbands and wives and between co-wives is frequent. Males, even when they belong to the same kin group, typically engage in agonistic relations, and the recurrence of internal low-level violence in social groups is high. Finally, Turkana males regularly engage in cattle rustling and retaliation raids against neighboring ethnic groups.

Stealing resources is not the only purpose of raiding. Neighboring ethnic groups tend to strike preemptively in order to diminish the risk of being attacked or to retaliate once they are in a position to do so after a previous aggression. The Turkana, as much as the surrounding populations of the area, must therefore be in a constant state of readiness to rebuff an aggression or to launch a punitive or preemptive raid.

This pattern of raiding and retaliation is especially important for bioarchaeologists working on ancient Native American societies because it mimics aspects of the interethnic relations found in North America prior to colonization. For instance, Maschner and Reedy-Maschner (1998) have acknowledged the prevalence and repetitive nature of raiding in North America (for the Northwest Coast specifically).

## Overall Findings: Injury and Trauma in the Sample Population

What are the main causes of typical nonlethal violence among the Turkana? Our research attempts to provide an answer to that question. Our study specifically focused on collecting data about subgroups at risk of repeated violence, about the accumulation of trauma and wounds throughout the course of a lifetime, and about injury-associated health problems. Special attention was paid to injury recidivism, a relatively well-known concept in the forensic and clinical literature (Caufeild et al. 2004; Hedges et al. 1995). The theory is that an individual who has been the victim of violence is more likely than the general population to experience it again.

The vast majority of the injuries sustained by the participants in the Turkana population were either accidental or occupational or were linked to violent acts. Accidental and occupational trauma include slips and falls, head injuries linked to falling objects, and livestock-related injuries.

The injuries related to violent acts fall into two broad categories: interpersonal conflict and raids. The former includes trauma sustained during fights with rivals, spouses, and co-wives or as the result of being disciplined by parents, siblings, and other members of the family or the community. The second category includes wounds and injuries contracted during raids against or by enemy tribes. Table 3.1 presents the trauma frequencies by categories (accident or occupational/aggression or violence). Gender (male/female) has no statistically significant effect on the frequency of accident-related trauma versus violence-related trauma ($p = 0.399$ using Fisher's exact [two-tailed] test). Because of the low rate of trauma and lack of exposure to violence in the adolescent subset of the sample population, the youngest participants were excluded from all subsequent analysis.

The adult males and females of our sample population had accumulated a fair amount of injury over their lifetimes (Table 3.2). Some of the nonlethal injuries were sustained as a result of accidents. Most females (85 percent) had healed injuries and occupational trauma related to herding and foraging activities. Sixty-eight percent of the males had evidence of occupational trauma and accidental injuries. Both sexes had a high rate of exposure to violence-related trauma: 71 percent of the females and 81 percent of the males presented evidence of violence-related trauma and injuries.

Table 3.1. Percent of adult females, adult males, and adolescents in a sample population of Turkana in northwest Kenya who sustained traumatic injuries by type of injury

| Cause of injury | Adult Females (N = 14) | Adult Males (N = 16) | Adolescents (N = 8) | Total (N = 38) |
|---|---|---|---|---|
| Accidental/occupational | 85.7 | 68.8 | 37.5 | 68.4 |
| Violence/interpersonal conflict | 71.4 | 81.3 | 25.0 | 65.8 |

Table 3.2. Percent of female and male adults in Turkana sample who sustained cranial and postcranial trauma

| Type of trauma | Adult Females (N = 14) | Adult Males (N = 16) | Total (N = 30) |
|---|---|---|---|
| Cranial | 64.3 | 68.8 | 66.7 |
| Postcranial | 21.4 | 43.8 | 33.3 |

Violence-Related Trauma

Data from body maps provided information on patterns of body wounds. The majority of traumatic wounds were located on the head. Sixty-five percent of both males and females had at least one cranial trauma. The head injuries ranged in severity from the presence of a scar to a deep depression. In contrast to head injuries, only 44 percent of males and 21 percent of females had postcranial traumas directly related to violence. The difference between cranial/postcranial trauma is statistically significant for females ($p = 0.054$ using Fisher's exact [two-tailed] test) but not for males ($p = 0.285$ using Fisher's exact [two-tailed] test).

In a male-dominated polygynous society, females are more likely to be systematically subjected to beatings that involve the head. This may explain the high prevalence of head wounds in females in the sample population. The cranial/postcranial violence-related injury ratio among females is strongly indicative of a situation that females typically face in male-dominated societies. The clinical and forensic literature suggests that the "logic" behind this high rate of cranial injury is that blows to the head serve as an effective way of quickly subduing an individual (Hadjizacharia et al. 2009; Shillingford 2001). Perpetrators choose trauma to

Table 3.3. Severity of injury, cranial region of injury, weapons used, and gender of victims who had cranial depression fractures in Turkana sample

| Injury Severity | Cranial Region | Weapon/Object | Gender |
|---|---|---|---|
| Deep depression | Not specified | Fighting stick | Male |
|  | Left side | Fighting stick |  |
|  | Left side | Wrist knife |  |
|  | Front | Bottle |  |
| Shallow depression | Not specified | Stone | Female |
|  | Right side | Cup |  |
|  | Front/left side | Stone |  |
|  | Front | Herding stick |  |
| Shallow depression | Back | Stone | Male |
|  | Front | Unidentified bone |  |
|  | Front/left side | Herding stick |  |
|  | Front | Herding stick |  |

the head and face because these wounds bleed easier and are more visible (Walker 1997, 160). Thus, cranial trauma serves as an effective means of marking a victim and establishing the perpetrator's dominance.

In societies such as the Turkana, males are likely to exhibit a more balanced ratio between cranial and postcranial violence-related injuries than females because their injuries are more likely to be associated with hand-to-hand combat situations in both individual conflicts and in warfare. An interesting finding supports this last claim (see Table 3.3). Males have more deep cranial depression fractures than females. These fractures are the result of the typical weapons used in dueling and close combat situations: fighting sticks and metal wrist knives. Fifty percent of the interviewed males affirm that they often fight, and 75 percent of those who do had deep head wounds. Of the males who did not report fighting often, most still had significant head wounds, hinting at the overall dangerous lifestyle of Turkana male warriors. In contrast, females had more evidence of shallow depression fractures inflicted by expedient weapons such as stones, cups and other utensils, or herding sticks.

Corporal Punishment, Domestic Abuse, Injury Recidivism, and Head Trauma

Research on injury recidivism has repeatedly shown that there is a strong correlation between rate of exposure to violence as a child and rate of exposure as an adult. Worldwide clinical data demonstrates that individuals who suffer significant injury are at a greater risk of future injuries (Blackmer and Marshall 1999; Caufeild et al. 2004; Hedges et al. 1995; Max et al. 2004; Roncadin et al. 2004; Wrightson, McGinn, and Gronwall 1995). One line of reasoning for why this pattern exists is that individuals who have survived a beating may have behavioral changes related to traumatic brain injury. A number of factors other than traumatic brain injury could explain the increased risk of violence. Personality disorders may hinder proper social interactions or social learning (Bandura 1973; Björkqvist 1997; Björkqvist and Österman 1992). A final component may be that an increased propensity for violence may be an adaptive response to particular environmental conditions (Buss and Todd 1997).

Male and female adults from the sample population were asked how frequently they had been beaten as children. About half of the females (57 percent) reported that they been subjected to systematic corporal punishment as children. In contrast, 81 percent of the males reported corporal punishment as children. This suggests a harsher disciplinary regime for boys than for girls and that boys were either more unruly than girls or that parents had little tolerance for the typical misbehavior of boys.

Among the individuals with a history of corporal punishment, 87 percent of the females and 69 percent of the males suffered head injuries as adults. In contrast, of the 43 percent of women who did not report having been subjected to systematic corporal punishment as children, 33 percent had cranial injuries as adults. These preliminary findings support injury recidivism on the female side of the sample population but not on the male side. Indeed, even if they were not beaten as children, males sustained a great amount of head traumas in adulthood (Tables 3.4a and 3.4b).

The difference in rates of cranial trauma between women who were exposed to systematic corporal punishment in childhood and those who were not is not statistically significant ($p = 0.091$ using Fisher's exact [two-tailed] test). One female in the sample was problematic. She first claimed that she had not been beaten systematically as a child, then qualified her response by saying that, yes, she had been subjected to corporal punishment but sparsely and only lightly. When we excluded this female from the sample because of this inconsistency, the difference in rates of cranial trauma between women exposed or not exposed to systematic corporal punishment in childhood became significant ($p = 0.021$ using Fisher's

Table 3.4a. Percent of adult females and adult males in Turkana sample who suffered corporal punishment in childhood and percent of that subgroup who later sustained cranial trauma

|  | Adult Females | Adult Males |
|---|---|---|
| Corporal punishment | 57.1 (8 of 14) | 81.3 (13 of 16) |
| Cranial trauma | 87.5 (7 of 8) | 69.2 (9 of 13) |

Table 3.4b. Percent of adult females and adult males in Turkana sample who did not suffer corporal punishment in childhood and percent of that subgroup who later sustained cranial trauma

|  | Adult Females | Adult Males |
|---|---|---|
| No corporal punishment | 42.9 (6 of 14) | 33.3 (2 of 6) |
| Cranial trauma | 18.7 (3 of 16) | 66.7 (2 of 3) |

exact [two-tailed] test). This result again lends support to the concept of injury recidivism and the use of head-bashing/beating to control members of dominated social groups (Tables 3.4a and 3.4b).

Domestic violence is typically underreported. In fact, less than 30 percent of the women from the sample reported that they had been systematically beaten by a spouse. However, of the women who reported such systematic abuse, 50 percent have cranial trauma. Women were also asked how often they had been beaten by co-wives. Remarkably, the same proportion of women who reported being beaten by husbands reported being beaten by co-wives. Of those who reported that specific form of abuse, one-third had cranial trauma (Table 3.5).

Of the individuals who sustained accidental injuries, approximately 74 percent had cranial injuries, and 70 percent of the individuals who sustained postcranial injuries had cranial injuries (Table 3.6). These trends could support the idea that cranial trauma may predispose people to other types of trauma. Well-documented sequelae linked to head trauma include cognitive, motor, and speech problems; migraines and dizziness; poor concentration; emotional instability; increased aggressiveness and antisocial behavior; and amnesia (Centers for Disease Control 2010; Cohen et al. 1999; Leon-Carrion and Ramos 2003; Brain Injury Association of Wyoming 2004). Through those lingering neurological and behavioral consequences, cranial trauma could have a decisive impact

Table 3.5. Percent of women in Turkana sample who suffered domestic abuse at the hands of husbands and co-wives and percent of those subgroups who also sustained cranial trauma

| Domestic Abuse | Domestic Abuse and Cranial Trauma |
| --- | --- |
| Husband-Wife | Husband-Wife |
| 28.6 (4 of 14) | 50 (2 of 4) |
| Co-wife | Co-wife |
| 21.4 (3 of 14) | 33.3 (1of 3) |

Table 3.6. Trauma co-occurrence in Turkana sample

| | Accidental / Cranial (%) | Postcranial / Cranial (%) |
| --- | --- | --- |
| Female (14) | 75.0 (9/12) | 66.7 (2/3) |
| Male (16) | 72.7 (8/11) | 45.5 (5/7) |
| Total (30) | 73.9 (17/23) | 70 (7/10) |

on an individual's functioning in society, eventually predisposing him/ her to more aggression and more accidents (Bazarian and Atabaki 2001; Glaesser et al. 2004; Hwang et al. 2008; Stern 2004; Zhang, Yang, and King 2004). Specific questions about the exact sequences of injuries and traumas were not part of the study, so there is no way to ascertain for the sample population if head traumas are indeed likely to predispose individuals to more injuries.

## Results and Discussion

For individuals living in prestate societies, everyday life involves a fair amount of accidental trauma. Most of it, though, affects only the soft tissue, and thus bioarchaeologists likely will not see these kinds of stresses and injuries on the human remains.

Injuries related to violence seem to be more severe and often result in trauma that affects the bone. Among both males and females in the Turkana sample there seems to be more trauma on the cranium (i.e., depression fractures) than on the postcranial skeleton related to violent interactions. Females seem to experience injury recidivism; they are likely to be influenced by an early exposure to violence during childhood. Females also sustain many injuries over a lifetime. Some females, however, have a much lower risk of trauma from any kind of aggressive violence. For males, there did not appear to be a strong relationship between childhood violence and adult injury, but there was a strong pattern of co-occurrence of injuries, an indication of repeated injuries. It is theorized that in this context, men are more violent and receive more injuries than females because of the nature of life in a raiding society.

Females (85.7 percent) are more likely than males (68.8 percent) to report accidental or occupational trauma. Plausibly this could be explained by the typical activities of women, which include milking big animals, collecting and carrying firewood, and constructing huts, shades, and kraals. Women use a wide range of potentially dangerous tools in these activities.

Among women, 21.4 percent reported injuries to the body and 64.3 percent reported injuries to the head linked to violence. Among men, 43.8 percent reported injuries to the body and 68.8 percent reported injuries to the head linked to violence. Over 80 percent of men (81.3 percent) were subjected to corporal punishment as children, and of that group 76.9 percent suffered additional injuries as adults. Similarly, about half of the female sample (57 percent) reported childhood corporal punishment, and among this group, 87.5 percent reported having suffered additional injuries as adults. These tantalizing preliminary results suggest a pattern of injury recidivism, but much more research into this is necessary.

These data demonstrate a number of cautionary points for bioarchaeologists. These include the need to avoid overinterpreting trauma as related to aggression, the fact that injury recidivism is sometimes underreported, and the need for a more nuanced approach to understanding sex differences in patterns of trauma. Our sample provides extensive evidence of trauma related to accidents and to occupation. If such prevalence is confirmed in populations living in nonmodern, nonindustrial environments, bioarchaeologists working on ancient societies should be wary of overinterpreting evidence of trauma as related to aggression. Our sample population also made clear that gender is an important factor when interpreting evidence of trauma on human remains. Furthermore, bioarchaeologists should use a more nuanced approach to analyzing trauma across age and sex categories and should place more emphasis on life history.

Violence is almost never a onetime event in a person's life. Analyzing nonlethal violence is one way to get at the complex biocultural processes that operate within social groups. In the case of the Turkana, violence is clearly linked to the nature of kinship, material culture, marriage patterns, housing, and status and wealth. An understanding of nonlethal violence should be attempted because it is the combination of these social factors that will explain how culturally sanctioned violence operates.

## Conclusion

The implication of this ethnobioarchaeological study is that working with living individuals can offer insight into the interpretation of trauma on skeletal remains of archaeological populations. Bioarchaeologists should report, analyze, and interpret the co-occurrence of body wounds associated with nonlethal trauma. Furthermore, bioarchaeologists should analyze traumas with an emphasis on life history trajectories. Finally, it is crucial that evidence of nonlethal violence be analyzed within broader inquiries about the use of lethal violence.

Much in the same way that ethnoarchaeologists gain insights into past tool use and typical daily activities by observing surviving populations, bioarchaeologists could become better informed about the nature of traumatic injury in past populations by collaborating with ethnographers who are working with modern societies still engaged in raiding and warfare.

## References Cited

Arkush, E. N., and M. W. Allen (editors)
2006    *The Archaeology of Warfare: Prehistories of Raiding and Conquest.* University Press of Florida, Gainesville.
Bandura, A.
1973    *Aggression: A Social Learning Process.* Prentice-Hall, Englewood Cliffs, N.J.
Bazarian, J. J., and S. Atabaki
2001    Predicting Postconcussion Syndrome after Minor Traumatic Brain Injury. *Academic Emergency Medicine* 8(8): 788–795.
Belay, K., F. Beyene, and W. Manig
2005    Coping with Drought among Pastoral and Agro-pastoral Communities in Eastern Ethiopia. *Journal of Rural Development* 28: 185–210.
Björkqvist, K.
1997    The Inevitability of Conflict, But Not of Violence: Theoretical Considerations on Conflict and Aggression. In *Cultural Variation in Conflict Resolution: Alternatives to Violence*, edited by D. P. Fry and K. Björkqvist, pp. 25–36. Lawrence Erlbaum Associates, Mahwah, N.J.
Björkqvist, K., and K. Österman
1992    Parental Influence on Children's Self-Estimated Aggressiveness. *Aggressive Behavior* 18: 411–423.

Blackmer, J., and S. C. Marshall
1999    A Comparison of Traumatic Brain Injury in the Saskatchewan Native North American and Non-Native North American Populations. *Brain Injury* 13(8): 627–635.

Brain Injury Association of Wyoming
2004    *Study of Undiagnosed Brain Injuries in Wyoming's Prison Population.* Edited by A. T. Force. Wyoming Department of Health Division Developmental Disabilities, Casper.

Bridges, P. S., K. P. Jacobi, and M. L. Powell
2000    Warfare-Related Trauma in the Late Prehistory of Alabama. In *Bioarchaeological Studies in the Age of Agriculture: A View from the Southeast,* edited by P. M. Lambert, pp. 35–62. University of Alabama Press, Tuscaloosa.

Buss, D. M., and K. Todd
1997    Human Aggression in Evolutionary Psychological Perspective. *Clinical Psychology Review* 17(6): 605–619.

Caufeild, J., A. Singhal, R. Moulton, F. Brenneman, D. Redelmeier, and A. J. Baker
2004    Trauma Recidivism in a Large Urban Canadian Population. *The Journal of Trauma: Injury, Infection, and Critical Care* 57(4): 872–876.

Centers for Disease Control
2010    Traumatic Brain Injury in Prisons and Jails: An Unrecognized Problem. Fact Sheet. Centers for Disease Control, Atlanta, Ga.

Chacon, R. J., and R. G. Mendoza (editors)
2007a   *Latin American Indigenous Warfare and Ritual Violence.* University of Arizona Press, Tucson.
2007b   *North American Indigenous Warfare and Ritual Violence.* University of Arizona Press, Tucson.

Chagnon, N. A.
1974    *Yaṇomamö.* Holt, Rinehart and Winston, New York.

Cohen, R. A., A. Rosenbaum, R. L. Kane, W. J. Wamken, S. Benjamin et al.
1999    Neuropsychological Correlates of Domestic Violence. *Violence and Victims* 14(4): 397–411.

Cybulski, J. S.
1992    A Greenville Burial Ground. In *Archaeological Survey of Canada Mercury Series, No. 146.* Canadian Museum of Civilization, Hull, Ontario.

Evans-Pritchard, E. E.
1940    The Political Structure of the Nandi-Speaking Peoples of Kenya. *Africa: Journal of the International African Institute* 13(3): 250–267.
1968    *The Neur: A Description of the Modes of Livelihood and Political Institutions of a Nilotic People.* Oxford University Press, New York.

Ferguson, R. B., and N. L. Whitehead (editors)
1992    *War in the Tribal Zone.* School of American Research Advanced Seminar Series. School of American Research Press, Santa Fe.

Fleisher, M. L.
2000    Kuria Cattle Raiding: Capitalist Transformation, Commoditization, and Crime Formation among an East African Agro-Pastoral People. *Comparative Studies in Society and History* 42(4): 745–769.

Gat, A.
2006    *War in Human Civilization.* Oxford University Press, Oxford.
Glaesser, J., F. Neuner, R. Lütgehetmann, R. Schmidt, and T. Elbert
2004    Posttraumatic Stress Disorder in Patients with Traumatic Brain Injury. *BMC Psychiatry* 4(5): 1–6.
Gould, R. A., and P. J. Watson
1982    A Dialogue on the Meaning and Use of Analogy in Ethnoarchaeological Reasoning. *Journal of Anthropological Archaeology* 1(4): 355–381.
Grauer, A. L., and C. A. Roberts
1996    Paleoepidemiology, Healing, and Possible Treatment of Traumas in the Medieval Cemetery Population of St. Helen-on-the-Walls, York, England. *American Journal of Physical Anthropology* 100: 531–544.
Gray, S., M. Sundal, B. Wiebusch, M. A. Little, P. W. Leslie, and I. L. Pike
2003    Cattle Raiding, Cultural Survival, and Adaptability of East African Pastoralists. *Current Anthropology* 44(S5): S3–S30.
Gulliver, P. H.
1951    *A Preliminary Survey of the Turkana: A Report Compiled for the Government of Kenya.* Communications from the School of African Studies, New Series 26. University of Capetown, Capetown.
Gunasekaran, S.
2007    Cattle Raiding and Heroic Tradition: Sedentary Pastoralism in Upland Tamil Nadu (Sixth to Tenth Century CE). *Indian Historical Review* 34: 91–124.
Haas, J.
1990    *The Anthropology of War.* Cambridge University Press, Cambridge.
Hadjizacharia, P., D. S. Plurad, D. J. Green, J. DuBose, R. Benfield, A. Shiflett, K. Inaba, L. S. Chan, and D. Demetriades
2009    Outcomes of Blunt Assault at a Level I Trauma Center. *The Journal of Trauma: Injury, Infection, and Critical Care* 66(4): 1202–1206.
Halbmayer, E.
2001    Socio-Cosmological Contexts and Forms of Violence: War, Vendetta, Duels and Suicide among the Yupka of North-Western Venezuela. In *Anthropology of Violence and Conflict,* edited by B. E. Schmidt and I. W. Schröder, pp. 49–75. Routledge, London.
Heald, S.
2000    Tolerating the Intolerable: Cattle Raiding among the Kuria of Kenya. In *Meanings of Violence: A Cross Cultural Perspective,* edited by J. Abbink and A. Göran, pp. 101–122. Berg, New York.
Hedges, B. E., J. E. Dimsdale, D. B. Hoyt, C. Berry, and K. Leitz
1995    Characteristics of Repeat Trauma Patients, San Diego County. *American Journal of Public Health* 85(7): 1008–1010.
Hendrickson, D., R. Mearns, and J. Armon
1996    Livestock Raiding among the Pastoral Turkana of Kenya: Redistribution, Predation and the Links to Famine. *IDS Bulletin* 27(3): 17–30.
Hwang, S. W., A. Colantonio, S. Chiu, G. Tolomiczenko, A. Kiss, L. Cowan, D. A. Redelmeier, and W. Levinson

2008    The Effect of Traumatic Brain Injury on the Health of Homeless People. *Canadian Medical Association Journal (CMAJ)* 179(8): 779–784.

Judd, M. A.
2002    Ancient Injury Recidivism: An Example from the Kerma Period of Ancient Nubia. *International Journal of Osteoarchaeology* 12: 89–106.

Judd, M. A., and C. A. Roberts
1999    Fracture Trauma in a Medieval British Farming Village. *American Journal of Physical Anthropology* 109: 229–243.

Jurmain, R.
1991    Paleoepidemiology of Trauma in a Prehistoric Central California Population. In *Human Paleopathology: Current Synthesis and Future Option,* edited by D. J. Ortner and A. C. Aufderheide, pp. 241–248. Smithsonian Institution Press, Washington, D.C.

Kelly, R. C.
2000    *Warless Societies and the Origin of War.* University of Michigan Press, Ann Arbor.

Kilgore, L., R. Jurmain, and D. P. Van Gerven
1997    Paleoepidemiological Patterns of Trauma in a Medieval Nubian Skeletal Population. *International Journal of Osteoarchaeology* 7: 103–114.

Koji, K.
1990    Deep Involvement in Social Interactions among the Turkana. *African Study Monographs* Supplemental 12: 51–58.

Lambert, P. M.
1994    War and Peace on the Western Front: A Study of Violent Conflict and Its Correlates in Prehistoric Hunter-Gatherer Societies of Coastal California. Ph.D. dissertation, University of California, Santa Barbara.
2007    The Osteological Evidence for Indigenous Warfare in North America. In *North American Indigenous Warfare and Ritual Violence,* edited by R. J. Chacon and R. G. Mendoza. University of Arizona Press, Tucson.

Lambert, P. M., and P. L. Walker
1991    Physical Anthropological Evidence for the Evolution of Social Complexity in Coastal Southern California. *American Antiquity* 65: 963–973.

Lamphear, J.
1988    The People of the Grey Bull: The Origin and Expansion of the Turkana. *Journal of African History* 29: 27–39.

Leon-Carrion, J., and F. J. Ramos
2003    Blows to the Head during Development Can Predispose to Violent Criminal Behaviour: Rehabilitation of Consequences of Head Injury Is a Measure for Crime Prevention. *Brain Injury* 17(3): 207–216.

Leslie, P. W., and M. A. Little
1999    *Turkana Herders of the Dry Savanna: Ecology and Biobehavioral Response of Nomads to an Uncertain Environment.* Research Monographs on Human Population Biology. Oxford University Press, Oxford.

Liénard, P., and F. Anselmo
2004    The Social Construction of Emotions: Gratification and Gratitude among the Turkana and Nyangatom of East Africa. In *At the Fringes of Modernity. People,*

*Cattle, Transitions,* edited by S. V. W. a. G. Verswijver, pp. 150–198. RMCA, Tervuren.

Lindner, R. P.
1981    Nomadism, Horses and Huns. *Past and Present* 92(1): 3–19.

Liston, M. A., and B. J. Baker
1996    Reconstructing the Massacre at Fort William Henry, New York. *International Journal of Osteoarchaeology* 6: 28–41.

Martin, D. L., and D. W. Frayer (editors)
1997    *Troubled Times: Violence and Warfare in the Past.* Gordon and Breach, Amsterdam.

Maschner, H. D. G., and K. L. Reedy-Maschner
1998    Raid, Retreat, Defend (Repeat): The Archaeology and Ethnohistory of Warfare on the North Pacific Rim. *Journal of Anthropological Archaeology* 17(1): 19–51.

Max, J. E., A. E. Lansing, S. L. Koele, C. S. Castillo, H. Bokura, and R. Schachar
2004    Attention Deficit Hyperactivity Disorder in Children and Adolescents Following Traumatic Brain Injury. *Developmental Neuropsychology* 25(1–2): 159–177.

McCabe, J. T.
2004    *Cattle Bring Us to Our Enemies: Turkana Ecology, Politics, and Raiding in a Disequilibrium System.* University of Michigan Press, Ann Arbor.

Milner, G. R.
1999    Warfare in the Prehistoric and Early Historic Eastern North America. *Journal of Archaeological Research* 7: 105–151.

Milner, G. R., E. Anderson, and V. G. Smith
1991    Warfare in Late Prehistoric West-Central Illinois. *American Antiquity* 56(4): 581–603.

Mulder, M. B.
1999    On Pastoralism and Inequality. *Current Anthropology* 40(3): 366–367.

Novak, S. A., T. Allen, and L. L. Bench
2007    Patterns of Injury: Accident or Abuse. *Violence Against Women* 13: 802–816.

Odegi-Awuondo, C.
1990    *Life in the Balance: Ecological Sociology of Turkana Nomads.* ACTS Press, Nairobi.

Owsley, D. W., and R. L. Jantz (editors)
1994    *Skeletal Biology in the Great Plains: Migration, Warfare, Health, and Subsistence.* Smithsonian Institution Press, Washington, D.C.

Pike, I. L.
2004    The Biosocial Consequences of Life on the Run: A Case Study from Turkana District, Kenya. *Human Organization* 63(2): 221–235.

Roncadin, C., S. Guger, J. Archibald, M. Barnes, and M. Dennis
2004    Working Memory after Mild, Moderate, or Severe Childhood Closed Head Injury. *Developmental Neuropsychology* 25(1–2): 21–36.

Schmidt, B. E., and I. W. Schröder (editors)
2001    *Anthropology of Violence and Conflict.* Routledge, London.

Shillingford, R.
2001    *The Elite Forces Handbook of Unarmed Combat.* St. Martin's Griffin, New York.

Stern, J. M.

2004    Traumatic Brain Injury: An Effect and Cause of Domestic Violence and Child Abuse. *Current Neurology and Neuroscience Reports* 4: 179–181.

Tornay, S.

1993    More Chances on the Fringe of the State? The Growing Power of the Nyangatom; a Border People of the Lower Omo Valley, Ethiopia (1970–1992). In *Conflicts in the Horn of Africa: Human and Ecological Consequences of Warfare,* edited by T. Tvedt, pp. 143–163. Department of Social and Economic Geography, Uppsala University, Uppsala.

2001    *Les Fusils jaunes: Générations et politiques en pays nyangatom (Éthiopie).* Société d'ethnologie, Nanterre.

Walker, P. L.

1989    Cranial Injuries as Evidence of Violence in Prehistoric Southern California. *American Journal of Physical Anthropology* 80: 313–323.

1997    Wife Beating, Boxing, and Broken Noses: Skeletal Evidence for the Cultural Patterning of Violence. In *Troubled Times: Violence and Warfare in the Past,* edited by D. L. Martin and D. W. Frayer, pp. 145–180. Gordon and Breach, Amsterdam.

2001    A Bioarchaeological Perspective on the History of Violence. *Annual Review of Anthropology* 30: 573–596.

Walker, P. L., L. S. Sugiyama, and R. J. Chacon

1998    Diet, Dental Health, and Cultural Change among Recently Contacted South American Indian Hunter-Horticulturists. In *Human Dental Development, Morphology, and Pathology: A Tribute to Albert A. Dahlberg,* edited by J. R. Lukacs, pp. 355–386. University of Oregon Anthropological Papers no. 54. Department of Anthropology, University of Oregon, Eugene.

Whitehead, N. L. (editor)

2004    *Violence.* School of American Research Press, Santa Fe, N.M.

Wilson, M., and M. Daly

1995    An Evolutionary Psychological Perspective on Male Sexual Proprietariness and Violence against Wives. *Violence and Victims* 8: 271–294.

Wrightson, P., V. McGinn, and D. Gronwall

1995    Mild Head Injury in Preschool Children: Evidence That It Can Be Associated with a Persisting Cognitive Defect. *Journal of Neurology, Neurosurgery, and Psychiatry* 59: 375–380.

Zhang, L., K. H. Yang, and A. I. King

2004    A Proposed Injury Threshold for Mild Traumatic Brain Injury. *Journal of Biomechanical Engineering* 126: 226–236.

# PART II

# SMALL-SCALE CONFLICT

# 4

## The Social and Cultural Implications of Violence at Qasr Hallabat

ROBERT T. MONTGOMERY AND MEGAN PERRY

### Introduction

Investigations of trauma in human skeletal remains can provide a wealth of information concerning the nature of human interactions during periods of expansion and conquest, changes in political regimes, and environmental fluctuations. Unfortunately for researchers, the discovery of human remains that display evidence of violent confrontations is rare because of problems with preservation or with locating gravesites. However, the reconstruction of life at Qasr Hallabat, an Umayyad desert castle (ca. AD 636–750) with a long history of previous occupation, provides an intriguing opportunity to examine the physical remains of violence from the Early Islamic period in Jordan.

The Spanish Archaeological Mission under the direction of Dr. Ignacio Arce discovered the remains of six individuals ($^{14}$C dated between cal. AD 772 and 895) in the main cistern at Qasr Hallabat in 2007 during their excavation and conservation of the site. Five of the six commingled individuals showed evidence of perimortem blunt force trauma to the head, and three of the six individuals showed signs of perimortem sharp force trauma to their appendages. Discovery of the human remains sparked interesting questions about who the individuals were, what happened to them during their lives, how they ended up in the bottom of the cistern, and what type of cultural and political climate would have led to this type of confrontation. Aside from this work's contribution to the anthropological study of violence and trauma, this is one of the first opportunities to examine human remains from the Early Islamic period. What had previously been known about this era comes from textual information shaped by the current political situation (and such texts were rarely translated from Arabic) or secondary source accounts based on analogies to modern-day inhabitants of the region (Jabbur 1995; Kennedy 2001, 2007; Schick 1998). Furthermore, historical and archaeological information concerning the sociopolitical characteristics of the Early Islamic period in Jordan, and more specifically the desert castles, have focused on the architectural and artistic qualities of physical buildings rather than on their inhabitants (Arce 2006, 2007, 2008; Bisheh 1993; Genequand 2006).

The aims of this study are to fully investigate the remains of the six individuals found within the cistern at Qasr Hallabat using physical anthropological methods to gain a better understanding of what happened to these individuals, how their experience would have been relatable to other groups in eighth–tenth centuries AD Levant, and the nature of the social and political climate that the inhabitants would have experienced. Furthermore, the analysis of trauma in these skeletal remains may add to the scope of the literature about warfare stratagems and weaponry. The pattern of trauma found in the individuals from Qasr Hallabat and the intent of the attackers to destroy a major water source points to a small-scale attack aimed at eliminating a group that was competing with the attackers for resources at a time when local groups had been left to fend for themselves (Jabbur 1995; Jordana et al. 2009).

## Description of the Physical and Environmental Site

Before delving into the nature of the trauma observed in this small sample of skeletal remains, it is important to have a basic understanding of the environmental landscape where Qasr Hallabat is situated. Qasr Hallabat is located approximately 60 kilometers east of the Jordanian capital Amman and approximately 12 kilometers east of the Via Nova Traiana (Arce 2008; see Fig. 4.1; Bisheh 1993, 49). The Via Nova Traiana served as a major north-south route through the eastern frontier of the Roman Empire and was protected by a series of fortifications known as the Limes Arabicus that were designed to fend off invaders and provide respite for pilgrims and merchants (Bowersock 1976; Parker 1986). Qasr Hallabat, which was

Fig. 4.1. Map of the region showing Qasr Hallabat in relation to Amman, Jordan.

originally constructed as one of these Roman fortifications, underwent major renovations in the years preceding the arrival of the Islamic caliphate (Arce 2006, 2007; Bisheh 1993). The arid steppe region where Qasr Hallabat is situated, known as the Badiya, has been long inhabited by Bedouin tribes who rely on a mixture of pastoralism, foraging, hunting, and small-scale agriculture for subsistence (Betts and Russell 2000, 24).

The most imposing aspect of the environmental landscape is the lack of the precipitation required for the subsistence of agricultural groups that began appearing with the arrival of the Umayyads in AD 636 (Jabbur 1995). The small amount of precipitation that falls annually in the region, which ranges from 50 to 200 millimeters, means that water collection and rationing is an extremely important aspect of survival in this harsh environment (Betts and Russell 2000, 30). To account for inevitable water shortages, numerous technological improvements were made to store and manage water resources that are still evident in the area today (e.g., AbdelKhaleq and Ahmed 2007). Qasr Hallabat's water system, which could hold millions of gallons, would accumulate water during the wet season and disperse rainwater throughout the remainder of the year to the palace and surrounding agricultural fields and encampments (AbdelKhaleq and Ahmed 2007, 90; Grabar 1963, 8; Haiman 1995, 35). An understanding of the environmental limitations imposed on the inhabitants of Qasr Hallabat underlines the impact of the contamination of an important water source with decomposing human remains.

In addition to potentially unstable political relations and the struggle to obtain necessary resources, earthquakes were a constant problem for those living in and around Qasr Hallabat throughout its occupation. Hallabat sits approximately 60 kilometers to the east of the tectonically active Dead Sea Rift, which encompasses the Jordan Valley and stretches southward into Africa as the Great Rift Valley. Approximately two years before the official transition from Umayyad to Abbasid control (ca. AD 750), a major earthquake affected large portions of the Levant and caused massive damage to Hallabat. The fact that rubble fell inside the qasr during the quake did not deter people from using the structure and the wells and cisterns it contained for years after the earthquake. Arce (2006) noted post-earthquake modifications to the structure, including construction of a bench, but the Qasr was never fully restored to its original status. The desire to reconstruct the structure seemed to have diminished with the resulting political takeover by the Abbasids and their move of the caliphate capital from Damascus to Baghdad (Blankinship 1994). Further tectonic activity in the region, which most likely occurred in the eleventh century AD, completely sealed the cistern and left it and parts of the qasr untouched until archaeological investigation (Ambraseys, Melville, and Adams 1994; Arce 2006; Guidoboni, Comastri, and Traina 1994).

The Ever-Changing History of Occupation

As previously stated, Qasr Hallabat was originally a fort that served as part of the Limes Arabicus fortification system (Genequand 2006; Harding 1959, 137–138). Over a period of a few centuries, the Byzantine Empire gave control to a group of Monophysite Christians, the Ghassanids. Eventually the leaders of the Byzantine Empire grew weary of their alliance with the foreign Ghassanids and began to lose faith in their willingness to protect the borderlands per their contract. Meanwhile, the Ghassanids were increasing their relations with the nomadic tribes by offering them support through the redistribution of resources (Arce 2006, 2007). Byzantine leaders began to expect that the Ghassanids would attempt to form an independent state because of their growing power and the support of the surrounding nomadic tribes (Arce 2007). The growing distrust between both the Ghassanids and Byzantines soon escalated, and the Ghassanids withdrew from the mutual alliance on two different occasions (once during the persecution of Monophysitism by the Chalcedonean orthodoxy and again under the control of Mundhir). This ultimately led to the dissolution of the Ghassanid's kingship in the Badiya. The fate of the final phylarch of the Ghassanids, Jabla, and many Monophysite Arabs was an eventual conversion to Islam following the Persian invasion in the early seventh century AD (Arce 2007).

The next phase of occupation at Qasr Hallabat took place after the Islamic conquest and the transition of the region from Byzantine to Umayyad leadership. The Umayyad reign, which lasted from the seventh to eighth centuries AD, displayed some similarities to the Ghassinids' methods in the way they obtained and asserted their power (Arce 2007, 2008). Following the Ghassanids' blueprint for control, the Umayyads redistributed wealth and goods, creating a dependency of the surrounding nomads upon the Islamic rulers for essential resources and adjudication in local disputes (Arce 2006, 2007). Amendments to the structure during this time seem to reflect this mutually beneficial existence between the Umayyad ruling elite and surrounding Bedouin people. The function of the inner sanctum of the original fort changed from a militarized zone into an accommodation for luxurious living, while the monastery was refurbished and reused as a dormitory with kitchen and storage space (Arce 2007; Genequand 2006, 17–20). However, more than just a luxurious retreat, Qasr Hallabat was a stopping point for merchants and travelers on pilgrimages and journeys to economic centers such as Jerusalem. In addition, the development of reservoirs and agricultural field systems suggests that the infrastructure provided by (or supported by) the Qasr facilitated the development of desert agriculture and that the Qasr residents controlled agricultural labor and consumed a portion of the agricultural product (AbdelKhaleq and Ahmed 2007; Haiman 1995; Harding 1959).

The Umayyad control of the region continued until the middle of the eighth century AD, when a new ruling family, the Abbasids, rebelled against the status quo and gained control of the Islamic territories (Blankinship 1994). This transition had a profound impact on the types of interactions between the urban population and the surrounding communities. Interactions between elites, local agricultural communities, and nomadic tribes became unstable and potentially volatile as a result of the deterioration of mutually beneficial relationships and the lack of dispute mediation after the Abbasids rose to power in ca. AD 750 (Blankinship 1994, 9). The onset of the Abbasid Caliphate resulted in the decline of urban centers east of the Jordan River, and administrative centers and many settlements (such as Qasr Hallabat) were abandoned. The dissolution of previously strong political and cultural bonds caused the Bedouin tribes to resort to raids and threats to communication and pilgrimage routes as a way to obtain the means of subsistence and express their dissatisfaction with the new political regime (Jabbur 1995, 484). This breakdown in control and intersocietal relationships led directly to the prevalence of violent conflicts. The resulting breakdown between elites and Bedouins and the movement of the capital essentially ended the occupation of the Qasr.

## Materials and Methods

Skeletal remains were discovered during the 2007 restoration of Qasr Hallabat conducted by the Spanish Archaeological Mission. The human remains were located at the bottom of the cistern underneath a covering of sediment and debris and were carefully removed from the cistern. However, no record of skeletal position, aside from the fact that the remains were commingled, was provided to the researchers (Arce personal communication). During the fall 2007 semester, the skeletal remains arrived at the East Carolina University Bioarchaeology Lab under a loan agreement with the Department of Antiquities of Jordan. Radiocarbon dating of skeletal samples (Geochron Laboratories: samples GX-33066 and GX-33006) indicates that these individuals perished and were deposited between cal. AD 772 and 895, after the qasr went out of official use with the end of Umayyad rule. The skeletons were located at the bottom of the cistern beneath the debris and sediment disturbance caused by an earthquake that destroyed the qasr, most likely in the tenth to eleventh centuries, and sealed the cistern in an undisturbed state (Guidoboni, Comastri, and Traina 1994; Karcz 2004).

The skeletal sample includes the commingled, well-preserved remains of a minimum of six individuals. Many of the postcranial remains could be separated into separate individuals because of morphological and taphonomic differences, but they could not be linked definitively to crania in the sample. Age and sex estimation was accomplished using morphological features of the skull and pelvis following Buikstra and Ubelaker (1994). Skeletal pathologies also were observed and recorded following Ortner (2003) and Aufderheide and Rodríguez-Martin (1998). Further indicators of health and quality of life were recorded and assessed using nonspecific indicators of stress such as dental enamel hypoplasias (DEHs), cribra orbitalia, porotic hyperostosis, and perisoteal infections.

Methods of Investigation

The patterns of trauma and pathology associated with these individuals were analyzed using macroscopic, microscopic, and radiographic techniques. Trauma in the skeletons was initially described in detail and scored according to the standards in Ortner (2003) and Aufderheide and Rodríguez-Martin (1998). Microscopic and radiographic investigation of trauma in the cranial and postcranial remains identified any healing at a trauma site that would indicate antemortem trauma (i.e., occurring before death) or unique breakage patterns that could indicate postmortem trauma (i.e., occurring after death) (Moraitis and Spiliopoulou 2006, 222; Ortner 2008; Walker 2001, 576). Additional radiographic examination was conducted on skeletal elements with evidence of perimortem trauma. Furthermore, any visible discolorations along the edges of the fractures in the skeletal remains were examined to investigate taphonomic influences on the bones (Behrensmeyer 1978). An assessment of antemortem and perimortem trauma patterns provided evidence for both accidental and violent incidents before or around the time of death (Finegan 2008). Finally, the morphology of the trauma was examined to try to determine the possible instruments used to cause them based on historical and archaeological evidence (Mitchell 2006; Mitchell, Nagar, and Ellenblum 2004, 2006; Rose et al. n.d.; Smith and Zegerson 1999). Lastly, the size of clearly defined impact sites were examined to give an estimation of the size and type of weapon used to create the trauma. Often the reconstruction of weapon injuries is difficult due to deformation at the impact site or destruction of the area altogether, and only rough estimates of weapon types concurrent with the military technology of the time will be expressed.

## Results

Demographic information can provide valuable information about the cultural circumstances surrounding the violent confrontation at Qasr Hallabat. Because of the amount of commingling and fragmentation and the lack of provenience information it was not possible to associate particular crania with a specific set of postcranial remains. The severe fragmentation of Crania 5 and 6 also prevented the recovery of any valuable demographic information in this study. Analysis of morphological characteristics of the crania and os coxae show that this sample was composed of 5 males and 1 female who were young to middle-aged adults (20–50 years old) at the time of death (Table 4.1).

### Description and Location of Cranial Trauma

Cranium 1 (a male 35–50 years old) displays perimortem blunt force trauma to both parietals (Fig. 4.2). The trauma to the left parietal appears as an impact site on the anterior portion with fractures radiating outward from the center. These radiating fractures extend to and follow along the coronal and squamosal sutures. As the fracture moves along the path of least resistance, it travels down the temporal bone through the sphenotemporal suture to the glenoid fossa. The right parietal displays a depression injury just posterior to the coronal suture that resulted in fracturing along the coronal suture and just posterior from the coronal suture just superior to the impact site.

Cranium 2 (a possible male aged 27–44 years) displays perimortem blunt force trauma on the posterior left side of the cranium and the left and right sides of the cranio-facial skeleton (Fig. 4.3). The posterior impact site is located along the lambdoidal suture near the asterion, and radiating fractures extend along this suture into the occipital bone and along the squamosal suture. Cranio-facial trauma resulted in fracturing along the right zygomatic sutures and of the ethmoid within the right eye orbit. Perimortem fracturing surrounds the left eye orbit, resulting in

Table 4.1. Descriptions of the individuals discovered in the Qasr Hallabat cistern

| | Age | Sex | Antemortem Trauma | Perimortem Trauma | Other Pathologies |
|---|---|---|---|---|---|
| Cranium 1 | 35–50 | M | Frontal (3 healed) | Left side of skull near pterion, right parietal near coronal suture | Caries RM$^2$, healed cribra orbitalia |
| Cranium 2 | 27–44 | M? | Frontal (2 healed) | Left posterior side of skull near asterion, left and right eye orbits and zygomatics | Dental calculus, dental caries, DEHs (RPM$^2$, RPM$^1$, RPM$^2$), healed cribra orbitalia |
| Cranium 3 | 35–50 | F? | Left parietal (1 healed) | Left posterior side of skull near asterion, right side resulting in removal of temporal | Cribra orbitalia, dental calculus |
| Cranium 4 | 35–50 | M? | None | Left side near squamosal suture involving left parietal and resulting in removal of temporal, trauma also may have resulted in destruction of craniofacial skeleton (unrecovered) | None |
| Cranium 5 | Indeterminate | M | Frontal (2 healed), occipital (1 healed) | Left parietal, occipital, left temporal, left side of frontal | Caries (RM$^2$), dental calculus |
| Cranium 6 | Indeterminate | Indeterminate | None | None | None |
| Postcrania 1 | 40–49 | M | None | None | Abnormal bone loss right humerus |
| Postcrania 2 | 40–44 | M | None | None | None |
| Postcrania 3 | 40–44 | M | None | Sharp force trauma left ulna | Active periostitis left femur |
| Postcrania 4 | 30–34 | M | None | None | Vertebral osteophytosis superior sacrum |
| Postcrania 5 | Indeterminate | M? | None | Sharp force trauma right femur and right tibia | None |
| Postcrania 6 | Indeterminate | F? | None | Sharp force trauma left tibia | Vertebral osteophytosis superior sacrum |

Note: Crania and postcrania from the sample could not be associated with each other due to similar age and sex profiles of the individuals, although Cranium 3 like associates with Postcrania 6 since they represent the only females in the sample. The final demographic breakdown of the sample is: one female 35–50 years old, one male 30–34 years old, three males 40–49 years old, and one male of indeterminate age.

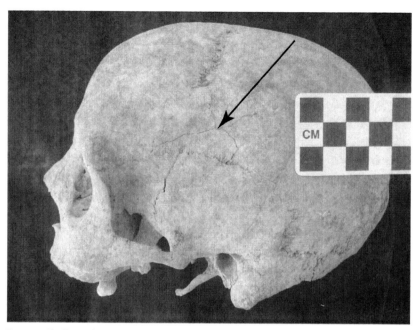

Fig. 4.2. Skull 1 with perimortem blunt force trauma to both parietals.

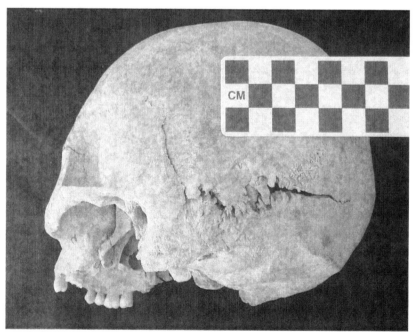

Fig. 4.3. Skull 2 with perimortem blunt force trauma on the posterior left side and in the craniofacial region.

fracturing between the zygomatic and the zygomatic process of the frontal and the greater wing of the sphenoid and between the ethmoid and the maxilla.

Cranium 3 (a possible female 35–50 years old) shows perimortem trauma on the posterior left side and on the right side that possibly resulted in removal of the temporal bone. The small fractures on the posterior left side originated from an impact site just inferior to the asterion. The right-side trauma extends from the squamosal suture all the way down to the foramen magnum. While the external auditory meatus is still slightly present, the temporal, the mastoids, and the entire zygomatic arch have been removed.

Cranium 4 (a possible male 35–50 years old) shows bilateral blunt force trauma. Along the right side there is some flaking along the coronal suture and along remnants of the inner table at the front of the trauma. Internal radiating fractures are also visible on the occipital and parietals. On each side, portions of the parietal, temporal, zygomatic, sphenoid, and the cranio-facial regions have been completely disarticulated. A linear fracture extends from the center of the left parietal toward lambda. Another radiating fracture extends from the anterior edge of trauma on the left side across the frontal bone to the right supraorbital notch. The inferior aspect of the trauma site has a radiating fracture line that cuts across the nuchal area of the occipital bone.

Cranium 5 (an adult male) required extensive assembling as a result of severe blunt force trauma. Extensive warping along the left side of the cranium made refitting the coronal suture and the squamosal suture difficult. A linear fracture extends from the left side along the lambdoidal suture and across the occipital bone. The left posterior cranio-facial portion, from the inferior aspect of the eye orbit to the alveolar bone, has been fractured off due to perimortem forces. An impact site with radiating fractures that are impeded by concentric ring fractures is present along the posterior portion of the sagittal suture just above lambda (Fig. 4.4). The entire right side of the braincase extending down to the inferior aspect of the cranium is absent and appears to have been fractured off along the sutures.

Cranium 6 (an adult of indeterminate sex) is composed only of portions of the calvarium. All of the broken edges of the calvarium are rounded. They show a great deal of flaking on both the inner and outer tables of the cranium. There does not appear to be any fracturing associated with

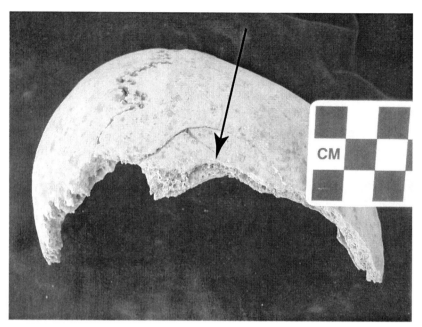

Fig. 4.4. Impact site with radiating fractures impeded by concentric ring fractures along the sagittal suture.

trauma within the remains, only the remnants of postmortem taphonomic processes.

Antemortem trauma is another readily visible aspect of the crania of four of the males from the cistern at Qasr Hallabat. Cranium 1 displays three separate depressions indicative of antemortem trauma along the frontal bone that shows signs of healing. Healed ovoid wounds were observed on the frontal bone, one ca. 5 mm above the right orbit, the other ca. 50 mm above the left orbit near the coronal suture. Cranium 3 displays a large depression that was caused antemortem along the sagittal suture, just behind bregma, that is 22.21 mm anterior to posterior and 29.08 mm laterally. Finally, Cranium 5 has a depression showing evidence of bone remodeling on the left portion of the frontal bone.

Description and Location of Postcranial Trauma

Postcranial trauma is present for only three of the individuals from the sample. Sharp force trauma is found in skeletons number three, five, and six, but there is no readily visible blunt force trauma in any of the

Fig. 4.5. Skeleton 3 showing defensive sharp force trauma to the right ulna.

postcranial remains. Skeleton number three (a male 40–44 years old) shows defensive sharp force trauma to the posterior of the right ulna (see Fig. 4.5). There are two wedge-shaped fractures with splintering, uniform coloring, and smooth edges. The proximal and distal wounds measure 11.81 mm by 6.2 mm and 15.53 mm by 7.86 mm, respectively. Skeleton five (a possible adult male) shows sharp force trauma in the right femur and tibia. Both cut marks show smooth edges, uniform coloration, and no signs of healing, which is indicative of perimortem trauma. Finally, skeleton number six (an adult female, probably associated with Cranium 3) shows sharp force trauma to the left tibia on the tibial tuberosity. There are no signs of healing and the wound displays sharply squared borders.

Nonspecific Indicators of Health

Macroscopic and microscopic investigation revealed a variety of pathologies in the dentition of this skeletal sample. Abnormalities and afflictions that were observed and recorded in the sample included carious lesions and dental enamel hypoplasias. Other nonspecific indicators that indicate nutritional deficiency in childhood or immunological breakdown include cribra orbitalia, periosteal infections, and vertebral pathologies associated with an active lifestyle.

Carious lesions have long been useful indicators of changes in a population's diet over time in archaeological settings (Larsen 1995). The frequencies of observed caries by tooth region can be beneficial in understanding the etiology of the plaque bacteria that creates the demineralization of enamel (Hillson 2008, 313). In the Qasr Hallabat sample, 31.6 percent of all the recovered teeth show carious lesions. The presence of dental enamel hypoplasias signifies a period of quantifiable stress within an individual's life (Hillson 2008). These enamel defects can be attributed to a specific age range because tooth development and amelogenesis occur at generally constant rates (Goodman and Rose 1990). Only Cranium 2 in this sample shows incidences of linear dental enamel hypoplasias. Three linear hypoplasias were discovered and measured from the midpoint of the buccal cemento-enamel junction to the most occlusal point of the defect (Buikstra and Ubelaker 1994, 56). One defect measured 3.3 mm on the upper right second premolar. Two other linear enamel hypoplasias were measured at 6.1 mm on the upper right and left first premolars. According to the linear regressions proposed by Goodman and Rose (1990, 98) this individual underwent two separate periods of stress at approximately 3 and 5 years of age. The age of 3 may correspond with physiological and psychological stresses related to weaning (Larsen 1995). An additional episode of stress at age 5 could have occurred from disease, malnutrition, or other stresses that are known to cause DEHs, possibly due to increased labor-related responsibilities of the child (Boyden and Levison 2000; Hawkes, O'Connell, and Blurton Jones 1995).

Another well-known indicator of general childhood stress and disturbance of immunological systems is anemia-related cribra orbitalia (Angel 1966; Stuart-Macadam 1985, 1987; Sullivan 2005; Wapler, Crubezy, and Schultz 2004). The presence of cribra orbitalia was observed in half of the sample. Crania 1, 2, and 3 show evidence of the distinctive bilateral pitting associated with cribra orbitalia in the roofs of the eye orbits. These lesions were no longer active but were in a state of healing; the lesions are partially filled in and show rounded margins.

In addition, the unassociated and commingled vertebrae were examined for the presence of any pathological conditions. The vertebrae were analyzed for the development of any Schmorl's nodes or the formation of osteophytes that may be indicative of age-related degenerative change or work-related stress. The sacrum of Skeleton 6 showed arthritic lipping with a sharp ridge that affected between one- and two-thirds of the circumference of the superior surface. All of the osteophyte formation for the vertebrae scored between a one and two, denoting that formations ranged from slight spicule formation to a slightly elevated ring (Buikstra and Ubelaker 1994). Thus the skeletal elements from the Qasr Hallabat sample demonstrate that these individuals were in fairly good health. The majority of pathological conditions recorded were caused by highly active lifestyles.

## Discussion

Examining these results within the cultural context of the eighth–tenth centuries AD in the Middle East can reveal the broader impacts of such incidents. The first objective is to discuss what the observed trauma explains about how these six individuals died and why they were deposited in a major source of water. The second objective is to examine the cultural context local inhabitants experienced to determine how social group interactions were affected by a changing political structure. The final goal is to compare trauma and pathology from Qasr Hallabat to similar populations to show how the experience of the individuals found at Qasr Hallabat was similar to or different from that of other contemporary groups.

### Differential Diagnosis of Violence at Qasr Hallabat

The first step in the process of understanding the cause of death of the individuals at Qasr Hallabat and the motivations of possible perpetrators is to determine what caused the trauma that is visible in their remains. Trauma in the cranium is often attributed to postmortem taphonomic modifications, accidental trauma, or trauma from interpersonal violence. Postmortem modifications to the bones caused by taphonomic processes that mimic trauma in the crania were ruled out for a number of reasons. Several characteristics of perimortem fractures distinguish them from postmortem breakages. They typically occur at acute or oblique angles to the bone, as opposed to the right angles seen in postmortem fractures, because of the living bone's relative plasticity (Walker 2001, 576). Perimortem fractures are also usually linear with sharp edges, whereas postmortem fractures appear with a more jagged edge (White and Folkens 2000, 409). The edges of postmortem fractures often appear lighter than the surrounding bone, while perimortem fracture edges are generally the same color (Walker 2001, 576). Another factor that distinguishes perimortem from postmortem defects is that postmortem trauma may show crumbling along the edges rather than fracturing (Galloway 1999, 16).

Observation of the trauma in the skeletons at Qasr Hallabat clearly demonstrates that the wounds were caused by perimortem forces in five of the six individuals.

Accidental trauma has been ruled out based on the location of cranial trauma above the brim level of a hat and the presence of appendicular sharp force trauma (Berryman and Symes 1998, 337–344). The presence of healed depressions in four of the six individuals suggests that this group had experienced less severe physical confrontations in the past that may have led to their last conflict. It is not possible to determine whether previous events were related to the most recent one, but it seems plausible that confrontations over resources or social relationships occurred regularly.

Finally, trauma resulting from being deposited in the cistern was eliminated as a possible cause because of the location and pattern of the blunt force trauma on the crania. Often, falls cause blunt force trauma that can be observed skeletally, though the degree of trauma is greatly affected by the age of the individual and how the individual falls. Vertical deceleration injuries are most often associated with falling or jumping from some height (Tomczak and Buikstra 1999, 254). Patterned fractures in the arms, legs, ribs, spinal column, and cranium would be expected after a fall from some height, but no blunt force injuries are found outside the crania of the individuals from Qasr Hallabat (Finegan 2008, 195). Even victims who may have been unconscious or already deceased at the time of the fall would be expected to show trauma in the form of compression fractures to the ribs and vertebrae; such fractures were not present in the individuals from Qasr Hallabat (Finegan 2008, 181; Spitz 1993, 244). Therefore, it is clear that the cranial blunt force trauma and postcranial sharp force trauma patterns indicate that the injuries were the result of intense interpersonal violence and not caused by an accident or by the process of depositing the individuals in the cistern.

The manner of death for five of the individuals (four males and one female) was determined to be homicide, as the wounds were not self-inflicted and presumably the individuals did not put themselves into the cistern willingly. The remaining male individual did not have visible perimortem trauma in the cranium, and because of our inability to associate the cranium with any postcranial remains, it was not possible to determine how he died. More detailed analysis of the pattern of trauma can lead to an assessment of how the attack against these six individuals was actually carried out.

## Cultural Implications for the Early Islamic Period

The presence of healed depression fractures in some of the crania suggests that the individuals that ended up in the cistern at Qasr Hallabat were no strangers to other, less severe violent confrontations. The frontal bone displays the highest percentage of healed blunt force trauma (50 percent), which is seen in Crania 1, 3, and 5. In addition, four of the six (66.6 percent) healed antemortem depressions are located on the left portion of the frontal bone. This location of healed trauma to the frontal bone tends to suggest a face-to-face skirmish that was not as violent as the event that ended the individuals' lives. Walker (1989, 319) discovered that individuals in antiquity most commonly survived wounds to the frontal bone but that survival rates for fractures elsewhere in the cranium were lower. However, the presence of these healed lesions cannot be ruled out as evidence of accidents such as falling onto a hard surface or accidentally hitting the head (Galloway 1999; Lovell 1997).

Although it seems clear that the cranial depressions seen in 66.6 percent of the sample were caused by violence, other possible sources for these pathologies exist. Ortner and Frohlich's 2008 work on Bab edh-Dra, an Early Bronze Age site in Jordan, suggests that sebaceous cysts caused by pressure-induced erosion of the outer table, can mimic healed antemortem trauma (Ortner and Frohlich 2008, 267). The lesions are almost always completely circular and affect only the outer table of the cranium (Ortner and Frohlich 2008, 267), which may help differentiate the two conditions. Even though radiographic examination was conducted on two of the crania with these lesions, it was not possible to determine if there was any reactionary response of the inner table of the cranium at the sites of the lesions. The form of the lesions in the Qasr Hallabat skeletal sample are never completely round; instead, they are more of an ovoid or oblong shape, which suggests that they are more likely the result of a strike that glanced off the individuals' skulls.

In addition, the sharp force trauma seen in three individuals clearly indicates interpersonal violence (Ghali 2008; Spitz 1993). The fact that these wounds showed no evidence of healing suggests that they occurred simultaneously with the cranial blunt force trauma. Some wounds apparently indicate defensive reactions of the victims, such as the scoop defect trauma on the ulna of Skeleton 3 that indicates a direct strike (Ghali 2008, 276; Judd 2008, 1658–1659; Walker 2001). Ghali (2008, 279) explains that scoop defects are generally observed in wounds created by long bladed weapons such as swords. The other sharp force traumas observed in the lower limbs are incised cut marks caused by smaller sharp objects that interrupt the bone's surface layer (Ghali 2008, 268).

All of this evidence tends to suggest that the Early Islamic period was not as tranquil as many historical sources claim. Historical and archaeological accounts of the Early Islamic period point to a relatively peaceful transition of power from the Umayyads to the Abbasids because of the fact that many Umayyad buildings were not destroyed and were used after the transition (Walmsley 2007). The trauma observed in the Hallabat sample contradicts this idea and suggests a view of the breakdown of social allegiances and struggle to obtain necessary resources in an environment of scarce resources. Because the Abbasids largely neglected the hinterlands, the rise of the Abbasid caliphate led to a loss of control of the hinterland regions and a renewal of tribal confrontations on a large scale (Blankinship 1994, 9; Lindsay 2005, 63). Raiding was a common practice in many societies under weak sociopolitical regimes and has been used to obtain scarce resources and to show superiority to other communities (Carman 1997, 11). Lindsay (2005, 62–63) explains that raiding other groups would have been a common occurrence in the Early Islamic periods for nomadic societies for these same reasons. Depositing six individuals in the main cistern at Qasr Hallabat would likely have been viewed as a way for an outside group to cripple a competing community and force them to work harder and possibly move out of the area.

## Comparisons to Relative Populations

An important step in contextualizing the events that occurred at Qasr Hallabat is to understand their life history before death. These individuals did not suffer extensively from poor health or nutrition while they were alive (see Fig. 4.6). Crusader period communities in Israel, such as Caesarea and Tel Jezreel, have notably lower frequencies of these conditions (Mitchell 2006; Smith and Zegerson 1999). The mostly subadult skeletons from the Crusader-era fortress at Al Wu'ayra, in contrast, had very high frequency of periostitis, probably due to the effects of scurvy and folic acid deficiency (Rose et al. n.d.). The individuals from Hallabat have almost no periosteal reactions or other signs of infection. Half of the individuals had at least one nonspecific indicator of stress, but these had

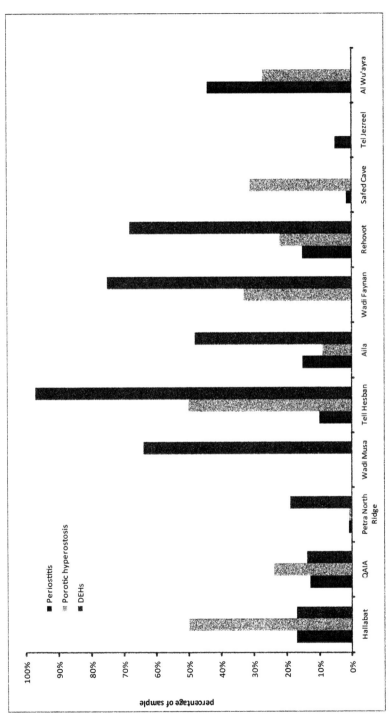

Fig. 4.6. Frequency of pathologies at different archaeological sites.

occurred during childhood or were inactive. The frequency of porotic hyperostosis is slightly higher in this group than among groups that date to the Roman and Byzantine periods, perhaps indicating an increase in iron deficiency during childhood. The lack of periostitis or DEHs may suggest (presuming that these are local individuals) that the political changes of the eighth century did not result in decreased access to resources in the region. Thus, the life history of these individuals does not indicate a greater susceptibility for violent death than for individuals from Roman, Byzantine, and medieval samples.

It is possible, however, that the type of trauma the individuals sustained may illuminate the social and cultural context in which their deaths occurred. The main studies dealing with trauma and warfare in the Near East have come from the examinations of urban and sedentary Crusader-period skeletal remains (Mitchell 2006; Mitchell, Nagar, and Ellenblum 2004, 2006; Rose et al. n.d.; Smith and Zegerson 1999). These accounts of trauma, combined with other accounts of the history of military science, can help to better define the situation encountered in the remains from Qasr Hallabat. For instance, military campaigns at Vadum Iacob Castle in Jerusalem exemplified a full-scale organized assault by Muslims that produced many bodies and destroyed the castle (Mitchell, Nagar, and Ellenblum 2006). The only injuries discovered in the skeletal remains from this skirmish consisted of sharp force trauma from swords to the arms and head and arrows to the abdomen and neck, a pattern that is distinctly different from the one at Qasr Hallabat.

The examination of trauma rates from the Crusader-period port city of Caesarea, in contrast, revealed no evidence of violent or weapon-related trauma (Rose et al. n.d.; Smith and Zegerson 1999), possibly because of the secure location of the site and an inhabitant's actions (Mitchell 2006). In addition, the analysis of the Roman-period sample of pastoral nomads from central Jordan identified very little trauma despite the group's supposed involvement with the Roman military (Perry 2007). Thus, other skeletal populations provide little evidence of intense interpersonal conflict in the Near East and instead reveal instances of healed trauma. This makes Qasr Hallabat a unique example.

The fact that the injuries documented in the Qasr Hallabat sample are mainly due to blunt force trauma and in a few instances to sharp force trauma suggests a nonmilitary attack during a period when the sword and the composite bow were popular and were becoming widely used by military forces. Examinations of technical military innovations during the Early Islamic period up to the period of the Crusades has revealed the adaptability of Muslim forces and the willingness of Muslim armies to adopt the newest and best military stratagems and technology (Alexander 1983; Hacker 1997; Jandora 1986; Nicolle 1999).

Detailed examinations of trauma patterns in the crania found at Qasr Hallabat further support the notion that the attacks were not organized by a military force. The cranial elements most affected by the perimortem blunt force trauma are the occipital (66.6 percent), followed by the parietals and temporals (58.3 percent), followed by the sphenoid and zygomatics (50 percent), and finally by the frontal and cranio-facial remains (33.3 percent). These findings suggest that the individuals who were the victims of violence were attacked from the sides or from behind. Such attacks would have affected the left side of the skull and the frontal and parietal bones; face-to-face combat would not have caused this type of damage (Inglemark 1939; Wakely 1997; Wenham 1989). In addition, the types of wounds found in the crania and postcrania do not reveal a clear pattern of attack that can be associated with formalized execution or torture (Asbridge 1999; Ibn Shaddād 2002; Mitchell 2006). Thus, the pattern of trauma observed in this sample seems to show that the victims were ill prepared to deal with the onslaught. These wounds are more characteristic of a surprise attack or a raid rather than an attack from an organized military.

Whether the violence at Qasr Hallabat was carried out by one of the nomadic pastoral groups in the region is not known. What is certain, though, is the intention of the attackers to decimate the population under attack, which is apparent in the intensity of violence inflicted upon them. This intention is further indicated by the fact that the dead bodies were put in the cistern, which would have destroyed the water source necessary for life in the region . These same tactics have been used in military invasions, such as those at Vadum Iacob Castle, to decimate the opposition and psychologically intimidate any that may have survived the attacks (Mitchell, Nagar, and Ellenblum 2006).

## Conclusions

Our investigation of archaeological and historical sources has shown that the circumstances surrounding the deaths of these six individuals were unique because of the way they were murdered and were then placed into a viable water source, especially when taking into consideration the political and social turmoil the region was experiencing. The fact that the individuals were deposited in the cistern shows the intention of the attackers to desecrate an important water source or to dispose of the bodies in secrecy. Most populations view bodies as unclean, so the disposal of six bodies in a main water source would have greatly affected any further attempts to use the Qasr and its resources.

Sources (Arce 2006; Harding 1959) indicate that the Umayyad ruling family occupied the Qasr from approximately 661 to 750 AD until the Abbasids gained control of the Islamic empire. The occupants of the Qasr were not limited to ruling elites looking for a desert retreat. Surrounding communities of pastoral nomads, who eventually became more sedentary as agricultural activity increased, were in constant interaction with the inhabitants of the Qasr and received support from the Qasr in the form of various goods (AbdelKhaleq and Ahmed 2007; Arce 2006). The period of political upheaval that resulted in the Abbasid takeover and the concomitant breakdown of allegiance to the surrounding communities (Jabbur 1995, 484) corresponds with the calibrated radiocarbon dates (eighth to ninth centuries AD) obtained from the skeletal remains of two of the deposited individuals. After Qasr was abandoned and the Abbasids rose to power around AD 750, violent interregional tribal confrontations took place. The historical and archaeological data suggest that the fact that the six individuals were deposited in the cistern at Qasr Hallabat was related to the social and political interactions of several groups whose relationships in a difficult environment were closely intertwined.

Finally, the presence of severe cranial blunt force trauma in five of the individuals and postcranial sharp force trauma in three of the individuals leads to the conclusion that these individuals were murdered. The pattern of the blunt force trauma in the crania and the absence of blunt force injuries to the postcrania suggest that the blunt force trauma was caused by violent conflict and not by accidental falls into the cistern (Berryman and Symes 1998; Spitz 1993). Though no specific weapons could be identified as having caused the injuries, we can speculate that they were moderately sized (based on the severity of trauma inflicted) and very portable. The severity of the events that caused the deaths of these six individuals was an unusual occurrence, even though the individuals had experienced violent interactions in the past (which is evident from healed cranial lesions). The combination of several types of analysis has allowed us to paint a much clearer picture of the events surrounding the deaths and interment of the six individuals at Qasr Hallabat.

We hope that this research will open new avenues of research in bio-archaeology in this region of the world and provide insight into this dynamic time period. The next step in analyzing the remains of these individuals would be to conduct stable isotope analysis of the bones. Such an analysis will allow researchers to determine if these individuals were local and if they had access to different dietary sources than other populations from this region of the Middle East. Another important aspect for future study would be the study of pathological conditions that may have affected individuals and the types of treatment that were available in the area at that time, especially given the presence of elites at this luxurious palatial settlement. Though the events that occurred at Qasr Hallabat in Jordan in the eighth to ninth centuries AD were unfortunate, they have resulted in an increased knowledge of the political and social interactions of the region and the time period.

## Acknowledgments

Thanks to Deb Martin and Ryan Harrod for putting together the symposium that led to the development of this book. We are grateful to Dr. Ignacio Arce of the Spanish Archaeological Mission for facilitating the study of these skeletal remains. Funding for the Qasr Hallabat restoration and excavation has been provided by the Spanish Agency for International Cooperation and the Spanish Institute for Cultural Heritage. This project would not be possible without the support of Dr. Fawwaz al-Khraysheh and the Jordanian Department of Antiquities. Jessica Walker assisted with the initial cleaning and analysis of the skeletal remains.

## References Cited

AbdelKhaleq, R. A., and I. A. Ahmed
2007    Rainwater Harvesting in Ancient Civilizations in Jordan. *Water, Science and Technology: Water Supply* 7(1): 85–93.
Alexander, D. G.
1983    Two Aspects of Islamic Arms and Armor. *Metropolitan Museum Journal* 18: 97–109.

Ambraseys, N., C. Melville, and R. Adams
1994    *The Seismicity of Egypt, Arabia, and the Red Sea: A Historical Review.* Cambridge University Press, Cambridge.

Angel, L. J.
1966    Porotic Hyperostosis, Anemias, Malarias, and Marshes in the Prehistoric Eastern Mediterranean. *Science* 153: 760–763.

Arce, I.
2006    Qasr Hallabat (Jordan) Revisited: Reassessment of the Material Evidence. In *Muslim Military Architecture in Greater Syria: From the Coming of Islam to the Ottoman Period,* edited by H. Kennedy, pp. 26–44. Brill Academic Publishers, Boston.
2007    Qaṣr Ḥallābāt: Continuity and Change from the Roman-Byzantine to the Umayyad Period. In *Studies in the History and Archaeology of Jordan IX,* edited by F. al-Khraysheh, pp. 325–344. Department of Antiquities, Amman.
2008    Hallabat: Castellum, Coenobium, Praetorium, Qasr: The Construction of a Palatine Architecture under the Umayyads. In *Residences, Castles, Settlements: Transformation Processes from Late Antiquity to Early Islam in Bilad al-Sham,* edited by F. al-Khraysheh, pp. 153–182. Colloquium on Late Antique and Early Islamic Archaeology in Bilad ash-Sham, Damaskus. Verlag Marie Leidorf, Rhaden.

Asbridge, T.
1999    *Walter the Chancellor's the Antiochene Wars.* Aldershot, Ashgate.

Aufderheide, A. C., and C. Rodríguez-Martin
1998    *The Cambridge Encyclopedia of Human Paleopathology.* Cambridge University Press, Cambridge.

Behrensmeyer, A. K.
1978    Taphonomic and Ecological Information from Bone Weathering. *Paleobiology* 4: 150–162.

Berryman, H. E., and S. A. Symes
1998    Recognizing Gunshot and Blunt Cranial Trauma through Fracture Interpretation. In *Forensic Osteology: Advances in the Identification of Human Remains,* 2nd ed., edited by K. J. Reichs, pp. 333–352. Charles C. Thomas, Springfield, Ill.

Betts, A. V. G., and K. W. Russell
2000    Prehistoric and Historic Pastoral Strategies in the Syrian Steppe. In *The Transformation of Nomadic Society in the Arab East,* edited by M. Mundy and B. Musallam, pp. 24–32. University of Cambridge Oriental Publications, Cambridge.

Bisheh, G.
1993    From Castellum to Palatium: Umayyad Mosaic Pavements from Qasr al-Hallabat in Jordan. *Muqarnas* 10: 49–56.

Blankinship, K. Y.
1994    *The End of the Jihād State: The Reign of Hishām ibn ʿAbd al-Malik and the Collapse of the Umayyads.* State University of New York Press, Albany.

Bowersock, G. W.
1976    Limes Arabicus. *Harvard Studies in Classical Philology* 80: 219–229.

Boyden, J., and D. Levison
2000    Children as Social and Economic Actors in the Development Process. Report prepared for the Expert Group on Development Issues (EGDI).
Buikstra, J. E., and D. H. Ubelaker
1994    Standards for Data Collection from Human Skeletal Remains (Buikstra and Ubelaker) Research Series no. 44. Arkansas Archaeological Survey, Fayetteville.
Carman, J.
1997    Introduction: Approaches to Violence. In Material Harm: Archaeological Studies of War and Violence, edited by J. Carman, pp. 1–24. Criuthne Press, Glasgow.
Finegan, O.
2008    Case Study: The Interpretation of Skeletal Trauma Resulting from Injuries Sustained Prior to, and as a Direct Result of Freefall. In Skeletal Trauma: Identification of Injuries Resulting from Human Remains Abuse and Armed Conflict, edited by E. H. Kimmerle and J. P. Baraybar, pp. 181–195. CRC Press, Boca Raton, Fla.
Galloway, A. (editor)
1999    Broken Bones: Anthropological Analysis of Blunt Force Trauma. Charles C. Thomas, Springfield, Ill.
Genequand, D.
2006    Umayyad Castles: The Shift from Late Antique Military Architecture to Early Islamic Palatial Building. In Muslim Military Architecture in Greater Syria: From the Coming of Islam to the Ottoman Period, edited by H. Kennedy, pp. 3–25. Brill Academic Publishers, Boston.
Ghali, B.
2008    Sharp Force Trauma. In Skeletal Trauma: Identification of Injuries Resulting from Human Remains Abuse and Armed Conflict, edited by E. H. Kimmerle and J. P. Baraybar, pp. 263–319. CRC Press, Boca Raton.
Goodman, A. H., and J. C. Rose
1990    Assessment of Systemic Physiological Perturbations from Dental Enamel Hypoplasias and Associated Histological Structures. Yearbook of Physical Anthropology 33: 59–110.
Grabar, O.
1963    Umayyad "Palace" and the "Abbasid Revolution." Studia Islamica 18: 5–18.
Guidoboni, E., A. Comastri, and G. Traina
1994    Catalogue of Ancient Earthquakes in the Mediterranean Area up to the 10th Century. Vol. 1. Istituto Nazionale di Geofisica, Rome.
Hacker, B. C.
1997    Military Technology and World History: A Reconnaissance. The History Teacher 30(4): 461–487.
Haiman, M.
1995    Agriculture and Nomad-State Relations in the Negev Desert in the Byzantine and Early Islamic Periods. Bulletin of the American Schools of Oriental Research 297: 29–53.

Harding, L.
1959    *The Antiquities of Jordan*. Thomas Y. Crowell Company, New York.
Hawkes, K., F. O'Connell, and N. G. Blurton Jones
1995    Hadza Children's Foraging: Juvenile Dependency, Social Arrangements, and Mobility among Hunter-Gatherers. *Current Anthropology* 36(4): 688–700.
Hillson, S. W.
2008    Dental Pathology. In *Biological Anthropology of the Human Skeleton*, 2nd ed., edited by M. A. Katzenberg and S. R. Saunders, pp. 301–340. John Wiley and Sons, Hoboken, N.J.
Ibn Shaddād, B.
2002    *The Rare and Excellent History of Saladin*. Translated by D. S. Richards. Ashgate, Aldershot.
Inglemark, B. E.
1939    The Skeletons. In *Armour from the Battle of Wisby, 1361*, edited by B. Thordemann, pp. 149–205. Vitterhets Historie och Antikvitets Akademie, Stockholm.
Jabbur, J.
1995    *The Bedouins and the Desert: Aspects of Nomadic Life in the Arab East*. State University of New York Press, Albany.
Jandora, J. W.
1986    Developments in Islamic Warfare: The Early Conquests. *Studia Islamica* 64: 101–103.
Jordana, X., I. Galtés, T. Turbat, D. Batsukh, C. García, A. Isidro, and P.-H. Giscard
2009    The Warriors of the Steppes: Osteological Evidence of Warfare and Violence from Pazyryk Tumuli in the Mongolian Altai. *Journal of Archaeological Research* 36(7): 1319–1327.
Judd, M. A.
2008    The Parry Problem. *Journal of Archaeological Science* 35: 1658–1666.
Karcz, I.
2004    Implications of Some Early Jewish Sources for Estimates of Earthquake Hazard in the Holy Land. *Annals of Geophysics* 47(2–3): 759–792.
Kennedy, H.
2001    *The Armies of the Caliphs: Military and Society in the Early Islamic State*. Taylor and Francis, London.
2007    *The Great Arabs Conquests: How the Spread of Islam Changed the World We Live In*. Da Capo Press, Cambridge.
Larsen, C. S.
1995    Biological Changes in Human Populations with Agriculture. *Annual Review of Anthropology* 24: 185–213.
Lindsay, J. E.
2005    *Daily Life in the Medieval Islamic World*. Greenwood Press, Westport, Conn.
Lovell, N. C.
1997    Trauma Analysis in Paleopathology. *Yearbook of Physical Anthropology* 40: 139–170.

Mitchell, P. D.
2006    Trauma in the Crusader Period City of Caesarea: A Major Port in the Medi-
        eval Eastern Mediterranean. *International Journal of Osteoarchaeology* 16(6):
        493–505.
Mitchell, P. D., Y. Nagar, and R. Ellenblum
2004    The Paleopathology of Skulls Recovered from a Medieval Cave Cemetery near
        Safed, Israel (Thirteenth to Seventeenth Century). *Levant* 36: 243–250.
2006    Weapon Injuries in the 12th Century Crusader Garrison of Vadum Iacob Castle,
        Galilee. *International Journal of Osteoarchaeology* 16(2): 145–155.
Moraitis, K., and C. Spiliopoulou
2006    Identification and Differential Diagnosis of Perimortem Blunt Force Trauma in
        Tubular Long Bones. *Forensic Science, Medicine, and Pathology* 2(4): 221–229.
Nicolle, D.
1999    Medieval Warfare: The Unfriendly Interface. *The Journal of Military History*
        63(3): 579–599.
Ortner, D. J.
2003    *Identification of Pathological Conditions in Human Skeletal Remains.* Academic
        Press, London.
2008    Differential Diagnosis of Skeletal Injuries. In *Skeletal Trauma: Identification of
        Injuries Resulting from Human Remains Abuse and Armed Conflict,* edited by E.
        H. Kimmerle and J. P. Baraybar, pp. 21–93. CRC Press, Boca Raton, Fla.
Ortner, D. J., and B. Frohlich
2008    *The Early Bronze Age I Tombs and Burials of Bâb edh-Drâ', Jordan.* AltaMira
        Press, Lanham, Md.
Parker, S. T.
1986    *Romans and Saracens: A History of the Arabian Frontier.* ASOR Dissertation
        Series No. 6. American Schools of Oriental Research (ASOR), Winona Lake,
        Ind.
Perry, M. A.
2007    Is Bioarchaeology a Handmaiden to History? Developing a Historical Bioar-
        chaeology. *Journal of Anthropological Archaeology* 26: 486–515.
Rose, J. C., F. Al-Awad, S. Al-Horani, and G. Vannini
n.d..    The Skeletons from Al-Wua'yra-Castellum Vallis Moysis. In author's possession.
Schick, R.
1998    Palestine in the Early Islamic: Luxuriant Legacy. *Near Eastern Archaeology*
        61(2): 74–108.
Smith, P., and T. Zegerson
1999    Morbidity and Mortality of Post-Byzantine Populations from Caesarea. In *Cae-
        sarea Papers 2: Herod's Temple, the Provincial Governor's Praetorium and Gra-
        naries, the Later Harbor, a Gold Coin Hoard, and Other Studies,* edited by K. G.
        Holum, A. Raban, and J. Patrich, pp. 433–440. Journal of Roman Archaeology,
        Portsmouth.
Spitz, W.
1993    *Spitz and Fisher's Medicolegal Investigation of Death: Guidelines for the Applica-*

*tion of Pathology to Crime Investigation.* 3rd ed. Charles C. Thomas, Springfield, Ill.

Stuart-Macadam, P.

1985    Porotic Hyperostosis: Representative of a Childhood Condition. *American Journal of Physical Anthropology* 66: 391–398.

1987    Porotic Hyperostosis: New Evidence to Support the Anemia Theory. *American Journal of Physical Anthropology* 74: 521–526.

Sullivan, A.

2005    Prevalence and Etiology of Acquired Anemia in Medieval York England. *American Journal of Physical Anthropology* 128: 252–272.

Tomczak, P., and J. E. Buikstra

1999    Analysis of Blunt Trauma Injuries: Vertical Deceleration versus Horizontal Deceleration Injuries. *Journal of Forensic Sciences* 44(2): 253–262.

Wakely, J.

1997    Identification and Analysis of Violent and Non-Violent Head Injuries in Osteo-Archaeological Material. In *Material Harm: Archaeological Studies of War and Violence,* edited by J. Carman, pp. 24–46. Criuthne Press, Glasgow.

Walker, P. L.

1989    Cranial Injuries as Evidence of Violence in Prehistoric Southern California. *American Journal of Physical Anthropology* 80: 313–323.

2001    A Bioarchaeological Perspective on the History of Violence. *Annual Review of Anthropology* 30: 573–596.

Walmsley, A.

2007    Developments and the Nature of Settlement in the Towns and Countryside of Syria-Palestine ca. 565–800. *Dumbarton Oaks Papers* 61: 318–352.

Wapler, U., E. Crubezy, and M. Schultz

2004    Is Cribra Orbitalia Synonymous with Anemia? Analysis and Interpretation of Cranial Pathology in Sudan. *American Journal of Physical Anthropology* 123: 333–339.

Wenham, S. J.

1989    Anatomical Interpretations of Anglo-Saxon Weapon Injuries. In *Weapons and Warfare in Anglo-Saxon England,* edited by S. C. Hawkes, pp. 123–139. Oxford University Press, Oxford.

White, T. D., and P. A. Folkens

2000    *Human Osteology.* 2nd ed. Academic Press, San Diego.

# 5

## Community Violence and Everyday Life

### Death at Arroyo Hondo

ANN M. PALKOVICH

## Introduction

Three young children—ages 3, 4, and 4 1/2—were interred together in the trash fill of a room at the fourteenth-century ancestral pueblo of Arroyo Hondo in the Northern Rio Grande. Their shared burial, their body positions (two were partly flexed but one individual was partly laid on top of the other two with the left arm extended above the head), and the fact that two large mano fragments are laid directly on the bodies are all unusual interment characteristics.

Beyond a common grave, these children share a pattern of skeletal injuries. Each died as a result of a forceful fatal blow to the crown of the head. In each case, these fractures centered on the sagittal suture and radiated downward, fracturing parietals and temporals; separating coronal, sagittal, occipital, and temporal sutures; and fracturing and separating the basicranium. Only one child, the four-year-old, showed evidence of facial trauma; three upper and two lower incisors were snapped off at the alveolus. All three children exhibited greenstick fractures of the ribs on both sides of their torsos, indicating that their bodies were also beaten or clubbed. Such disquieting forensic data suggest that these three children may have been killed in a single violent act and that their bodies were then disposed of in a common grave without ceremony. The mano fragments that were recovered above their bodies may have served as the instrument of their deaths.

The well-preserved partial remains of a 13-year-old adolescent—an articulated right leg, an articulated left arm, and bits of the right forearm—were also recovered with these children. It is difficult to fully account for this partial skeleton. No additional bone fragments or evidence of weathering were noted for this adolescent's skeleton, nor was there any cutting, marring, or other manipulation of these remains. There is no skeletal evidence of physical violence directed at this individual. Though this adolescent—either as a whole body or as partial articulated remains—appears to have been interred at the same time with the three children, what he or she represents in this multiple interment is uncertain.

The deaths of the three young children are further contextualized by number of other informal interments noted at Arroyo Hondo. The remains of six adults, five on or near the floor and one in the trash fill, were recovered from Kiva G-5. Four adults were recovered from the floors of two rooms in Roomblock 16. In addition, skull fragments exhibiting drybone fracturing and kerf marks on a radius and ulna found scattered on the floor in Roomblock 18 represent at least two adults whose remains were manipulated postmortem. Together, these three children, one adolescent, and 12 adults were subject to acts of violence or postmortem manipulation during the 20 years this area of Arroyo Hondo was inhabited.

Aggression and violence experienced within ancestral Puebloan communities (see chapters 1 and 6 this volume), including Arroyo Hondo, have been variously interpreted as an expression of broad-scale power relations. Such violence may include acts of social dominance or intimidation such as nonlethal abuse (Kantner 1997, 1999; Kuckelman et al. 2000; Martin 1997), cannibalism (e.g., Turner and Turner 1999; White 1992; see also Walker 2008), or systematic genocide (Komar 2008; Potter and Chuipka 2010). Yet community violence can also represent culturally embedded acts in which aggression in response to calamitous everyday events are framed by the group's world view, beliefs, and practices. Within the limits of our ability to reconstruct past behavior, the context and patterns of violence can provide us with insights into what the deaths of these children could have represented to those who resided at Arroyo Hondo.

Witchcraft currently is one of the most persuasive interpretations for some acts of violence noted in ancestral Pueblo villages. Discussions of witchcraft are found throughout the published literature and in ethnographies of various Puebloan groups (e.g., Anderson et al. 1989; Cushing 1967 [1882–1883]; Hawley 1950; Hill and Lange 1982; Hoebel 1952; Lummis 1894;

Ortiz 1969; Parsons 1927a, 1927b, 1939; Simmons 1974; Smith and Roberts 1954; Stevenson 1904; Titiev 1972; White 1935, 1942, 1962). Witches were personifications of evil in Puebloan society and were held responsible for drought, illness, and other misfortunes, from minor to catastrophic. In Puebloan beliefs, witches were spirits that preyed upon the "unexpired lives" of those who had died but whose spirits had not yet been freed to return to the underworld (Ortiz 1969, 140). These witch spirits took human form by occupying the bodies of the living. Ethnographic accounts indicate that the killing of witches was a dangerous, heavily ritualized task that was undertaken only by those in specific ritual societies (for example, the Bear Society at Santa Clara [Hill and Lange 1982]; the Flint, Giant, and Fire societies at Zia [White 1930, 1962]; and the Medicine Society at Isleta [Ellis 1979]). Various forms of interrogation and ritualized violence were directed at those suspected of being witches, including clubbing, torture, bludgeoning, execution, dismemberment, defleshing, cutting, body pounding, crushing of body parts, and burning (Darling 1998; Ellis 1951, 1968, 1970; Goldfrank 1967). Witches could ultimately be destroyed if one turned their spirit to dust (*nag opah,* Ortiz 1969, 40). The greater, more common social concern was that a witch's spirit had been prohibited from returning to the underworld (Simmons 1942) and instead lingered among the living, waiting for the opportunity to possess another human (Goldfrank 1967; Ortiz 1969). Since witches usually appeared in human form (Parsons 1939), physical trauma to the body rendered it useless to the witch's spirit (Goldfrank 1967; Ortiz 1969). Acts of aggression and violence (for example, the ritual handling and speaking to arrows for protection and strength) and acts of curing and purification (for example, the use of ashes) were all measures used to drive away, to protect against, or to outright to kill witches (Darling 1998).

Witches were dangerous in part because they could be anyone. Witches could be male or female, young or old. Witchcraft knowledge and power could be passed through families or passed on to individuals who were recruited. Witches could also organize themselves into societies much like other ritual groups. Witches could act alone, though long-established familial relationships sometimes resulted in multiple executions that included children (Darling 1998). The archaeological context and forensic assessment used to interpret the deaths of the three children at Arroyo Hondo appear to be consistent with the ethnographic information on witchcraft accusations.

These childhood deaths also lead us to consider the relationship between "personhood" at fourteenth-century Arroyo Hondo and the meaning of community and ritualized violence. Generally, Western societies
view "persons" as individuals fixed by a physical body and by an identity
shaped by social interactions into a fully integrated, complete individual
who has personal agency. However, the concept of personhood is not necessarily coincident with the concept of individual in some Melanesian
societies, such as those in Highland New Guinea, where people exist as
"dividual" and "partible" (Fowler 2004, 15). In these cultures, a person is
not contained in one physical body; aspects of the person reside in social
interactions, substances, objects, animals, and other relations outside the
body. In this sense, a person is relational and is defined by context and
actions, and interactions with "things" convey elements of personhood to
the individual. Fowler (2004) has suggested ideas of personhood that may
provide insights about the past, for example, how persons are embodied in part by their interactions with fur-bearing mammals in Mesolithic
Scandinavia.

It appears that Puebloan cosmology may have similarly shaped people
as relational persons. Ethnographers have noted that Puebloans distinguish between kinds of beings (see Ellis 1951; Ortiz 1969; White 1962),
including everyday individuals (according to Ortiz, "Dry Food People," or
weed people), individuals who fulfill particular secular or ritual functions
(Ortiz's Towaʾe), and Made people, or those with a special status related
to moieties (Ortiz's Patowaʾe). These kinds of beings have parallel forms
in the spiritual world, and upon death, one becomes the same kind of being in the underworld. The interplay between earthly existence and the
underworld and the melding of these two planes of spiritual existence are
evident in several ways. For example, during annual ritual cycles, Made
people appear as underworld deities, literally becoming the personifi-
cation of these deities; the underworld spirit is embodied in its earthly
counterpart. In the case of the recently deceased, the spirit leaves the body
and remains in the village for four days before taking up permanent residence in the underworld. In this situation, the person is the spirit that
is making the transition from earthly existence to the underworld and
the physical body retains no special significance. Each of these instances
suggests that a Puebloan person is centered in a spiritual existence that is
fluid and relational, in the context of both moments of ritual performance
and transitions between earthly and underworld beings.

Of interest here are two categories of being, innocents (or "not *seh t'a*") and witches ("*chuge ing*") (Ortiz 1969, 140). Children younger than six years are considered to be innocents whose existence is still within the realm of the underworld, and they are therefore not yet persons. As Ortiz has noted, "to be not yet *seh t'a* is to be innocent or not yet knowing. . . . To be innocent is to be not yet Tewa; to be not yet Tewa is to be not yet human; and to be not yet human is to be, in this use of the term, not entirely out of the realm of spiritual existence" (ibid.)

Young children retain an ambiguous status as persons; their earthly existence is recognized through a naming ceremony after four days of life, and a water-giving ceremony at one year recognizes the infant as a part of a moiety within the village's social structure. It is not until the water-pouring ceremony that occurs between 6 and 10 years of age and the finishing ceremony that occurs at 10 years that a child's existence is recognized as fully incorporated into an earthly person. Only when an individual becomes Towa'e (a Dry Food Person), at which point gender roles are given and one is formally incorporated into a moiety, is he or she finally considered fully human. This is when the individual becomes a person.

Witches are a different category of beings. Like children, they are individuals who contain a spirit, but they are never persons. They are unwanted and dangerous spirits who bring ill fortune to those who are considered persons.

> Witches do not exist . . . independently of the three living categories of being, because they recruit their members from the living and lead a parallel existence with them in this life. Because witches live on the unexpired lives of their victims, it is believed they must continually kill or perish themselves. Thus witchcraft is a shadowy but parallel partner in this life; it is a spectre which stands ever ready to invade the other three human categories. (Ortiz 1969, 140)

The earthly presence of witches and their ability to take physical form as individuals renders the representation of "person" within Puebloan cosmology both fluid and potentially fraught with danger. Unlike children, whose ritual path eventually incorporates them into Puebloan society by endowing them with personhood, witches represent an evil influence that threatens to disrupt and destabilize the orderliness of Puebloan society and cosmology.

This perception of personhood has interesting implications for our understanding of community violence and ritualized violence. Violent, ritualized acts as responses to everyday stresses may not necessarily have been untaken or understood in the same way as other violent events, particularly when directed at members of a social group who were suspected of witchcraft. It is possible that at Arroyo Hondo, once stresses such as disease, illness, crop failure, and drought were perceived to be the result of witchcraft, individuals were scrutinized and accusations were made. Suspected individuals were likely members of the community yet at some point were no longer perceived as "persons" within the realm of cosmology but rather as some other form of evil being . From this perspective, it is possible that the three young children in the trash fill at Arroyo Hondo were perceived as threats, as somehow dangerous because the community believed that witch spirits had entered their bodies. As innocents—beings not of this world—they were particularly susceptible to possession by evil influences. They may have been targeted for ritualized acts of violence—the fatal blows to the crowns of their heads, the breaking of their teeth, and the clubbing of their torsos—because they were not perceived as members of the village or as "persons" within the Puebloan cosmology. This violent act may have served to protect "persons" within the village by damaging the bodies of the children and thus rendering them no longer usable by witches. Perhaps the violence was performed as a ritualized and perhaps even an obligatory responsibility. If that is the case, these were not acts of social domination. The deaths of these three children at Arroyo Hondo may have been purposeful, necessarily violent acts that were shaped by and understood within an understanding of personhood as a fluid category that carried the responsibility for discovering and dealing with nonpersons responsible for evil deeds.

By any measure, the fourteenth-century village of Arroyo Hondo was an ancestral Pueblo under severe stress, particularly because dietary limitations had a profound impact on the health of the villagers. The pueblo had been founded around AD 1300 at a time of relative abundance for the Galisteo Basin. But after that time, rainfall declined steadily, which necessitated dry farming and the exploitation of locally available plant and animal resources. These resources were not enough for more than a marginal existence. Temperature declines in the period may also have affected the length of growing seasons and the amount of crop production. Scurvy and megablastic anemia were common among the villagers at Arroyo Hondo.

Rickets—which is usually observed only in isolated cases in ancestral Puebloan groups—was pervasive at Arroyo Hondo. Nine adults and four children recovered during excavations exhibited skeletal deformation and patterned porosities associated with rickets. These individuals would have experienced lifelong physical limitations from limb deformation. A young woman severely affected by developmental field defects and delays as well as a case of anencephaly were also present in the population. The height of these health stresses and the violence events evident from many informal interments occurred in the same time span of roughly 30 years. It is possible that health issues related to insufficient food resources were among the stresses that led to and triggered the violence events that lead to the deaths of the three children at Arroyo Hondo. I suggest that cosmology shaped not just the lives of these people but their understanding of this violence as well.

Archaeologists have explored the similarities and differences between the ethnohistorical record and earlier ancestral Puebloan villages in many ways. It is clear that many aspects of Puebloan cosmology that we find in historical accounts were practiced at fourteenth-century northern Rio Grande settlements such as Arroyo Hondo. Yet the material evidence we note archaeologically is more than patterns of behavior that we can link to the ethnographic past. The parallels evident between fourteenth-century Puebloan life and ethnohistorical accounts suggest that fundamental aspects of the Puebloan world view and cosmology that ethnologists have described defined the nature of good and evil in ancient Pueblo groups and likely underpinned appropriate, sanctioned, ritualized responses to misfortune. Variability in these patterns in the region and across time (especially comparing Arroyo Hondo with the Southwest sites discussion by Pérez this volume) are intriguing and provide a cautionary note about generalizations. Both the anomalies we see in the unusual interments at Arroyo Hondo and the individuals who died violently point to categories of nonpersons within ancestral Puebloan society and suggest that not all violence acts at villages such as Arroyo Hondo carried the same meaning. It is possible that some community violence may have been ritualized, perhaps obligatory acts directed at those who were not "persons" and thus were perceived to be threats to the well-being of the community. These violent acts may well have been attempts to deal with evil influences that were affecting the village instead of the result of power struggles between competing groups. What we see materially at Arroyo Hondo is evidence not just of violence but of events whose meaning is both nuanced by and deeply embedded in a cosmology that shaped and gave meaning to the lives and deaths of these past people.

## References Cited

Anderson, I. F., K. J. Crichton, T. Grattan-Smith, R. A. Cooper, and D. Brazier
1989    Osteochondral Fractures of the Dome of the Talus. *The Journal of Bone and Joint Surgery* 71(8): 1143–1152.
Cushing, F. H.
1967 [1882–1883]    *My Adventures in Zuni.* Filter Press, Palmer Lake.
Darling, A. J.
1998    Mass Inhumation and the Execution of Witches in the American Southwest. *American Anthropologist,* n.s. 100(3): 732–752.
Ellis, F. H.
1951    Patterns of Aggression and the War Cult in Southwestern Pueblos. *Southwestern Journal of Anthropology* 100(3): 732–752.
1968    An Interpretation of Prehistoric Death Customs in Terms of Modern Southwest Parallels. In *Collected Papers in Honor of Lyndon Lane Hargrave,* edited by A. H. Schroeder, pp. 57–76. Papers of the Archaeological Society of New Mexico no. 1. Museums of New Mexico Press, Albuquerque.
1970    Pueblo Witchcraft and Medicine. In *Systems of North American Witchcraft and Sorcery,* edited by D. E. Walker, pp. 37–72. vol. 1. Anthropological Monographs of the University of Idaho. University of Idaho Press, Moscow.
1979    Isleta Pueblo. In *Southwest,* edited by A. Ortiz, pp. 351–365. Vol. 19 of *Handbook of North American Indians.* Smithsonian Institution Press, Washington, D.C.
Fowler, C.
2004    *The Archaeology of Personhood: An Anthropological Approach.* Routledge, London.
Goldfrank, E. S.
1967    *The Artist of "Isleta Paintings" in Pueblo Society.* Smithsonian Contributions to Anthropology no. 5. Smithsonian Institution Press, Washington, D.C.
Hawley, F. M.
1950    The Mechanics of Perpetuation in Pueblo Witchcraft. In *For the Dean: Essays in Anthropology in Honor of Byron Cummings on His Eighty-Ninth Birthday,* edited by E. K. Reed and D. S. King, pp. 143–158. Hohokam Museums Association and Southwestern Monuments Association, Tucson.
Hill, W. W., and C. H. Lange
1982    *An Ethnology of Santa Clara Pueblo.* University of New Mexico Press, Albuquerque.
Hoebel, E. A.
1952    Keresan Witchcraft. *American Anthropologist* 54: 586–589.

Kantner, J.
1997    Survival Cannibalism or Sociopolitical Intimidation? Explaining Perimortem
        Mutilation in the American Southwest. Paper presented at the 62nd Annual
        Meeting of the Society for American Archaeology, Nashville, Tennessee, April.
1999    Survival Cannibalism or Sociopolitical Intimidation? Explaining Perimortem
        Mutilation in the American Southwest. *Human Nature* 10(1): 1–50.
Komar, D.
2008    Patterns of Mortuary Practice Associated with Genocide: Implications for Ar-
        chaeological Research. *Current Anthropology* 49(1): 123–133.
Kuckelman, K. A., R. R. Lightfoot, and D. L. Martin
2000    Changing Patterns of Violence in the Northern San Juan Region. *Kiva* 66(1):
        147–165.
Lummis, C. F.
1894    *The Man Who Married the Moon and Other Pueblo Indian Folk-Stories.* The
        Century Co., New York.
Martin, D. L.
1997    Violence against Women in the La Plata River Valley (A.D. 1000–1300). In *Trou-
        bled Times: Violence and Warfare in the Past,* edited by D. L. Martin and D. W.
        Frayer, pp. 45–75. Gordon and Breach, Amsterdam.
Ortiz, A.
1969    *The Tewa World.* University of Chicago Press, Chicago.
Parsons, E. C.
1927a   Witchcraft among the Pueblos: Indian or Spanish? *Man* 27 (6): 106–12.
1927b   Witchcraft among the Pueblos: Indian or Spanish? *Man* 27 (7): 125–28.
1939    *Pueblo Indian Religion.* 2 vols. University of Chicago, Chicago.
Potter, J. M., and J. P. Chuipka
2010    Perimortem Mutilation of Human Remains in an Early Village in the American
        Southwest: A Case for Ethnic Violence. *Journal of Anthropological Archaeology*
        29(4): 507–523.
Simmons, L. W.
1942    *Sun Chief: The Autobiography of a Hopi Indian.* Yale University Press, New Ha-
        ven, Conn.
Simmons, M.
1974    *Witchcraft in the Southwest: Spanish and Indian Supernaturalism on the Rio
        Grande.* University of Nebraska Press, Lincoln.
Smith, W., and J. M. Roberts
1954    *Zuni Law: A Field of Values.* Papers of the Peabody Museum of American Ar-
        chaeology and Ethnology, Vol. 43, No. 1. Harvard University Press, Cambridge.
Stevenson, M. C.
1904    *The Zuni Indians: Their Mythology, Esoteric Fraternities and Ceremonies.* Bureau
        of American Ethnology Bulletin no. 23. Smithsonian Institution Press, Wash-
        ington, D.C.
Titiev, M.
1972    *The Hopi Indians of Old Oraibi.* University of Michigan Press, Ann Arbor.

Turner, C. G., II, and J. A. Turner
1999    *Man Corn: Cannibalism and Violence in the Prehistoric American Southwest.* University of Utah Press, Salt Lake City.

Walker, W. H.
2008    Witches, Practice, and the Context of Pueblo Cannibalism. In *Social Violence in the Prehispanic American Southwest,* edited by D. L. Nichols and P. L. Crown, pp. 143–183. University of Arizona Press, Tucson.

White, L. A.
1930    A Comparative Study of Keresan Medicine Societies. In *Proceedings of the 23rd International Congress of Americanists,* pp. 604–619. International Congress of Americanists, New York.
1935    *The Pueblo of Santa Domingo, New Mexico.* Memoirs of the American Anthropological Association no. 43. American Anthropological Association, Menasha.
1942    *The Pueblo of Santa Ana, New Mexico.* Memoirs of the American Anthropological Association no. 60. American Anthropological Association, Menasha.
1962    *The Pueblo of Sia.* Bureau of American Ethnology Bulletin no. 184. Smithsonian Institution Press, Washington, D.C.

White, T. D.
1992    *Prehistoric Cannibalism at Mancos 5MTUMR-2346.* Princeton University Press, Princeton, N.J.

# 6

Bioarchaeological Signatures of Strife
in Terminal Pueblo III Settlements
in the Northern San Juan

KRISTIN A. KUCKELMAN

## Introduction

Ancestral Pueblo farmers inhabited the northern San Juan area of the American Southwest for two millennia before completely and permanently vacating the region about AD 1280. The catalysts and societal context for this population movement, which brought about monumental changes in the Pueblo world, have been the subject of speculation by archaeologists and the public for many decades. Recent research into the causes of this complete depopulation has revealed some factors responsible for this exodus, including a complex array of conditions that began to render the region inhospitable, if not uninhabitable, by the mid-1270s. Numerous and interrelated factors such as severe drought, dense population, resource depletion, cooler temperatures, disrupted seasonal precipitation patterns, truncated growing seasons, environmental degradation, dietary stress, social turmoil, and outbreaks of violence have all been implicated (Ahlstrom, Van West, and Dean 1995; Benson 2006; Cameron 1995; Cameron and Duff 2008; Cordell 1997, 365–397; Cordell et al. 2007; Dean et al. 2000; Dean and Van West 2002; Glowacki 2006, 2010; Kohler 2000, 2010; Kohler, Varien, and Wright 2010; Kohler et al. 2008; Kuckelman 2002, 2006, 2010a, 2010b; Kuckelman, Lightfoot, and Martin 2002; Larsen et al. 1996; Lipe 1995; Lipe and Varien 1999, 339–343; Petersen

1994; Petersen and Matthews 1987; Salzer 2000; Van West and Dean 2000; Varien et al. 1996; Varien et al. 2007; Wright 2006, 2010).

Perhaps the most direct and intriguing evidence of the circumstances associated with this depopulation can be found on the remains of Pueblo residents themselves, those who perished in their villages as migrations from the region were under way. Recent bioarchaeological and contextual analyses of human remains from terminal Pueblo III sites in the northern San Juan region reveal abundant and compelling evidence of conflict and other turmoil associated with regional depopulation. In this chapter, I review the evidence of strife on human remains found in abandonment contexts from sites that have been conclusively dated to the terminal portion of the Pueblo III period. I then examine what these data suggest about the roles of violence and aggression in late Pueblo society in the northern San Juan.

Recent excavations by the Crow Canyon Archaeological Center at the sites of three distinct villages that were constructed, occupied, and vacated during the final 20 to 30 years of regional occupation have yielded bioarchaeological, taphonomic, and contextual evidence of a significant level of strife and other hardship just before the region was depopulated, about AD 1280. Human remains from the Sand Canyon, Castle Rock, and Goodman Point pueblos, located in what is today the Four Corners area of the U.S. Southwest, exhibit evidence of trauma associated with depopulation. This evidence and additional indicators of violence and strife reveal that the occupations of these villages ended as a result of devastating attacks that were probably perpetrated with multiple goals in mind.

The human remains found in abandonment contexts at these three sites that exhibit evidence of violence are the only published assemblages that have been firmly tree-ring-dated to the final few decades of regional occupation. The osteological and taphonomic evidence of strife on these remains thus reflects turmoil that can be firmly associated temporally with the complete depopulation of the region. The associated stratigraphic, depositional, architectural, contextual, and tree-ring data offer unparalleled and invaluable insights about those who perished as well as the societal contexts, conditions, actions, and events that ended the occupations of individual villages and the region as a whole.

Evidence of various forms of strife that might have resulted from discord associated with regional depopulation has been found on human remains from numerous other sites, such as La Plata 23 (White 1992, 367–368), La Plata 33 (Morris 1939, 82), Long House (Nordenskiöld 1979 [1893], 170), Charnel House Tower (Turner and Turner 1999, 141–143), Alkali Ridge Site 13 (Brues 1946, 328), San Juan River NA7166 (Turner and Turner 1999, 335), Site 5MT9943 (Lambert 1999), and Salmon Pueblo (Akins 2008; Shipman 2006; Turner and Turner 1999). I excluded these cases from this study because of outdated or ambiguous analytic data, or because dating was too imprecise to confidently attribute these incidents to the final few years of regional occupation.

At Site 5MT9943, for example, on the Ute Mountain piedmont, three juveniles and an older adult female all perished from blows to the cranium (Lambert 1999). The adult female, whose remains were left on a structure floor, had suffered extensive skull fracturing. The remains of the juveniles had been placed in a pit: one body had been left exposed to the elements before it was put into the pit, and the cranium of another bore cut marks indicative of scalping. However, these incidents of violence cannot be dated more precisely than sometime between AD 1225 and 1280 (Lambert 1999, 217–218, 225) and thus might have occurred many years before final regional depopulation.

And at Salmon Pueblo, along the San Juan River in northwestern New Mexico, some form of strife might have been a factor in the charring and commingling of the remains of at least 25 individuals, mostly children, in the collapsed roofing material of a structure referred to as the Tower Kiva (Akins 2008). Although this event has been firmly tree-ring dated to the terminal portion of the Pueblo III period, after AD 1263, the analytic data, taphonomic interpretations, and resulting conclusions of the numerous osteologists who have studied these remains vary widely (cf. Akins 2008; Turner and Turner 1999). Inferences include accident, warfare, considerate cremation, and cannibalism (Akins 2008; Shipman 2006; Turner and Turner 1999). The ambiguity of the data and the conflicting interpretations compel me to exclude the assemblage from the Salmon Tower Kiva from this study.

From AD 1260 to 1280, Sand Canyon Pueblo and Goodman Point Pueblo were probably the two largest settlements in the region; each housed 500 to 800 residents. Like many villages built in the mid-1200s in this region, these pueblos were constructed around springs at the heads of canyons and were largely enclosed by massive one-story-tall stone walls. Multiple lines of evidence suggest that these walls served defensive purposes (Kenzle 1993; Kuckelman 2002; Kuckelman et al. 2007, paras. 172–175; Kuckelman, Lightfoot, and Martin 2002). Castle Rock Pueblo, a contemporaneous but smaller village located in McElmo Canyon 7.5 km southwest of Sand Canyon Pueblo, was constructed in a defensive posture on and around the base of a narrow, prominent butte. It was home to 75 to 150 residents.

Tree-ring data indicate that a drought referred to by archaeologists as the Great Drought descended on the northern San Juan by AD 1276 and persisted until 1299. Other research indicates that the area suffered a variety of deleterious climatic and other environmental changes (Kohler, Varien, and Wright 2010) as well as an unprecedented population density during this time (Kohler et al. 2007; Varien et al. 2007).

A recent study revealed that the residents of the Sand Canyon, Castle Rock, and Goodman Point pueblos suffered dietary stress just before the occupations of those villages ended and the region was depopulated (Kuckelman 2008, 2010a, 2010b). That study compared food remains recovered from middens, or refuse deposits, to food remains left in abandonment contexts—for example, in collapsed roofing debris, on floor surfaces, or in the fills of cooking hearths. The remains in the middens tell us what the residents ate during most of the span of village occupation, whereas the remains left in abandonment contexts reveal the contents of the final meals consumed by the residents of these villages before they either migrated or were killed by attackers. The comparison of food remains indicates that just before regional depopulation maize and other crops failed and flocks of domesticated turkeys, which provided essential animal protein, were much diminished. The populace subsisted primarily by hunting and gathering whatever wild foods could be obtained across the depleted and drought-ravaged landscape. They competed with the residents of other communities for the same scanty resources.

Osteological and taphonomic analyses of human remains found in abandonment contexts at the Sand Canyon, Castle Rock, and Goodman Point pueblos reveal numerous types of trauma, modifications, and other evidence of aggression that indicate village-wide attacks. Tree-ring dates tie this lethal violence to the depopulation of the northern San Juan. The villages were attacked sometime after the latest tree-ring date for each site—AD 1277 for Sand Canyon, 1274 for Castle Rock, and 1269 for Goodman Point Pueblo. These dates thus temporally associate the evidence of strife on the human remains in abandonment contexts with the depopulation of these villages and the region about AD 1280.

In all likelihood, the attackers were other Pueblo residents of the region (Bradley 2002; Kuckelman 2002, 245–246, 2006, 134; Kuckelman et al. 2007, para. 201; Lightfoot and Kuckelman 2001, 64; Linton 1944; Lipe and Varien 1999, 341). Further, the human remains found in abandonment contexts at each of these three sites appear to be those of residents of the pueblos rather than the remains of attackers. When occupations of these villages ended, a minimum of 35 individuals had died at Sand Canyon Pueblo, at least 41 residents of Castle Rock Pueblo had died, and a minimum of 11 villagers had died at Goodman Point Pueblo.

## Methods

The Crow Canyon Archaeological Center conducted excavations at Sand Canyon Pueblo from 1984 to 1993, during which 5 percent of the site was excavated (Kuckelman 2007). We conducted fieldwork at Castle Rock Pueblo from 1990 through 1994, during which 5 percent of the site was excavated (Kuckelman 2000). Our research at Goodman Point Pueblo occurred from 2005 through 2008, during which slightly less than 1 percent of the site was excavated (Kuckelman, Coffey, and Copeland 2009). The human remains discovered during excavations at the Sand Canyon and Castle Rock pueblos were analyzed by various osteologists: J. Michael Hoffman, David A. Kice, M. Anne Katzenberg, Cynthia S. Bradley, Debra L. Martin, and Alan H. Goodman (Kuckelman and Martin 2007, Table 5). Kathy Mowrer performed in-field analysis on remains at Goodman Point Pueblo (analytic records on file at the Crow Canyon Archaeological Center). Excavation methods used at the Sand Canyon and Castle Rock pueblos are described in an early version of Crow Canyon's *Field Manual* (Bradley and Lightfoot 1986), and methods used at Goodman Point Pueblo are outlined in a later version of that manual (Crow Canyon Archaeological Center 2001b). Electronic site reports and databases contain plan maps and descriptions of remains found at Sand Canyon Pueblo (Crow Canyon Archaeological Center 2004; Kuckelman 2007; Kuckelman and Martin 2007) and Castle Rock Pueblo (Crow Canyon Archaeological Center 2001a); a comprehensive site report for Goodman Point Pueblo is in preparation as of this writing.

## Results

Recent bioarchaeological and contextual analyses of human remains from these terminal Pueblo III sites in the northern San Juan reveal a variety of lethal and nonlethal trauma and other evidence of aggression, including antemortem and perimortem cranial depression fractures, broken noses, teeth fractured from blows to the mouth, modifications indicative of trophy taking, nonformal disposition of remains, postmortem neglect, disarticulation, spiral fracturing, cut marks, burning, and incomplete and commingled remains of multiple individuals (Kuckelman 2008, 2010a, 2010b; Kuckelman, Lightfoot, and Martin 2002; Kuckelman and Martin 2007; Mowrer 2010). Some of these bioarchaeological signatures of strife can be categorized as evidence of aggression and others as evidence of anthropophagy (the consumption of human flesh). Also, some villagers might have died of starvation. However, starvation cannot be reliably assessed from skeletal remains (White 1992, 363). Aggression is directly indicated on these remains by the following evidence: cranial depression fractures, nasal fractures, teeth broken from blows to the mouth, a variety of postcranial fractures, face removal, cranial cut marks indicative of scalping, and articulated remains thermally altered by exposure to burning roof timbers.

Aggression is indirectly indicated by postmortem neglect; that is, remains that were either left or deposited in abandonment contexts (on floors, roofs, or prehistoric ground surface) and by remains that are disarticulated, weathered, or damaged by carnivores. Postmortem neglect was the most prevalent indicator of aggression at all three sites under study. Articulated remains in sprawled positions are also indicative of violent death (Figs. 6.1 and 6.2); many bodies at the Sand Canyon and Castle Rock pueblos were apparently deposited through a convenient doorway or roof hatchway. After suffering blunt force trauma to the cranium, the individual in Figure 6.2 was apparently thrown head-first down the kiva hatchway, the cranium further shattering as it struck the vertical slab deflector.

Specific evidence of anthropophagy includes cut marks, chop marks, percussion striae, inner conchoidal fracture scars, spiral fractures, reaming, end polish or pot polish, thermal alteration of disarticulated remains (especially of the articular ends of long bones), deposits of incomplete and

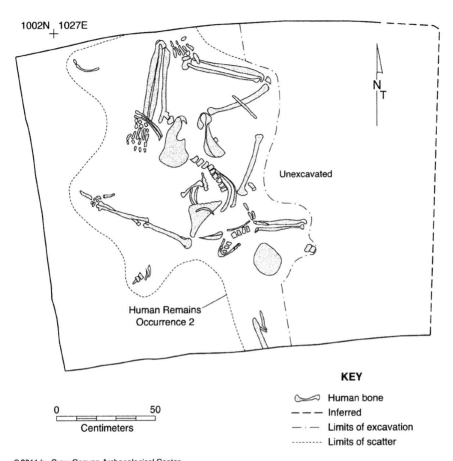

1002N 1027E
+

Unexcavated

N
↑

Human Remains
Occurrence 2

**KEY**

⌒⌒⌒ Human bone
— — — Inferred
— · — Limits of excavation
·········· Limits of scatter

0 _____ 50
Centimeters

Fig. 6.1. Plan map of Human Remains Occurrence 2, Room 105.

commingled remains of multiple individuals (Fig. 6.3), and the presence of human myoglobin in two cooking jars and a mug (Kuckelman, Lightfoot, and Martin 2002). The most compelling evidence of widespread anthropophagy was found at Castle Rock Pueblo (ibid.). This anthropophagy might have been prompted by dietary stress, competition for resources, and widespread societal turmoil that immediately preceded the depopulation of the region (Kuckelman 2010b).

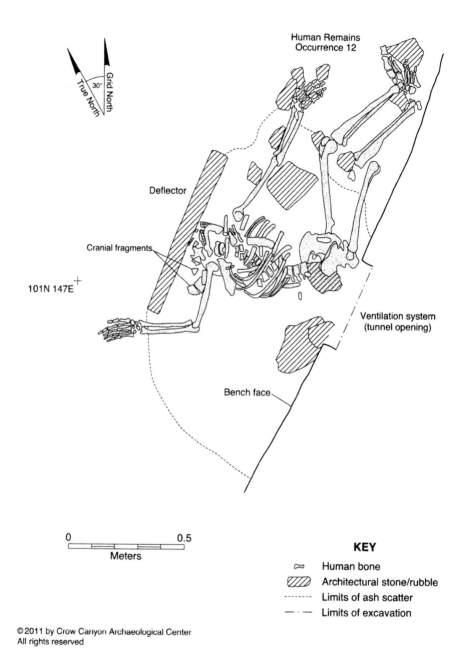

Human Remains
Occurrence 12

Grid North

True North

30°

Deflector

Cranial fragments

101N 147E

Ventilation system
(tunnel opening)

Bench face

0                  0.5
Meters

**KEY**

Human bone

Architectural stone/rubble

- - - - - - - Limits of ash scatter

— · — Limits of excavation

Fig. 6.2. Plan map of Human Remains Occurrence 12, Kiva 103.

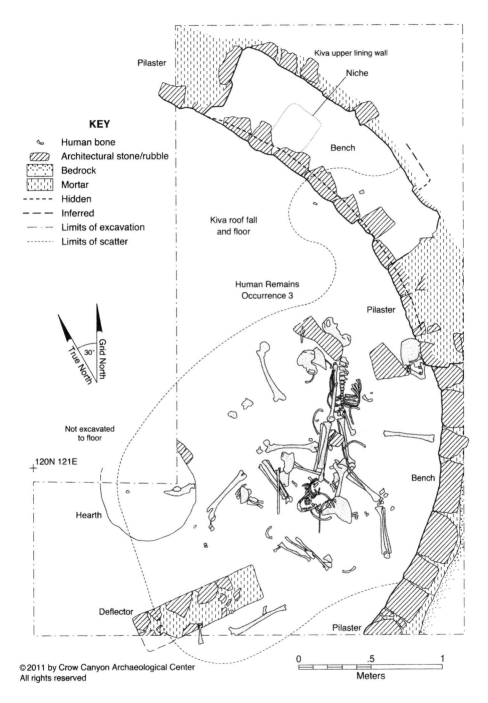

KEY

| | |
|---|---|
| 👃 | Human bone |
| ▨ | Architectural stone/rubble |
| ⬚ | Bedrock |
| ⬚ | Mortar |
| - - - - - | Hidden |
| — — — | Inferred |
| —·—·— | Limits of excavation |
| ·········· | Limits of scatter |

Pilaster

Kiva upper lining wall

Niche

Bench

Kiva roof fall
and floor

Human Remains
Occurrence 3

Pilaster

Grid North

30°

True North

Not excavated
to floor

+120N 121E

Hearth

Bench

Deflector

Pilaster

0   .5   1

Meters

Fig. 6.3. Map of Human Remains Occurrence 3, Kiva 302.

## Discussion

The foregoing bioarchaeological, taphonomic, and contextual data associate strife with the depopulation of the region in the late AD 1200s in the following forms: nonlethal aggression in the form of postcranial fractures, lethal aggression in the form of perimortem cranial fractures, ritual aggression in the form of trophy taking, and anthropophagy. These bioarchaeological signatures of strife reveal a great deal about the roles of aggression and violence in Ancestral Pueblo society during the depopulation of the northern San Juan.

In the context of the widespread deterioration of climatic and other environmental conditions, aggression would have served to relieve subsistence stress by intimidating and inhibiting the mobility of those competing for wild resources. Lethal violence would have reduced the number of individuals competing for limited stored and wild food resources. The remains of few men in their prime were found in abandonment contexts; the fact that most of the remains found were those of women, children, and the ill and the incapacitated suggests that young, able-bodied men were absent from the villages during the attacks and that the motive for the attacks was the elimination of competition rather than military.

Aggression would have also served to relieve subsistence stress by enabling access to consumables such as turkeys and stored food in settlements. Had the goal been merely to neutralize competitors—a far safer strategy and one that would have required significantly fewer warriors—the aggressors would have ambushed small parties as they ventured outside the pueblos. Thus, attacks on these fortified settlements suggest that entry into the villages and access to stored provisions was a primary goal of the aggression. Lethal aggression would also have served to relieve subsistence stress by enabling the victors to engage in anthropophagy, which could have been prompted by severe, drought-related food shortages.

Two types of aggression were less clearly associated with the relief of subsistence stress. Trophy taking, such as scalping, face removal, and decapitation, can be interpreted as politico-ritual acts of triumph that were intended to display dominance over enemies and might also have functioned to intimidate and demoralize potential adversaries. These acts might thus have been distinct from the strictly pragmatic elimination of competitors for resources. However, among Pueblo Indians ethnohistorically, the taking of scalps has been associated with promoting or ensuring precipitation (Ellis 1979, 444–445; Parsons 1939). Parsons (Parsons 1929, 138) states that "at Zuni and presumably in all the pueblos the scalps are rain senders." Thus, the conflict and the associated taking of scalps that occurred just before the depopulation of the northern San Juan region might have been an attempt to lessen or end the droughty conditions that plagued the residents of the region in the late 1270s.

Second, the motivations behind and the actions that resulted in the deposition of charred cranial fragments found on extramural surfaces in Architectural Blocks 700 and 1200 at Goodman Point Pueblo (Kuckelman, Coffey, and Copeland 2009, Fig. 6.2) are unclear. Block 700 was a distinctive, planned, multistory, D-shaped, biwall structure on the canyon rim in the center of the village. This complex was probably designed and used for special purposes by ritual or political leaders. Charred cranial fragments were found in a fire pit dug into a prehistoric ground surface a few meters north of the structure, and additional fragments were scattered on an extramural surface just outside a doorway in the west wall of the structure and in midden deposits southwest of the structure. No charred cranial fragments or human bones of any type were found in any thermal feature at Castle Rock or Sand Canyon Pueblo, nor were any such fragments found on any extramural surface at either of those sites. The presence of the remains in these particular contexts at Goodman Point Pueblo thus raises the possibility that the charring and depositing of the remains were in some manner associated with special use of the D-shaped block.

An additional charred cranial fragment—an upper eye orbit of an adult that exhibited a perimortem fracture (Mowrer 2010)—was found in a shallow midden deposit in Architectural Block 1200. This large block contains two public buildings—a great kiva and a pre-planned, four-kiva complex encircled by biwall rooms (Kuckelman, Coffey, and Copeland 2009, Fig. 6.2). No burned human remains were found in midden deposits at Sand Canyon or Castle Rock Pueblo, and the presence of such remains in midden contexts in Blocks 700 and 1200 at Goodman Point Pueblo suggests that these fractured and burned remains were deposited by the residents of Goodman Point Pueblo itself rather than by attackers who, one might argue, would have been unlikely to observe the customary discard locations of village residents.

The disarticulation and charring of these remains clearly were caused by human actions. It is not impossible that these actions stemmed from starvation or revenge anthropophagy perpetrated by the attackers of these villages, which appears to have been the case with the disarticulated remains found at Castle Rock and possibly at Sand Canyon Pueblo. However, the fragments were not accompanied by other bones, were located in ambiguous contexts that might not have been associated with abandonment, and were found near public architecture. The fact that some fragments were in a fire pit and others were in middens suggest an alternative possibility—that these fragments indicate actions with the remains of enemies perpetrated by the residents of Goodman Point Pueblo late in the occupation of the village instead of indicating actions of attackers after they overran the village. Thus, these fragments might have been deposited by residents of Goodman Point Pueblo as a result of ritual activity by leaders or other privileged individuals and might have involved trophy remains of enemies that had been brought back to Goodman Point Pueblo. Such actions, instead of being part of a strictly secular survival strategy, could have served to gain political or ritual power or prestige or to display dominance over "others."

## Conclusion

Although the level of conflict perpetrated by the Ancestral Pueblo residents of the northern San Juan was small in scale compared to the types of warfare waged by the highly trained and organized standing armies of nations of other times and places, the events recounted here nevertheless illustrate widespread violent and desperate actions that affected many people and had profound societal consequences. Empirical evidence of trauma associated with depopulation, as well as additional indicators of conflict that were revealed during excavations at the Sand Canyon, Castle Rock, and Goodman Point pueblos, suggest that violent attacks on these terminal Pueblo III villages might have served numerous purposes: to eliminate or reduce competition for limited resources; to gain access to consumables such as turkeys and stored food within settlements; to intimidate, demoralize, and display dominance over other Pueblo communities; to engage in anthropophagy; or to engage in magico-religious acts designed to lessen or end the drought.

This study of the bioarchaeological signatures of strife on the remains of Pueblo residents of the northern San Juan who perished during the depopulation of the region about AD 1280 reveals a variety of aggressive actions involving the residents of multiple villages across the region. In the context of drought, resource depletion, and crop failure in the mid-1270s, many of these actions could have been motivated by the need to mitigate effects of subsistence stress and might have functioned to put the limited resources that were available into the hands of the most able and aggressive members of society. In other words, these actions might have enabled the survival of a cultural group. Although this mechanism was probably beneficial from the standpoint of societal survival, it clearly undermined the welfare of members of subordinate groups who were the primary victims of aggression. Other actions, such as trophy taking, stemmed from more subtle and nuanced aspects of Pueblo society and cosmology at the time, illustrating perhaps a drive to exert or gain control over enemy competitors through ritual and symbolic displays of dominance or to bring an end to droughty climatic conditions.

These bioarchaeological signatures of strife on the human remains from terminal Pueblo III villages in the northern San Juan region thus shed light on important aspects of the depopulation of the region and complex facets of the cultural roles of violence and aggression in ancient Pueblo society during migrations from the region late in the thirteenth century. The bioarchaeological evidence of strife temporally associated with regional depopulation thus illuminates crucial and fundamental aspects of the cultural role of aggression and violence at an especially significant hinge point in Pueblo prehistory.

## References Cited

Ahlstrom, R. V. N., C. R. Van West, and J. S. Dean
1995    Environmental and Chronological Factors in the Mesa Verde–Northern Rio Grande Migration. *Journal of Anthropological Archaeology* 14: 125–142.
Akins, N. J.
2008    Human Remains Recovered from the Tower Kiva at Salmon Ruins. In *Chaco's Northern Prodigies: Salmon, Aztec, and the Ascendancy of the Middle San Juan Region after AD 1100*, edited by P. Reed, pp. 140–164. The University of Utah Press, Salt Lake City.
Benson, R.
2006    *The Just War Theory: A Traditional Catholic Moral View.* The Tidings, Los Angeles.

Bradley, B. A., and R. R. Lightfoot
1986    *Field Manual.* Crow Canyon Archaeological Center, Cortez.
Bradley, C. S.
2002    Thoughts Count: Ideology and the Children of Sand Canyon Pueblo. In *Children in the Prehistoric Puebloan Southwest,* edited by K. A. Kamp, pp. 169–195. University of Utah Press, Salt Lake City.
Brues, A.
1946    Alkali Ridge Skeletons, Pathology and Anomaly. In *Archaeology of Alkali Ridge, Southeastern Utah,* edited by J. O. Brew, pp. 327–329. Papers of the Peabody Museum of American Archaeology and Ethnology, vol. 21. Harvard University Press, Cambridge, Mass.
Cameron, C. M.
1995    Migration and the Movement of Southwestern Peoples. *Journal of Anthropological Archaeology* 14: 104–124.
Cameron, C. M., and A. I. Duff
2008    History and Process in Village Formation: Context and Contrasts from the Northern Southwest. *American Antiquity* 73(1): 29–57.
Cordell, L. S.
1997    *Archaeology of the Southwest.* 2nd ed. Academic Press, San Diego.
Cordell, L. S., C. R. Van West, J. S. Dean, and D. A. Muenchrath
2007    Mesa Verde Settlement History and Relocation: Climate Change, Social Networks, and Ancestral Pueblo Migration. *Kiva* 72: 379–405.
Crow Canyon Archaeological Center
2001a   The Castle Rock Pueblo Database. Crow Canyon Archaeological Center. Available at http: //www.crowcanyon.org/ResearchReports/dbw/dbw_chooser. asp?Site=5MT1825. Accessed August 4, 2010.
2001b   The Crow Canyon Archaeological Center Field Manual. Crow Canyon Archaeological Center. Available at http: //www.crowcanyon.org/ResearchReports/ FieldManual/fm_titlepage.asp. Accessed July 30, 2010.
2004    The Sand Canyon Pueblo Database. Crow Canyon Archaeological Center. Available at http: //www.crowcanyon.org/ResearchReports/dbw/dbw_chooser. asp?Site=5MT765. Accessed August 4, 2010.
Dean, J. S., G. J. Gumerman, J. M. Epstein, R. L. Axtell, A. C. Swedlund, M. T. Parker, and S. McCarroll
2000    Understanding Anasazi Culture Change through Agent-Based Modeling. In *Dynamics in Human and Primate Societies: Agent-Based Modeling of Social and Spatial Processes,* edited by T. A. Kohler and G. J. Gumerman, pp. 179–205. Oxford University Press, New York.
Dean, J. S., and C. R. Van West
2002    Environment-Behavior Relationships in Southwestern Colorado. In *Seeking the Center Place: Archaeology and Ancient Communities in the Mesa Verde Region,* edited by M. D. Varien and R. H. Wilshusen, pp. 81–99. University of Utah Press, Salt Lake City.

Ellis, F. H.
1979    Laguna Pueblo. In *Southwest*, edited by A. Ortiz, pp. 438–449. Vol. 19 of *Handbook of North American Indians*. Smithsonian Institution Press, Washington, D.C.

Glowacki, D. M.
2006    The Social Landscape of Depopulation: The Northern San Juan, A.D. 1150–1300. Ph.D. dissertation, Arizona State University.
2010    The Social and Cultural Contexts of the Thirteenth-Century Migrations from the Central Mesa Verde Region. In *Leaving Mesa Verde: Peril and Change in the Thirteenth-Century Southwest*, edited by T. A. Kohler, M. D. Varien, and A. M. Wright, pp. 200–221. University of Arizona Press, Tucson.

Kenzle, S. C.
1993    Enclosing Walls: A Study of Architectural Function in the American Southwest. M.A. thesis, University of Calgary.

Kohler, T. A.
2000    The Final 400 Years of Prehispanic Agricultural Society in the Mesa Verde Region. *Kiva* 66: 191–204.
2010    A New Paleoproductivity Reconstruction for Southwestern Colorado, and Its Implications for Understanding Thirteenth-Century Depopulation. In *Leaving Mesa Verde: Peril and Change in the Thirteenth-Century Southwest*, edited by T. A. Kohler, M. D. Varien, and A. M. Wright, pp. 102–127. University of Arizona Press, Tucson.

Kohler, T. A., C. D. Johnson, M. D. Varien, S. G. Ortman, R. G. Reynolds, Z. Kobti, J. Cowan, K. Kolm, S. Smith, and L. Yap
2007    Settlement Ecodynamics in the Prehispanic Central Mesa Verde Region. In *The Model-Based Archaeology of Socionatural Systems*, edited by T. A. Kohler and S. van der Leeuw, pp. 61–104. School for Advanced Research Press, Santa Fe.

Kohler, T. A., M. D. Varien, and A. M. Wright (editors)
2010    *Leaving Mesa Verde: Peril and Change in the Thirteenth-Century Southwest*. University of Arizona Press, Tucson.

Kohler, T. A., M. D. Varien, A. M. Wright, and K. A. Kuckelman
2008    Mesa Verde Migrations: New Archaeological Research and Computer Simulation Suggests Why Ancestral Puebloans Deserted the Northern Southwest United States. *American Scientist* 96: 146–153.

Kuckelman, K. A.
2002    Thirteenth-Century Warfare in the Central Mesa Verde Region. In *Seeking the Center Place: Archaeology and Ancient Communities in the Mesa Verde Region*, edited by M. D. Varien and R. H. Wilshusen. University of Utah Press, Salt Lake City.
2006    Ancient Violence in the Mesa Verde Region. In *The Mesa Verde World: Explorations in Ancestral Pueblo Archaeology*, edited by D. G. N. Noble, pp. 127–136. School of American Research Press, Santa Fe.
2008    An Agent-Based Case Study of the Depopulation of Sand Canyon Pueblo. In

*The Social Construction of Communities: Agency, Structure, and Identity in the Prehispanic Southwest,* edited by M. D. Varien and J. M. Potter, pp. 109–121. Altamira, Boulder, Colo.

2010a   Catalysts of the Thirteenth-Century Depopulation of Sand Canyon Pueblo and the Central Mesa Verde Region. In *Leaving Mesa Verde: Peril and Change in the Thirteenth-Century Southwest,* edited by T. A. Kohler, M. D. Varien, and A. M. Wright, pp. 180–199. University of Arizona Press, Tucson.

2010b   The Depopulation of Sand Canyon Pueblo, a Large Ancestral Pueblo Village in Southwestern Colorado. *American Antiquity* 75(3): 497–525.

Kuckelman, K. A. (editor)

2000   *The Archaeology of Castle Rock: A Late-Thirteenth-Century Village in Southwestern Colorado.* Crow Canyon Archaeological Center, Cortez. Available at http://www.crowcanyon.org/publications/castle_rock_pueblo.asp. Accessed July 27, 2010.

2007   *The Archaeology of Sand Canyon Pueblo: Intensive Excavations at a Late-Thirteenth-Century Village in Southwestern Colorado.* Crow Canyon Archaeological Center, Cortez. Available www.crowcanyon.org/sandcanyon. Accessed July 27, 2010.

Kuckelman, K. A., B. A. Bradley, M. J. Churchill, and J. H. Kleidon

2007   A Descriptive and Interpretive Summary of Excavations, by Architectural Block. In *The Archaeology of Sand Canyon Pueblo: Intensive Excavations at a Late-Thirteenth-Century Village in Southwestern Colorado,* edited by K. A. Kuckelman. Crow Canyon Archaeological Center, Cortez. Available at www.crowcanyon.org/sandcanyon. Accessed July 30, 2010.

Kuckelman, K. A., G. D. Coffey, and S. R. Copeland

2009   *Interim Descriptive Report of Research at Goodman Point Pueblo (Site 5MT604), Montezuma County, Colorado, 2005–2008.* Crow Canyon Archaeological Center, Cortez. Available at http://www.crowcanyon.org/ResearchReports/GoodmanPoint/interim_reports/2005_2008/GPP_interim_report_2005_2008.pdf. Accessed July 28, 2010.

Kuckelman, K. A., R. R. Lightfoot, and D. L. Martin

2002   The Bioarchaeology and Taphonomy of Violence at Castle Rock and Sand Canyon Pueblos, Southwestern Colorado. *American Antiquity* 67: 486–513.

Kuckelman, K. A., and D. L. Martin

2007   Human Skeletal Remains. In *The Archaeology of Sand Canyon Pueblo,* edited by K. A. Kuckelman. Crow Canyon Archaeological Center, Cortez. Available at www.crowcanyon.org/sandcanyon. Accessed July 30, 2010.

Lambert, P. M.

1999   Human Skeletal Remains. In *Environmental and Bioarchaeological Studies,* edited by B. R. Billman. Vol. 5 of *The Puebloan Occupation of the Ute Mountain Piedmont.* Publications in Archaeology no. 22. Soil Systems, Phoenix.

Larsen, D. O., H. Neff, D. A. Graybill, J. Michaelsen, and E. Ambos

1996   Risk, Climatic Variability, and the Study of Southwestern Prehistory: An Evolutionary Perspective. *American Antiquity* 6(2): 217–241.

Lightfoot, R. R., and K. A. Kuckelman
2001    A Case of Warfare in the Mesa Verde Region. In *Deadly Landscapes: Case Studies in Prehistoric Southwestern Warfare,* edited by G. E. Rice and S. A. LeBlanc, pp. 51–64. University of Utah Press, Salt Lake City.

Linton, R.
1944    Nomad Raids and Fortified Pueblos. *American Antiquity* 10(1): 28–32.

Lipe, W. D.
1995    The Depopulation of the Northern San Juan: Conditions in the Turbulent 1200s. *Journal of Anthropological Archaeology* 14: 143–169.

Lipe, W. D., and M. D. Varien
1999    Pueblo III (A.D. 1150–1300). In *Colorado Prehistory: A Context for the Southern Colorado River Basin,* edited by W. D. Lipe, M. D. Varien, and R. H. Wilshusen, pp. 290–352. Colorado Council of Professional Archaeologists, Denver.

Morris, E. H.
1939    *Archaeological Studies in the La Plata District, Southwestern Colorado and Northwestern New Mexico.* Carnegie Institution of Washington Publication no. 519. Carnegie Institution of Washington, Washington, D.C.

Mowrer, K.
2010    Notes and Analytic Records on File, pp. 279–415. Crow Canyon Archaeological Center, Cortez.

Nordenskiöld, G.
1979 [1893]    *The Cliff Dwellers of the Mesa Verde, Southwestern Colorado: Their Pottery and Implements.* Translated by D. L. Morgan. Rio Grande Press, Glorieta, N.M.

Parsons, E. C.
1929    *The Social Organization of the Tewa of New Mexico.* Memoir of American Anthropological Association no. 36. American Anthropological Association, Menasha.
1939    *Pueblo Indian Religion.* University of Chicago, Chicago.

Petersen, K. L.
1994    A Warm and Wet Little Climate Optimum and a Cold and Dry Little Ice Age in the Southern Rocky Mountains, U.S.A. *Climatic Change* 26: 243–269.

Petersen, K. L., and M. H. Matthews
1987    Man's Impact on the Landscape: A Prehistoric Example from the Dolores River Anasazi, Southwestern Colorado. *Journal of the West* 26(3): 4–16.

Salzer, M. W.
2000    Temperature Variability and the Northern Anasazi: Possible Implications for Regional Abandonment. *Kiva* 65(4): 295–318.

Shipman, J. H.
2006    A Brief Overview of Human Skeletal Remains from Salmon Ruins. In *Introduction, Architecture, Chronology, and Conclusions,* edited by P. F. Reed, pp. 327–330. Vol. 1 of *Thirty-Five Years of Archaeological Research at Salmon Ruins, New Mexico.* Center for Desert Archaeology and Salmon Ruins Museum, Bloomfield, N.M.

Turner, C. G., II, and J. A. Turner
1999    *Man Corn: Cannibalism and Violence in the Prehistoric American Southwest.*
        University of Utah Press, Salt Lake City.

Van West, C. R., and J. S. Dean
2000    Environmental Characteristics of the A.D. 900–1300 Period in the Central Mesa
        Verde Region. *Kiva* 66: 19–44.

Varien, M. D., W. D. Lipe, M. A. Adler, I. M. Thompson, and B. A. Bradley
1996    Southwest Colorado and Southwestern Utah Settlement Patterns: A.D. 1100 to
        1300. In *The Prehistoric Pueblo World, A.D. 1150–1350,* edited by M. A. Adler, pp.
        86–113. University of Arizona Press, Tucson.

Varien, M. D., S. G. Ortman, T. A. Kohler, D. M. Glowacki, and C. D. Johnson
2007    Historical Ecology in the Mesa Verde Region: Results from the Village Ecody-
        namics Project. *American Antiquity* 72(2): 273–299.

White, T. D.
1992    *Prehistoric Cannibalism at Mancos 5MTUMR-2346.* Princeton University Press,
        Princeton, N.J.

Wright, A. M.
2006    A Low-Frequency Paleoclimatic Reconstruction from the La Plata Mountains,
        Colorado, and Its Implications for Agricultural Paleoproductivity in the Mesa
        Verde Region. M.A. thesis, Washington State University.

2010    The Climate of the Depopulation of the Northern Southwest. In *Leaving Mesa
        Verde: Peril and Change in the Thirteenth-Century Southwest,* edited by T. A.
        Kohler, M. D. Varien, and A. M. Wright, pp. 75–101. University of Arizona Press,
        Tucson.

# PART III

# WARFARE

# 7

## The Space of War

### Connecting Geophysical Landscapes with Skeletal Evidence of Warfare-Related Trauma

HEATHER WORNE, CHARLES R. COBB, GIOVANNA VIDOLI,
AND DAWNIE WOLFE STEADMAN

## Introduction

Warfare is a cultural process that has significant ramifications for many aspects of everyday life. Milner (1995, 221) defines warfare as "purposeful violence calculated to advance the ambitions of separate political factions, regardless of who was involved, the regularity of fighting, the number of participants, or specific combat tactics." Bioarchaeological analysis has revealed that warfare in prehistoric eastern North America was widespread and varied, ranging from small-scale ambushes involving a few individuals to large-scale massacres (Milner, Anderson, and Smith 1991). Archaeological and skeletal evidence of interpersonal violence has been found in many populations throughout the prehistoric eastern United States.

Like other regions in the Eastern Woodlands, archaeological evidence of social stress exists in the Middle Cumberland Region (MCR) of Tennessee during the Mississippian period (ca. AD 1000–1450) in the form of palisades and artwork. Direct evidence of the type and intensity of warfare can be found in human skeletal remains, including trophy taking, scalping, and projectile wounds. While individual cases of scalping or projectile wounds are documented in the MCR, no synthetic analysis of the nature of warfare exists for this area. Documenting the incidence and frequency of warfare-related trauma is a necessary first step of a larger regional project on the interrelationships among agricultural sedentism, warfare, and health in the MCR. This study looks at the geographic pattern of warfare from a number of cultural and ecological perspectives in order to identify possible correlates of warfare, concentrating specifically on thirteen skeletal samples from Mississippian sites throughout the Middle Cumberland Region of Tennessee.

## The Middle Cumberland Region

The Middle Cumberland Region is located in the Nashville Basin, or Central Basin, of Tennessee. Made up of three distinct physiographic regions (the Highland Rim, the Outer Basin, and the Inner Basin), the MCR provided a unique environment for the development of local Mississippian groups (Miller 1974; Smith 1992) (Fig. 7.1). The Central Basin is an elevated depression made up of the Inner and Outer Basins and is surrounded by the Highland Rim, a low plateau. Although the Inner Basin and Highland Rim have many faunal and floral resources, agricultural productivity is low because of the low phosphate content of the soils. The Outer Basin is higher in elevation and more rugged than the Inner Basin. The floodplains of the Cumberland River and its major tributaries provide soils high in nutrients, but poorly developed terraces hinder long-term occupation because of periodic flooding. Many civic-ceremonial centers were located in more remote locations along secondary tributaries with better-developed terraces, presumably to reduce the risk of costly flooding (Smith 1992). Although Mississippian communities in the MCR used a mixed hunting-and-gathering and horticultural subsistence strategy, isotopic analysis suggests that the intensification of maize agriculture there was "rapid and extreme" compared to other Mississippian populations (Buikstra et al. 1988, 248). Middle Cumberland Region groups had access to various local lithic and chert gravel resources as well as saline springs (Smith 1992; Smith and Moore 1996).

Small autonomous polities emerged along the western rim of the Central Basin around AD 1000. Local mound centers were positioned along major tributaries, which most likely provided "social mechanisms for integrating dispersed egalitarian farming populations" (Smith 1992, 364–365). Site placement was probably influenced by the natural arrangement of river divisions and by the proximity of high-phosphate soils in the Outer Basin. This site arrangement created "a substantial area surrounded

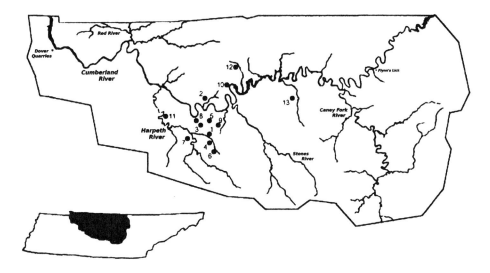

Fig. 7.1. Cumberland Region and study sites, modified from Smith and Moore (2005).

by a 'shield' of palisaded mound centers, protecting what essentially can be defined as an unmodified hunting and gathering territory" (Smith 1992, 365). Analysis of artifact assemblages suggests that these independent polities had continual interaction with one another (Smith 1992).

Despite a lack of studies focused primarily on the topic of warfare in the MCR, considerable evidence implies that conflict did affect groups in the region. Smith (1992) suggests that settlement patterns likely are the result of a compromise between access to natural resources and defensibility. Many sites were located in highly defensible positions such as on steep embankments or within meandering bends. Evidence for palisade construction is present for at least nine of the thirteen sites included in this study. The absence of evidence that palisades were built at some of these sites is likely attributable to incomplete excavations or excavations that were not conducted systematically. Skeletal evidence of interpersonal violence, including scalping and inflicted projectile wounds, has been documented for multiple MCR sites (e.g., Averbuch [40Dv60], Arnold [40Wm5], and Gordontown [40Dv6]; Berryman 1981; Smith 1992). A number of artistic representations of warfare also exist from the MCR (Smith 1992). For example, the Myer Gorget from Castalian Springs depicts what appears to be a warrior or a deity who is holding a decapitated head in one hand and a ceremonial mace in the other hand. The Thruston

Tablet, also from the Castalian Springs area, illustrates two individuals engaged in conflict. A petroglyph mace is located on a bluff top overlooking the Mound Bottom site.

Geophysical analysis of prehistoric landscapes can aid in bioarchaeological studies of warfare by mapping conflict on the terrain in order to synthesize patterns of settlement and behavior that may indicate violent conflict. Understanding how communities interact with the landscape that surrounds them can provide information not only about subsistence needs or the importance of natural resources but also about sociopolitical relationships. Interactions between communities in a region, whether they were hostile or not, surely informed settlement choices. For instance, allies may have chosen to have a clear line of sight to facilitate rapid communication. During times of political instability, communities likely made settlement location choices that increased site defensibility, even at the expense of access to natural resources. This study uses two geophysical variables, site visibility and waterway size, to provide information about settlement choices and how such choices may have influenced or been informed by warfare in the MCR.

## Methods

The ultimate cause of warfare in prehistoric (or even contemporary) populations is difficult, if not impossible, to ascertain. Motivations for engaging in conflict vary over time and between groups and individuals. Individuals in positions of power have different motives than other community members. Factors that influence the escalation of violence may affect individuals differently. This is not to say that determining the cause of war is unimportant but rather that a more informative and attainable goal might be to identify the consequences warfare has for a region, for a community, or for individuals. The purpose of this study is not just to document the presence and frequency of warfare-related trauma in the MCR but also to identify possible correlates or consequences. Which communities in the region were targeted? Who in each community was affected? What was the spatial distribution of warfare-related trauma, and how did people use space or the landscape in relation to warfare?

In order to address these questions, we conducted bioarchaeological analysis on over 1,700 skeletal remains from thirteen Mississippian sites. We determined sex and age following "Standards for Data Collection

Table 7.1. Sample size of each of the 13 MCR sites in this study

| Site | Sample Size |
| --- | --- |
| Arnold (40Wm5) | 122 |
| Averbuch (40Dv60) | 340 |
| Bowling Farm (40Dv426) | 50 |
| Cain's Chapel (40Dv3) | 48 |
| Fewkes (40Wm1) | 13 |
| Ganier (40Dv15) | 40 |
| Gordontown (40Dv6) | 64 |
| Gray's Farm (40Wm11) | 28 |
| Jarman (40Wm210) | 72 |
| Moss Wright (40Su20) | 47 |
| Mound Bottom (40Ch8) | 13 |
| Rutherford-Kizer (40Su15) | 15 |
| Sellers (40Wi1) | 18 |
| TOTAL | 870 |

from Human Skeletal Remains" (Buikstra and Ubelaker 1994). Individuals of all ages with at least 25 percent of the skull present were included in the sample (N = 870). Of the 522 adults (>18 years) whose sex we know, 43.5 percent (N = 227) were female and 56.5 percent (N = 295) were male. See Table 7.1 for subsample sizes by site. We then compared the results of the bioarchaeological analysis to geophysical characteristics of the landscape. In particular, this study focuses on measures of visibility and the size of local waterways to address how social stress in the form of violent trauma may have influenced decisions about where to locate a site.

Following previous bioarchaeological research in warfare, we used conservative criteria to identify warfare-related trauma. These criteria included 1) cut marks associated with scalping; 2) evidence of decapitation or dismemberment; 3) blunt force trauma to the cranium; and 4) projectile point injuries (Milner 1998, 1999; Steadman 2008). Information about burial context was also collected, when available, including the location of the remains in the cemetery, the number of individuals in the grave, and the presence or type of burial goods interred with the deceased.

Cut marks associated with scalping, a form of trophy taking, usually consist of thin, straight cuts located circumferentially around the cranium, often in areas of greatest muscle attachment (Owsley and Berryman 1975). These cut marks may vary in length, density, or location. Scalping does not always leave evidence in the bone (Hamperl 1967). Furthermore, not all victims of scalping die immediately or even from the scalping incident itself. Victims are often immobilized first, which may prove fatal (Owsley and Berryman 1975). There are also several documented historic and prehistoric cases of individuals surviving a scalping event (Aufderheide and Rodríguez-Martin 2003; Berryman 1981; Hamperl 1967; Ortner 2003; Owsley and Berryman 1975; Smith 2003; Willey 1990). Cases of healing after scalping, which usually show unique patterns of healing and/or secondary infection, were also considered.

Other forms of trophy taking (i.e., decapitation or dismemberment) often leave cut marks on or adjacent to the element removed, such as on the occipital bone, the mandible, or the cervical vertebrae for decapitation or circumferential cut marks around the articular ends of long bones (Mensforth 2007; Raemsh 1993). The absence of a bone is not, however, enough to indicate dismemberment, as the element may have been removed or disarticulated during reburial or looting of a grave. We took care to distinguish between perimortem dismemberment and postmortem curation, such as flesh removal, by carefully documenting the patterns of cut marks observed on the bones (Raemsh 1993).

Projectile point injuries are difficult to diagnose without an embedded point, as the insult to the bone may be similar to any number of other trauma, depending upon the size, directionality, and velocity of the point. The presence of a projectile point alone is not sufficient to diagnose a projectile point injury. For instance, a point discovered in the chest cavity may have been placed on the chest of the deceased as an offering and migrated to its final location during decomposition. Not all projectile point injuries leave evidence in the bone; only an estimated 25–33 percent of projectile injuries actually strike bone (Lambert 1997, 93; Milner 2005, 150). This suggests that most projectile point injuries are not visible in the bioarchaeological record.

Both antemortem and perimortem cranial blunt force trauma are often considered to be evidence of violent trauma (Milner, Anderson, and Smith 1991; Smith 2003; Steadman 2008; Willey 1990). The shape of the wound, the location on the skull, and the degree of healing can all help researchers distinguish between intentional and accidental trauma, determine the weapon used, and suggest whether the injury was a product of intragroup or intergroup violence (Smith 2003; Walker 1989; Walker 1997). Postcranial fractures, including parry fractures, were not considered warfare-related trauma in this study, as accidental causes usually cannot be ruled out.

Table 7.2. Definitions of waterway ranks

| Waterway Rank | Waterway Definition |
| --- | --- |
| 4 | Major river |
| 3 | Secondary tributary |
| 2 | Tertiary tributary |
| 1 | Creek |

Site visibility and the size of waterways near a site were the key geo-physical variables addressed in this study. Local waterways were ranked by size using a variation of the Strahler system (Table 7.2), ranging from "1" (creeks/streams) to "4" (the Cumberland River or its major tributaries). Local waterways affect communities in a number of important ways. Rivers offer a means for transportation; they not only provide access to natural resources, they also provide the means for groups to interact. Rivers also provide routes for importing and exporting trade items; they offer protection from attacks by limiting land attacks; they supply necessary water to agricultural fields; and they are associated with abundant faunal and floral resources. Large rivers, especially those with steep banks located next to communities, may provide added protection by forming geographic barriers that limit the available entryways for land attacks. Large rivers would also allow for more efficient transportation between neighboring allies in times of need, not to mention potential escape routes. Smaller rivers or streams would make travel to and from allied communities more difficult and would provide less of an obstacle for assailants on foot.

Site visibility not only provides information about how much of the landscape was visible from a community and how visible the community was to the surrounding area, it also serves as a correlate of physical terrain. Site visibility is measured as the percent of the landscape that is visible from a given site location within a defined area; for this study, the area was a 1,000-meter radius. Using a 1 kilometer viewshed for each site, we measured visibility as the percentage of the landscape surface that was visible from the site location. Thus, high values correspond with a flat environment and low values indicate a more rugged terrain. The more rugged the landscape, the lower the visibility will be for the site because steep ridges may block entire portions of the surrounding terrain from view. The ruggedness of the terrain affects the ability of a community to find suitable agricultural land and may also affect the ability of people to traverse the surrounding landscape. Site visibility, or the amount of the surrounding terrain that is visible from a site and vice versa, could affect community security or defensibility in a number of ways. If a community is not visible to potential attackers, then a surprise attack would be difficult if the attackers are not familiar with the landscape. Having a greater percentage of the surrounding landscape visible from a site, especially between neighboring populations, could allow allies to communicate in times of need and allow the community to see attackers approaching. However, sentinels on raised platforms, trees, or bluffs could provide such a warning without necessitating visibility between sites on the ground.

## Results

We combined the numbers of scalpings, dismemberments or decapitations, cranial blunt force traumas, projectile point injuries, and sharp force traumas to arrive at an overall trauma frequency for the MCR sample of 5.4 percent (N = 47) (Tables 7.3, 7.4). Only four of the thirteen site subsamples (Bowling Farm, Fewkes, Ganier, and Mound Bottom) had no skeletal evidence of warfare-related trauma. Of the 522 adults of known sex, 4.6 percent of females (8/227) and 13.1 percent of males (32/295) exhibited evidence of violent trauma. Chi square analysis showed that males had a significantly greater frequency of trauma than females ($p < 0.002$). One juvenile showed clear evidence of warfare-related trauma, a child 4–8 years old from the Sellars site with cut marks on the cranium consistent with scalping. Of the 20 cases of scalping from eight MCR sites, six showed evidence of subsequent infection, an indication that the individual survived for a period of time after the scalping incident. There were three cases of sharp force trauma, two projectile point injuries, and one possible decapitation (Figs. 7.2–7.4). The most common injury encountered in the MCR sample was cranial blunt force trauma; 27 victims from seven of the site subsamples exhibited this injury. Twenty-five individuals, or 53 percent (25/47) of the violent trauma cases, had at least one healed depression fracture on the cranium; six individuals had two (Table 7.5). We used chi-square tests to detect significant differences between males and females for the location (anterior, posterior, lateral, superior) of cranial blunt force trauma ($p = 0.045$). We also found significant differences between males and females when only anterior and posterior cranial locations were considered ($p = 0.029$).

Table 7.3. Trauma frequencies at each of the 13 sites in this study

| Site | Trauma (N) | Trauma Frequency (%) |
|---|---|---|
| Arnold (40Wm5) | 6/122 | 4.9 |
| Averbuch (40Dv60) | 19/340 | 5.6 |
| Bowling Farm (40Dv426) | 0/50 | 0 |
| Cain's Chapel (40Dv3) | 6/48 | 12.5 |
| Fewkes (40Wm1) | 0/13 | 0 |
| Ganier (40Dv15) | 0/40 | 0 |
| Gordontown (40Dv6) | 6/64 | 9.4 |
| Gray's Farm (40Wm11) | 2/28 | 7.1 |
| Jarman (40Wm210) | 4/72 | 5.6 |
| Moss Wright (40Su20) | 2/47 | 4.2 |
| Mound Bottom (40Ch8) | 0/13 | 0 |
| Rutherford-Kizer (40Su15) | 1/15 | 6.7 |
| Sellers (40Wi1) | 1/18 | 5.6 |
| TOTALS | 47/870 | 5.4 |

Table 7.4. Number of warfare-related traumas by site and type of trauma inflicted

| Site | Trauma Total | CBFT | Scalp | Decap | Proj Pt | SFT |
|---|---|---|---|---|---|---|
| Arnold (40Wm5) | 6 | 3 | 3 | 0 | 0 | 0 |
| Averbuch (40Dv60) | 19 | 12 | 6 | 0 | 1 | 2 |
| Bowling Farm (40Dv426) | 0 | 0 | 0 | 0 | 0 | 0 |
| Cain's Chapel (40Dv3) | 6 | 3 | 4 | 0 | 0 | 0 |
| Fewkes (40Wm1) | 0 | 0 | 0 | 0 | 0 | 0 |
| Ganier (40Dv15) | 0 | 0 | 0 | 0 | 0 | 0 |
| Gordontown (40Dv6) | 6 | 4 | 1 | 1 | 0 | 1 |
| Grays Farm (40Wm11) | 2 | 2 | 0 | 0 | 0 | 0 |
| Jarman (40Wm210) | 4 | 2 | 3 | 0 | 1 | 0 |
| Moss Wright (40Su20) | 2 | 1 | 1 | 0 | 0 | 0 |
| Mound Bottom (40Ch8) | 0 | 0 | 0 | 0 | 0 | 0 |
| Rutherford-Kizer (40Su15) | 1 | 0 | 1 | 0 | 0 | 0 |
| Sellers (40Wi1) | 1 | 0 | 1 | 0 | 0 | 0 |
| TOTALS | 47 | 27 | 20 | 1 | 2 | 3 |

*Note*: Multiple individuals show evidence of more than one type of trauma. CBFT = cranial blunt force trauma; Scalp = scalping; Decap = decapitation; Proj Pt = projectile point injury; SFT= sharp force trauma (not including scalping).

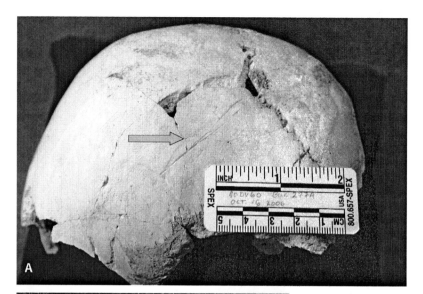

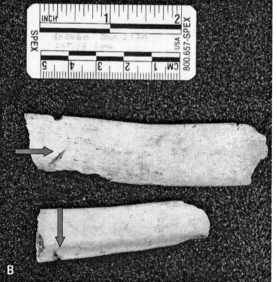

Fig. 7.2. Individual 277A from
the Averbuch sample showing
A) evidence of scalping;
B) sharp force trauma to several ribs; and C) an embedded
projectile point in a cervical
vertebra.

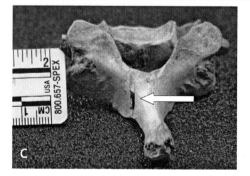

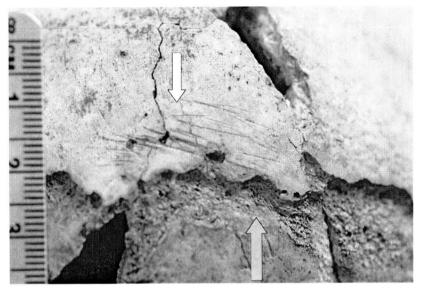

Fig. 7.3. Burial 15Misc, an adult of indeterminate sex from the Arnold sample with the right parietal showing cut marks (white arrow) and a lytic line (gray arrow) due to subsequent infection.

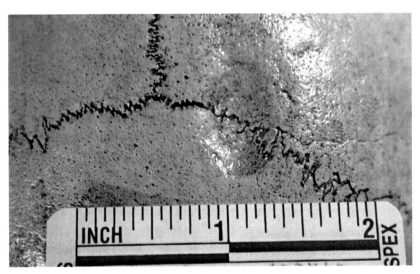

Fig. 7.4. Burial 121B, a probable male from the Averbuch sample with a healed cranial depression fracture on the left coronal suture.

Table 7.5. Location of healed cranial depression fractures by sex

|  |  | Location on Cranium |  |  |  |  | Total |
|  |  | Anterior | L Lateral | R Lateral | Superior | Posterior |  |
|---|---|---|---|---|---|---|---|
| Sex | Female | 0 | 0 | 0 | 1 | 5 | 6 |
|  | Male | 9 | 4 | 1 | 2 | 4 | 20 |
|  | Unknown | 2 | 1 | 0 | 2 | 0 | 5 |
| Total |  | 11 | 5 | 1 | 5 | 9 | 31 |

Table 7.6. Summary of GIS variables for each of the sample sites

| Site | Waterway Rank | Visibility (ratio) |
|---|---|---|
| Arnold (40Wm5) | 1 | 0.39 |
| Averbuch (40Dv60) | 1 | 0.41 |
| Bowling Farm (40Dv426) | 1 | 0.33 |
| Cain's Chapel (40Dv3) | 1 | 0.13 |
| Fewkes (40Wm1) | 1 | 0.22 |
| Ganier (40Dv15) | 4 | 0.41 |
| Gordontown (40Dv6) | 1 | 0.31 |
| Gray's Farm (40Wm11) | 3 | 0.20 |
| Jarman (40Wm210) | 1 | 0.39 |
| Moss Wright (40Su20) | 1 | 0.42 |
| Mound Bottom (40Ch8) | 3 | 0.28 |
| Rutherford-Kizer (40Su15) | 1 | 0.43 |
| Sellers (40Wi1) | 1 | 0.41 |

In order to determine how social stress in the form of warfare-related trauma may have affected community choices about where to settle, we compared waterway size and visibility scores of MCR sites with subsample trauma frequencies using linear regression. The waterway rank and visibility ratios for each of the thirteen sites are given in Table 7.6.

Among the thirteen MCR sites included in this study, ten were located along small waterways categorized as streams. Only three sites were located along larger waterways: Ganier was located along the Cumberland River and Mound Bottom and Gray's Farm were situated along the Harpeth River, a major tributary of the Cumberland River. We recategorized waterway rank as "small" (streams ranked as "1") or "large" (the Cumberland or major tributaries with rankings of "4" or "3") and then compared small and large waterways by the absence or presence of trauma using Fisher's exact test. Sites that showed no evidence of trauma

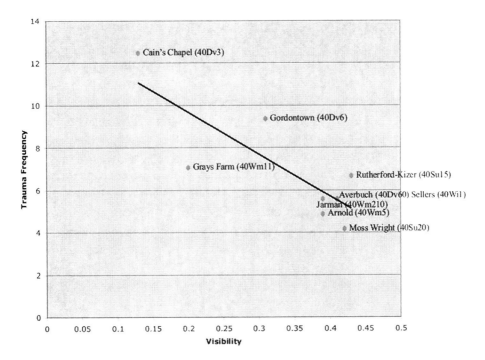

Fig. 7.5. Trauma frequency and visibility.

were significantly ($p = 0.035$) more likely to exist along larger waterways, whereas sites that provided evidence of warfare-related trauma present were more often located along streams.

Visibility scores ranged from 0.13 for Cain's Chapel to 0.43 for Rutherford-Kizer. We compared the trauma frequencies of the nine sites that exhibited warfare-related trauma to visibility scores using linear regression analysis. A significant negative correlation was detected ($R = -0.826$, $p = 0.003$). Sites with higher trauma frequencies had lower visibility, meaning that a smaller percentage of the surrounding landscape was visible from the sites with higher rates of trauma (Fig. 7.5).

## Discussion

The results indicate that the decision about where to locate a site in the MCR was, as Smith (1992) has suggested, a compromise between access to natural resources and the ability to defend the site. The presence of palisade construction at nine of the thirteen sites suggests that the threat of violence from outside attacks was at least perceived throughout the region and that the threat was great enough for communities to invest the time and labor necessary to build and maintain such defensive structures. There is a strong negative correlation between trauma frequency and the amount of the surrounding terrain that is visible from a site, meaning that sites where visibility was lower had higher rates of violent trauma. Furthermore, sites with skeletal evidence of violent trauma were significantly more likely to be located along smaller waterways or streams.

Because visibility is a proxy for roughness of terrain, decreased visibility would also suggest that sites with higher trauma rates were situated in areas with rougher terrain, perhaps to discourage outsiders from approaching on foot. Sites situated on small streams would provide further obstacles for aggressors. While remote locations in difficult-to-traverse areas could discourage potential attackers, such a location could affect a number of aspects of community life negatively. Larger waterways provide efficient travel routes for trade and for procuring natural resources. Water is also necessary for agricultural fields and provides habitats for plant and animal species. Large waterways can also offer a protective boundary against land attacks. Correlation does not imply causation, however. It is not clear what the relationship between warfare-related trauma, visibility from a site, and stream size entails. Unexamined factors may be involved. Perhaps locating a site in the hinterland increases the risk of violence by reducing a community's ability to rally allies or detect approaching attackers.

The purpose of this study is not to address the ultimate cause of warfare but to identify potential geophysical correlates of violent conflict. The results of the bioarchaeological and geophysical analysis suggests that not only were communities in the MCR affected physically by social stress, as is apparent from skeletal evidence of violent trauma and death, but that settlement location choices were actually correlates of such stress. Nine of the thirteen site subsamples showed skeletal evidence for violent conflict in the form of scalping, cranial blunt force trauma, projectile injuries, sharp force trauma, or decapitation. While males were significantly more likely to be victims of violence than females, both sexes and at least one juvenile were affected. This suggests that all members of the community were potential targets. There is no evidence for large-scale massacres in the MCR. Intergroup violence was likely characterized by intermittent attacks or ambushes on small groups or individuals.

While intergroup violence was present throughout the region, some evidence suggests intragroup violence was present as well. The high rates of healed cranial depression fractures in the MCR samples are similar to rates seen in prehistoric groups from the California coast (Lambert 1997; Walker 1989) and East Tennessee (Smith 2003). High rates of healed cranial blunt force trauma are attributed in these cases to ritualized or codified violence. In these studies, males tended to have higher incidences of antemortem depression fractures than females. The injuries were also more often present on the frontal bone, suggesting that victims were facing their attackers, whereas there was little pattern to where injuries were located in females. The wounds were usually round or ellipsoid, suggesting that the weapon was perhaps a war club. Table 7.7 gives comparable trauma rates for a number of regions in the Southeast, including healed blunt force trauma in the cranium. Whatever the cause, the frequency of healed cranial blunt force trauma among remains in the MCR is

Table 7.7. Comparisons of violent trauma frequencies by region

| Site | Trauma rates for all ages (percent within region) | Antemortem cranial blunt force trauma (percent within trauma rate subgroup) | Source |
|---|---|---|---|
| MCR (Mississippian) | 5.4 (47/870) | 53.2 (25/47) | Worne (2011) |
| Norris Farms (Oneonta) | 22 (58/264) | 25.9 (15/58) | Milner, Anderson, and Smith (1991); Milner and Smith (1990) |
| Orendorf (Mississippian) | 9.3 (25/268) | 20 (5/25) | Steadman (2008) |
| Koger Island (Mississippian) | 9.2 (10/108) | 30 (3/10) | Bridges (1996) |
| East Tennessee, Dallas phase (Mississippian) | 3.9 (10/259) | 78 (7/9) | Smith (2003) |
| East Tennessee, Mouse Creek phase (Mississippian) | 7.3 (20/273) | 60 (12/20) | Smith (2003) |

comparable to frequencies attributed elsewhere to intragroup violence. Smith (2003, 303) suggests that the lack of an "overarching civil authority," as was likely the case in the MCR, may have contributed to the need for dispute resolution in the form of sanctioned violence. Sex differences in location of wounds could be attributed to gender role differences during attacks on a community. When a small group of individuals are under attack, perhaps women flee to protect the children or to avoid being taken captive while men face their attackers as they attempt to protect the group.

Whatever the source, violence was a threat to community safety for Mississippian groups in the MCR. The consequences are evident in the compromises made between how much terrain was visible from a site, how much access a site had to large waterways, and how much time and effort it would require to construct protective walls. Perhaps a lack of the resources that would have been needed to protect a more optimal site near a large waterway or one that offered higher visibility led to the decision of many MCR communities to locate their site in the hinterland.

## Conclusion

This study is unique in both the regional approach and in its inclusion of geophysical data. The results suggest not only that warfare and violence were present during the Mississippian period in the MCR but also that settlement choices were affected or influenced by patterns of violence. It is not clear whether groups that lived in remote settings chose such sites because of the social stress of warfare or if an isolated location increased a community's risk for violent attacks. Though the relationship between warfare-related violence and local waterway size and visibility is perhaps still underdefined, it is important to pursue further investigation of the connections between local ecology, human settlement patterns, and conflict. Further studies in the MCR currently under way include incorporating the variables of community health and biodistance, which may further highlight regional patterns of warfare and its correlates. The goals of the larger NSF-funded project, of which this study is a part, are to identify the interrelationships among sedentary agriculture, community health, and warfare in the Middle Cumberland Region. The region is unique because most mound centers are located in more remote locations than Mississippian communities in other regions. Studies in regions outside the MCR may also provide insight into a broader interregional pattern of settlement choice and warfare.

## Acknowledgments

A special thanks to the following people and institutions for their help and for granting us permission to analyze skeletal collections from the Middle Cumberland Region of Tennessee: Michael C. Moore, Aaron Deter-Wolf, and John Broster at the Tennessee Division of Archaeology; Boyce N. Driskell and Jennifer McDonough at the University of Tennessee Archaeological Research Laboratory; Lynne Sullivan at the Frank H. McClung Museum at the University of Tennessee; Tiffiny A. Tung at Vanderbilt University; and Michele Morgan and Olivia Herschensohn at the Peabody Museum of Archaeology and Ethnology at Harvard University. Thanks also to Kevin E. Smith of Middle Tennessee State University and Tennessee State Archaeologist Michael Moore for sharing their knowledge and expertise about Mississippian period Middle Cumberland Region archaeology. We would also like to thank Debra L. Martin, Ryan P. Harrod, and Ventura Pérez for the invitation to contribute to this volume. This project was supported by an NSF grant awarded to D. W. Steadman and C. C. Cobb (BCS-0613173).

## References Cited

Aufderheide, A. C., and C. Rodríguez-Martin
2003    *The Cambridge Encyclopedia of Human Paleopathology.* Cambridge University Press, Cambridge.
Berryman, H. E.
1981    The Averbuch Skeletal Series: A Study of Biological and Social Stress at a Late Mississippian Period Site from Middle Tennessee. Ph.D. dissertation, University of Tennessee.
Bridges, P. S.
1996    Warfare and Mortality at Koger's Island, Alabama. *International Journal of Osteoarchaeology* 6: 66–75.
Buikstra, J. E., W. Autry, E. Breitburg, L. E. Eisenberg, and N. van der Merwe
1988    Diet and Health in the Nashville Basin: Human Adaptation and Maize Agriculture in Middle Tennessee. In *Diet and Subsistence: Current Archaeological Perspectives: Proceedings of the 19th Annual Chacmool Conference,* edited by B. V. Kennedy and G. M. LeMoine, pp. 243–259. Archaeological Association of the University of Calgary, Calgary.

Buikstra, J. E., and D. H. Ubelaker

1994 *Standards for Data Collection from Human Skeletal Remains.* Arkansas Archaeological Survey Research Series no. 44. Arkansas Archaeological Survey, Fayetteville.

Hamperl, H.

1967 The Osteological Consequences of Scalping. In *Diseases in Antiquity,* edited by D. R. Brothwell and A. T. Sandison, pp. 630–634. Charles C. Thomas, Springfield.

Lambert, P. M.

1997 Patterns of Violence in Prehistoric Hunter-Gatherer Societies of Coastal Southern California. In *Troubled Times: Violence and Warfare in the Past,* edited by D. L. Martin, pp. 77–109. Gordon and Breach, Amsterdam.

Mensforth, R. P.

2007 Human Trophy Taking in Eastern North America during the Archaic Period: The Relationship to Warfare and Social Complexity. In *The Taking and Displaying of Human Body Parts as Trophies by Amerindians,* edited by R. J. Chacon and D. H. Dye, pp. 222–277. Springer, New York.

Miller, R. A.

1974 *The Geological History of Tennessee.* State of Tennessee, Department of Conservation, Division of Geology, Nashville.

Milner, G. R.

1995 An Osteological Perspective on Prehistoric Warfare. In *Regional Approaches to Mortuary Analysis,* edited by L. A. Beck, pp. 221–244. Plenum Press, New York.

1998 Archaeological Evidence for Prehistoric and Early Historic Intergroup Conflict in Eastern North America. In *Deciphering Anasazi Violence: With Regional Comparisons to Mesoamerican and Woodland Cultures,* edited by P. Y. Bullock, pp. 69–91. HRM Books, Santa Fe.

1999 Warfare in the Prehistoric and Early Historic Eastern North America. *Journal of Archaeological Research* 7: 105–151.

2005 Nineteenth-Century Arrow Wounds and Perceptions of Prehistoric Warfare. *American Antiquity* 70(1): 144–156.

Milner, G. R., E. Anderson, and V. G. Smith

1991 Warfare in Late Prehistoric West-Central Illinois. *American Antiquity* 56(4): 581–603.

Milner, G. R., and V. G. Smith

1990 Oneota Human Skeletal Remains. In *Archaeological Investigations at the Morton Village and Norris Farms 36 Cemetery,* pp. 111–148. Reports of Investigations no. 45. Illinois State Museum, Springfield.

Ortner, D. J.

2003 *Identification of Pathological Conditions in Human Skeletal Remains.* Academic Press, London.

Owsley, D. W., and H. E. Berryman

1975 Ethnographic and Archaeological Evidence of Scalping in the Southeastern United States. *Tennessee Archaeologist* 31: 41–60.

Raemsh, C. A.
1993    Mechanical Procedures Involved in Bone Dismemberment and Defleshing in Prehistoric Michigan. *Midcontinental Journal of Archaeology* 18(2): 217–244.

Smith, K. E.
1992    The Middle Cumberland Region: Mississippian Archaeology in North Central Tennessee. Ph.D. dissertation, Vanderbilt University.

Smith, K. E., and M. C. Moore
1996    On the River and Up the Creek: Contrasting Settlement Patterns in the Cumberland Valley. Paper presented at the 53rd Annual Meeting of the Southeastern Archaeological Conference, Birmingham, Alabama.

Smith, M. O.
2003    Beyond Palisades: The Nature and Frequency of Late Prehistoric Deliberate Violent Trauma in the Chickamauga Reservoir of East Tennessee. *American Journal of Physical Anthropology* 121(4): 303–318.

Steadman, D. W.
2008    Warfare Related Trauma at Orendorf, a Middle Mississippian Site in West-Central Illinois. *American Journal of Physical Anthropology* 136(1): 51–64.

Walker, P. L.
1989    Cranial Injuries as Evidence of Violence in Prehistoric Southern California. *American Journal of Physical Anthropology* 80: 313–323.
1997    Wife Beating, Boxing, and Broken Noses: Skeletal Evidence for the Cultural Patterning of Violence. In *Troubled Times: Violence and Warfare in the Past,* edited by D. L. Martin and D. W. Frayer, pp. 145–180. Gordon and Breach, Amsterdam.

Willey, P. S.
1990    *Prehistoric Warfare on the Great Plains: Skeletal Analysis of the Crow Creek Massacre Victims.* Garland Publishing, New York.

Worne, H.
2011    Conflicting Spaces: Bioarchaeological and Geophysical Perspectives on Warfare in the Middle Cumberland Region of Tennessee. Ph.D. dissertation, Binghamton University.

# 8

## Where Are the Warriors?

### Cranial Trauma Patterns and Conflict among the Ancient Maya

VERA TIESLER AND ANDREA CUCINA

## Introduction

Missionary Juan de Torquemada vividly recounts a dramatic encounter between European and Maya militias during the early sixteenth century. Spanish explorer Francisco Hernández de Córdoba and his party were making landfall on the Yucatecan coast near Champotón when they suddenly found themselves in the middle of a skirmish with Maya natives:

> The Indians were painted, armed with arrows and with all the appearance of being ready to fight, and they ordered the artillery to be discharged from the ships in order to frighten them. The Indians were much astonished at the fire and smoke. And were somewhat confused at the sound, but they did not fly but instead attacked with spirit and boldness and with great unanimity and making loud cries, and throwing stones, sticks and arrows. . . . The Indians, although they never had received such fierce wounds [as from metal swords and fire weapons], still stood in the fight with great courage, animated by the presence and spirit of their captain and lord, until they won the battle. And in the chase and in the embarkation [of the Spaniards], they killed with arrows forty-seven Spaniards and wounded more than fifty. (Torquemada quoted in Tozzer 1941, 11–12)

Among the mortally wounded was Francisco Hernández himself. He received several arrow wounds during the battle, and he died soon afterward. Also two of the Spanish survivors who were captured by Champotón's warlord still alive, joined their companions in death. Both were sacrificed by the natives to their gods, as was the local custom.

This colonial incident illustrates why the European subjugation of the Maya heartlands was so different from the conquest of the Aztec-dominated Central Highlands, where the Spaniards' strategic alliances and surprise attacks led to the swift overthrow of the Aztec empire and the instauration of colonial rule within just two years. Domination of the Maya territories took decades, really centuries. Officially, at least, European control over Yucatan was accomplished by the late 1540s, after enormous efforts by the Spanish crown and a series of unsuccessful previous campaigns (*entradas*) in which the Spaniards were worn down by a multifront guerrilla war in a decentralized political landscape. The natural geography of impenetrable brush and forests and an absence of rivers made things even worse for the Spaniards and kept them from effectively controlling the Maya sector of the colonies. Here, rebellious outbreaks were the order of the day and culminated in the so-called Caste War, a prolonged native revolt against the exploitation and cruelty of the Yucatecans of European descent that lasted more than fifty years (1847–1901).

Scholarship on ancient Maya conflict and war tactics has relied heavily on iconography (Fig. 8.1), epigraphy, ethnohistory, and archaeological data sets. These sources of information stress the use of astronomy as a way to organize time, specific ecological and ideological undercurrents of warfare, and economic and political motivations for ancient Maya battles and other forms of organized violence (Foster 2002; Freidel 1986; O'Mansky and Demarest 2007; Pagliaro, Garber, and Stanton 2003). Current interpretations emphasize the forging of political alliances, economic tributes, and control of trade routes as reasons to go to war instead of focusing on territorial expansion as the sole explanation for warfare (Foster 2002; O'Mansky and Demarest 2007). A significant increase in military action is discernable for the second half of the first millennium in the Maya world, accompanied by the dramatic collapse and abandonment of most Lowland city kingdoms and a regrouping into a new political order at the beginning of the Postclassic. Humiliation and ritual slaughter of captives and ostentatious displays of supreme military leadership seem to have been essential aspects of institutionalized conflict for the Maya. If these displays weren't due to propaganda statements and rulers' self-acclaim, the increase in military action indeed implies that Maya rulers

Fig. 8.1. Scene painted on a Classic period ceramic vessel, showing three armed warriors with prisoner. "Trophy masks" hang from the belts of two of the warriors. Kerr (2000), 962; redrawn by M. Sánchez.

had not only declared war on their enemies and commanded their armies but were also possibly actively engaged on the battlefields (Fig. 8.1).

Apart from what we know about the existence and goals of organized violence, we understand surprisingly little about actual tactics the Maya used in battle. We also do not know how specialized (or unspecialized) troops were recruited and transported or even how large typical Maya armies were. Other unanswered questions include how ancient weapons were used and how deeply violence was embedded in civilian society. How important was interregional violence compared to intraregional violence? How important were attacks by raiding, and how dominant was open army combat in winning military conflicts?

Bioarchaeological approaches have great potential for offering new and unique insights on some of these questions. Skeletal evidence of specific healed and unhealed trauma patterns provide information about the types of interpersonal violence used in Maya society and the weaponry that was used to accomplish that violence, thus complementing conventional interpretations derived from the material record or from Maya

imagery. Sex, age, and status attributions of injured individuals are informative about the victims' role in society and provide clues about the type
of violence suffered and the social cost of interpersonal aggression. We
think that bioarchaeological data sets go beyond adding new empirical
information. The bodies of those who suffered violent wounds add a human dimension to our understanding of violence and tell us something
about how deeply that violence was embedded in a society. This chapter
offers a fresh look at human conflict and how institutionalized it was in
the Maya realm, using a data source that has been underexplored so far
(see Pérez-Flores 2006).

## Material and Methods

For the purposes of this study, we selected a cohort of 1,103 Maya skeletons
with at least part of the frontal bone intact from a sample of 3,000 systematically scored skeletal individuals, most of which were deteriorated
or incomplete. These skeletons belong to a number of series recovered
from 63 mostly residential burial collections. The largest skeletal series
document the large Classic-period urban center of Copán, Honduras; the
peninsular coastal ports of Xcambó and Jaina; and the ritual sinkhole (the
Sacred Cenote) at Chichen Itzá (Figs. 8.2 and 8.3). At least one quadrant of
the frontal bone could be scored from each skeletal individual included in
this study. We scored these frontal bones for type and presence of lesions
per quadrant. This established an initial inventory of traumatic skull lesions, most of which consist of healed blunt force trauma. In a subsequent
phase of this study, we extrapolated from this group 725 individuals that
presented a complete and intact frontal bone and were thus suitable for
subsequent comparisons of the frequency of and patterns of distribution
of traumatic injuries.

We chose the frontal bone as the basic unit of analysis for two reasons.
First, its morphological attributes make it relatively resistant to degradation; and second, most skulls were much too deteriorated to permit an
overall evaluation that included parietal, temporal, and occipital bones or
facial segments. An additional consideration was that forehead injuries
seem to be suitable indicators of face-to-face aggression, especially since
we know that Maya warriors appear to have worn relatively light head
protection during combat. Iconography of battle scenes depicts them ei-

Fig. 8.2. Map of Maya area showing archaeological sites mentioned in the text.
Underlined place-names indicate sites dated to the Postclassic period.

Fig. 8.3. Sacred Cenote, Chichén Itzá. Photo by V. Tiesler.

ther without any head covering or wearing pillbox helmets or cloth wraps (Foster 2002, 147).

At the outset of this study, we assumed that different forms of interpersonal violence and weaponry use should leave distinctive marks in the frontal bone. These marks should reveal data about the distribution patterns and forms of the wounds, differences by sex and age, and other contextual considerations. We acknowledge that other causes, such as accidents or domestic violence, might have also produced traumatic injuries on the frontal bone, although we pose that their proportion should be constant within each analyzed category.

In what follows, we describe the morphology and patterns of lesions on frontal bones and suggest several hypothetical scenarios based on comparisons of different age classes and differing patterns of injury by sex. We compare the frequency of trauma for individuals in urban and rural settings, for individuals found at inland and coastal sites, and for individuals from different time periods. The chronology of our study encompasses four periods: the Preclassic to Early Classic periods (before AD 600); the Late Classic period (AD 600–800), when institutional violence is presumed to have increased (O'Mansky and Demarest 2007); the Terminal Classic period (AD 800–900), when most Maya kingdoms declined; and the Postclassic era (AD 900–1519), when a new political organization was installed and pan-regional trade dynamics developed under the leadership of the Mesoamerican Quetzalcoatl cult.

Finally, we compare the funerary status of individuals within each site as a way of exploring differences in social rank (see Cucina and Tiesler 2007; Krejci and Culbert 1995; Tiesler 2007). We looked at the possibility that remains recovered from ritual depositories in karstic sinkholes (cenotes) believed to be postsacrificial, such as the Sacred Cenote at Chichén Itzá, are those of warriors or captives (Fig. 8.3). These remains cannot be sorted into particular segments of a society. Submerged sinkhole deposits cannot be controlled for any contextual attribute such as chronology, residence, or status. Instead, they designate only a rather nonspecific cohort of individuals who were selected at different times and under different cultural circumstances for ritual deposit. Because of these contextual limitations, we decided to treat individuals from the large cranial sample from the Sacred Cenote of Chichén Itzá as a separate category and to remove human deposits in dry caves from our sample altogether.

## Results

We initially sorted our data by the four quadrants of the frontal bone— upper right, upper left, lower right, and lower left. In our initial subset, 1,103 individuals presented at least one quadrant. In this group, 5.7 percent of the specimens exhibited one or more wounds in the lower left quadrant, 4.8 percent exhibited wounds in the lower right quadrant, 3.2 percent exhibited wounds in the upper right quadrant, and 2.46 percent exhibited wounds in the upper left quadrant (Fig. 8.4). The distribution of these lesions on the frontal bone suggests that blows to the lower half were more common than blows to the upper half.

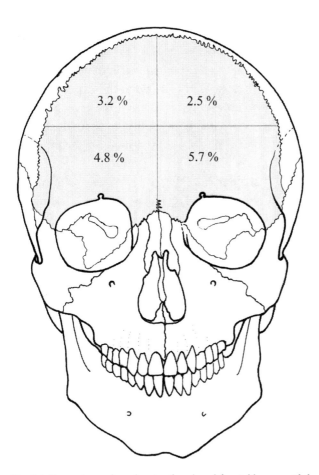

Fig. 8.4. Percentage of quadrants of analyzed frontal bones with lesions.

When we looked at the data another way—by comparing the number of injuries of the left and right sides of the frontal bone—there were no significant differences. For this reason, and because many individuals in our initial sample were represented by only one frontal fragment, we decided to focus only on individuals that were represented by the whole frontal bone. The decreased our sample size to 725 individuals, which is still large enough to be further divided by sex and age, time period, location, status, and contextual classes. Obviously, because of the specific nature of the sample, not all the specimens were characterized by all parameters.

We assumed that if the data showed more injuries to the left side of the face than to the right, that would be an indication of face-to-face combat. Since most humans are right-handed, blows should impact the left side of the frontal bone more often. However, we found that the distribution of the marks in the 121 frontal bones that exhibited marks of violent trauma only slightly (and not significantly) corresponded to the expected close-combat pattern. In fact, only 57 specimens (47.0 percent) had injuries on the left side only (regardless of the quadrant), while 49 individuals (40.5 percent) had injuries on the right side only. The remaining 15 specimens (12.4 percent) had marks on both sides.

A comparison of individuals from different time periods showed a more distinct difference. Those from the Pre-Classic–Early Classic sample presented the lowest rate of injuries (10.77 percent of the skulls had at least one scar). Individuals from Late Classic, Terminal Classic, and Postclassic exhibited a different pattern; in each of these three chronological groups, about 16 percent of the skulls had at least one scar (Table 8.1). The sample from the Sacred Cenote at Chichén Itzá (Fig. 8.3) presented a rate of injury of 20.14 percent. These last values are on average four times as high as the values for the individual quadrants, because in this analysis the unit corresponds to the whole frontal bone, thus providing a larger surface for observable injuries.

As expected, adults were more likely than subadults to have scars on the frontal bone. Among the specimens from the Preclassic, 13.3 percent of adults had scars, and the range increased to more than 18 percent in the later periods. Twenty-five percent of adults in the cenote sample had lesions (Table 8.1). Nonetheless, it is noteworthy that subadults (many of which were infants) were not spared. Leaving the cenote sample aside, more than 11 percent of Late Classic period subadults presented frontal

Table 8.1. Rate of injuries in four chronological periods and at the Sacred Cenote at Chichén Itzá by age and sex

| | Preclassic–Early Classic | | Late Classic | | Terminal Classic | | Postclassic | | Chichén Itzá Sacred Cenote | |
|---|---|---|---|---|---|---|---|---|---|---|
| | % | N | % | N | % | N | % | N | % | N |
| Subadults | 5.00 | 20 | 11.59 | 69 | 6.67 | 15 | 7.69 | 26 | 15.79 | 76 |
| Females | 18.75 | 16 | 12.20 | 82 | 16.22 | 37 | 15.79 | 38 | 12.00 | 25 |
| Males | 5.41 | 37 | 24.18 | 91 | 16.07 | 56 | 17.65 | 51 | 28.57 | 56 |
| All adults | 13.33 | 45 | 18.18 | 154 | 18.18 | 88 | 18.39 | 87 | 25.00 | 68 |
| Total population | 10.77 | 65 | 16.14 | 223 | 16.50 | 103 | 15.79 | 114 | 20.14 | 144 |

Note: The cenote sample is considered as an independent unit of analysis because it is not possible to assign dates to any of the specimens.

bones with lesions, while between 5 percent and 7 percent of the infants and juveniles who lived before or after that period had injuries to their foreheads.

Dividing our sample by sex also produced evidence of a significant pattern. Males show an equal or higher frequency of wounds than females in almost every time period except the earliest time range for this study, namely the combined Preclassic–Early Classic period, when women surpass men in terms of frequency of injury. For females, we found no statistically significant differences across the four time periods (chi square = 0.846, $p$ = 0.932), but the lower frequency among males in the Preclassic–Early Classic segment is at the edge of a significant difference from males in the other periods (chi square = 9.228, $p$ = 0.056). However, it must be noted that data from the earliest period is not clearly indicative of sex-related exposure to violence because the sample size is smaller and a chi-square analysis between males and females is not significant (1.028, $p$ = 0.311, likely due to the small number of females [16] in this subgroup). The Late Classic is the period with the major gender difference in trauma frequencies, while the following chronological periods manifested a more equal exposure between the sexes. Finally, the greater rate of injuries among males in the cenote sample approximates the rate of injury among males in the Late Classic subgroup (Table 8.1).

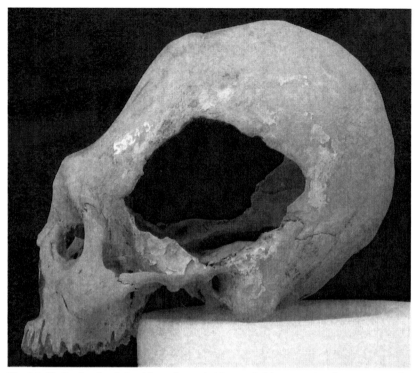

Fig. 8.5. Skull of male adult with perforated sides, probably stemming from *tzompantli* exposition, Sacred Cenote, Chichén Itzá. Peabody Museum, Harvard University, no. 5824-3. Photo by V. Tiesler.

The frontal bones of males were also more likely than those of females to show evidence of posthumous scalping, defleshing, or *tzompantli* (skull rack) exhibition (Fig. 8.5), practices that Mayanist scholarship has associated with warrior or ancestor status. Of the 21 complete skulls with postmortem cut marks made by slicing (mostly belonging to the Sacred Cenote skeletal series), some 13 belonged to males and only two to females. Among the skulls that had been manipulated after death, only males bore traces of trauma on the forehead.

Most warriors are depicted in Maya iconography as members of the elite. When we analyzed lesions according to status (as indicated by funerary attire and burial architecture; see Krecji and Culbert 1995), we found that the frontal bones of 22.2 percent of upper elite (grades 4–5) individuals and 22.7 percent of lower elite (grades 2–3) individuals showed evidence of violent impact, in contrast to a much lower statistic of 13.6 percent among commoners.

Table 8.2. Rate of lesions for coastal and inland Mayans by sex

|  | Coastal Mayans | Inland Mayans |
|---|---|---|
| Males | 22.00 | 14.46 |
| Females | 16.48 | 11.32 |

Looking at the sample by geographical distribution highlights distinctive patterns during the Classic period. Most of the individuals in the regional comparison are from the Classic period in our cohort and the Postclassic period is incompletely covered in this analysis. The distribution of violent injuries to the frontal bone is fairly even and differences are not statistically significant when populations from urban centers and the hinterland (periphery) are compared (11.13 percent versus 13.23 percent). Generally speaking, both males and females in coastal populations appear to have suffered a higher rate of lesions than their counterparts in inland populations (see Table 8.2). The two major coastal collections analyzed here are from Xcambó and Jaina, small commercial ports located at strategic points along the coastal trade route of the peninsula (Fig. 8.6).

One last point that deserves attention is the morphology and state of healing of the documented traumatic lesions. We documented 97 wounds, but only three individuals had sustained wounds shortly before death. These fresh penetrating cuts were up to nine centimeters wide. In general, depressions with circular and oval outlines appear to prevail (see 37 and 38, Fig. 8.6). Both the oval and circular outlines are relatively small (on average 13.6 mm and 20.7 mm in diameter, respectively). Almost all of the oval wounds were detected on the left side of the frontal bone, whereas the circular wounds were equally distributed on the left and right sides. We also found 14 instances of healed longitudinal grooves that measured half an inch long on average; these were found on both sides of the frontal bone. The distribution and frequency of the few semicircular depression fractures are different: most of these are more than an inch in diameter and appear on the left side of the forehead.

To synthesize: the majority of wounds are completely healed and their morphology denotes impacts from small, pointed objects on both sides of the forehead that are consistent with arrow or spear points or perhaps even small stones from slingshots. Comparatively few lesions seem to have been inflicted by heavy weapons used at close range. Most of these wounds were large, and some of them were clearly lethal; they exhibit

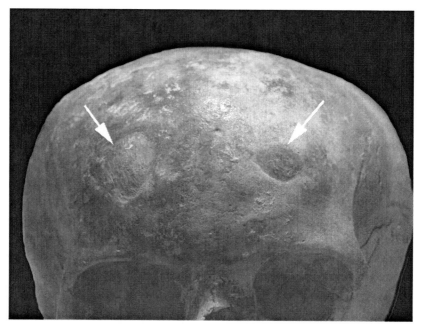

Fig. 8.6. Skull from Jaina, Campeche, with two healed frontal lesions with roughly oval outlines. Dirección de Antropología Física, INAH.

no signs of bone remodeling. These wounds are examples of both blunt force and sharp force trauma and appear to have been inflicted by knives, spiked obsidian clubs, or axes.

## Discussion

In our regional analysis, both blunt force and sharp force trauma occurred with similar frequency in both men and women from burials all over the Maya Lowlands, at least in the anatomical segment under study. These wounds were distributed on the different locations of the frontal bones of the individuals in roughly equal proportions, with a slight increase in the lower left quadrant. This overall trend speaks categorically against a scenario of standing armies of warriors involved in face-to-face combat, in which case we would expect a strong predominance of traumatic lesions among males and more injuries on the unprotected left side of the forehead than on the right side.

In order to highlight the bioarchaeological trends encountered in this study, let us compare our results with those documented for other traditional societies. For comparison, we will focus on selected pre-Hispanic Andean sites, where frontal lesions have been recorded systematically. Thanks to the good preservation that prevails in the Andean area, frontal lesions have been registered mostly as part of more comprehensive counts that include all of the neurocranium or the cranium (including the face). Frontal lesions account for 15.7 percent of the total traumas in San Pedro de Atacama (Torres-Rouff and Junqueira 2006, 67), for example, and for 51.9 percent of the total number of head wounds at Wari sites (Tung 2007, 946). These frequencies give us reason to believe that the total number of head lesions among the Maya skulls in our sample should be much higher than the counts of forehead injuries, on which we focused in this study.

In the Wari Empire, frontal injuries appear to center strongly in the lower left quadrant of the forehead (Tung 2007, 948–952). This pattern suggests that many of the inflicted lesions should have stemmed from direct (person-to-person) combat in the documented Wari sites, a trend that differs from the Maya sample, with its rather uniform anatomical distribution. The differences in the anatomical topography of the marks between the Andean foreheads (predominantly on the left lower quadrant of the frontal bone) and our results for the Maya area (which suggest a more homogeneous distribution) are matched by differences in the frequency of frontal trauma by sex. While the Andean studies (Torres-Rouff and Junqueira 2006; Tung 2007) generally highlight a clear male dominance in lesions, in the Maya population under study, the proportion of injured males and females was more balanced, with the exception of the specific mortuary contexts of the Sacred Cenote context and the Late Classic sample. Compared to the Andean trauma patterns described here, the Maya trends align more with scenarios of unrelated accidents, interpersonal violence, and raiding than with a scenario of male-dominated armies engaged in face-to-face combat.

Let us examine further the trends within the documented Maya sample, where significant differences in frequency and types of lesions are evident. Individuals recovered from the nonfunerary context of the Sacred Cenote sustained head injuries at a rate that was up to twice that of individuals from proper burials that indicate reverential, ancestral treatment. This rate of injury pertains to skinned or defleshed trophy heads and other examples of postmortem manipulation, most of which were recovered from the Sacred Cenote at Chichén Itzá (Fig. 8.5). These differences could point to the presence of the "warriors" we were looking for at the outset of this study, although the archaeological record provides no clear clues about the degree and form of organization of violent conflicts.

Speaking of warriors, our results also suggest that Maya paramounts did indeed participate in battlefield conflict and that rulers were involved actively in interpersonal violence. The fact that high-status skeletons had a higher proportion of lesions than commoners in our sample is an indication that these individuals did not take safe positions behind the front lines but, at least in some cases, were actively involved in the fighting (Foster 2002), although low sample numbers limit our ability to make generalizations. Some of the wounds we recorded are associated with known rulers of the Classic period. Such is the case of the skull that is presumed to be that of Lord Sky Witness of the Kaan dynasty from Dzibanché, who ruled Calakmul during the decade from AD 561 to 572 (Martin and Grube 2008; Velásquez-García 2005). This skull exhibits multiple depression fractures in a healed state on both sides of the forehead (Fig. 8.7). Conversely, Janaab' Pakal of Palenque had no traces of trauma on his well-preserved skull that would point to interpersonal violence. The mortal remains of this paramount, who the inscriptions hail as a victorious Late Classic warlord, were thoroughly studied in 1999 as part of an on-site study at the Temple of the Inscriptions at Palenque (Tiesler 2006).

Despite the profiling of those individuals who suffered the most traumatic injuries, the combined bioarchaeological and contextual evidence is insufficient to yield clear indications that would suggest a specialized standing army in the Maya region, as has been documented from other data sources for the Aztecs or the Inca. Indeed, the contextual information, the distribution of the documented lesions, and the sex and age distribution of the injured individuals in our sample point to armed raids of settlements rather than any institutionalized mass violence exerted between professional armies. Such raids appear to have been as common in the small hinterland communities as in the urban seats of political power. These affected females and also minors to a considerable degree, indicating the high social cost the general population had to pay.

In addition to scars inflicted by raids and battles, some of the wounds we documented are surely the result of domestic accidents or interpersonal aggression. At the outset of the study, we assumed that these injuries would have been constant over time and across cultures, but we must acknowledge that trauma related to domestic incidents introduces an

Fig. 8.7. Skull presumed to pertain to Lord Sky Witness, Dzibanché's Early Classic ruler, showing at least four healed frontal lesions. Proyecto Arqueológico Sur de Quintana Roo, INAH. Photo by V. Tiesler.

element of uncertainty into any attempt to interpret trauma as evidence of warfare or even as an expression of other forms of institutionalized, social, or structural violence.

For now, at least, the types of injuries to the frontal bones and the ways they were distributed indicate that most of the wounded individuals analyzed in this study were the victims, not the perpetrators, of violence and were not active participants in person-to-person combat. The lesions appear with almost equal frequency on the right and the left sides of the frontal bone. The clues these wounds provide suggest that most of them were inflicted by long-range arrows, spears, or stones from slingshots. Different types of weapons were used in close-range combat, such as knives, axes, and obsidian-spiked clubs and spears (Foster 2002). It is very likely that such razor-sharp weapons inflicted wound patterns that are different from the general wound patterns observed, specifically sharp force trauma in the form of cuts and semicircular depressions. We found only a small proportion of such wounds in our skeletal cohort.

Scholars have long argued that institutional violence in the Maya realm, at least before the collapse of Maya society, was waged by centrally controlled political entities to acquire allies, tribute, and access to basic and exotic commodities (Martin and Grube 2008; O'Mansky and Demarest 2007). From this standpoint, the high number of traumas we recorded in the small coastal sites comes as a surprise at first glance, as one would expect such high levels of violence in and around a central inland stronghold that held control of these trade routes. Although we can only speculate about the exact reasons for the high levels of interpersonal violence at coastal sites, we pose that economics are a strong motive for violent conflict, either armed robbery or the defense of highly valued foreign goods during transport to markets.

Lastly, differences are also evident when the sample is divided by time period. A peak in social violence is evident during the Terminal Classic period, a century that saw dramatic social change, invasions, and political breakdown, at least in the Central Maya Lowlands. Such events doubtless took a toll on the local population, which was reduced or exterminated or had to relocate in distant territories. These dynamics likely were accompanied by conflict and collective violence, as other types of evidence for the so-called collapse appear to indicate (Webster 2002).

## Conclusion

In closing, we think bioarcheological approaches have much to offer in the research of the ancient Maya and warfare, despite the limitations this type of research does have, particularly when analyzing ambiguous or isolated bone assemblages, as shown above. The lack of clear distinctions in many human clusters can make clear analysis difficult. Also, most of the signatures of organized conflict and violence may have been the products of ritual behaviors or domestic conflict or accidents. These caveats and the incompleteness of the archaeological record imply the need for careful case-by-case discussions of relevant data sets.

Our systematic examination of skeletal trauma in frontal bones, which included the remains of children, women, and men from different social sectors, cultural contexts, and time periods, has provided novel insights, along with new points of departure for further assessing the roles and the extent of violence in ancient Maya society. Our evidence suggests that violence in the Maya realm was present and affected all segments of society, although not all of them equally. Regarding the implication of the extent of interpersonal violence and its potential institutionalized quality, the documented evidence speaks against any scenario of organized combat of large standing armies and instead suggests middle-range skirmishes and community raids. This conclusion brings us back to the ideas expressed in the introduction about native Maya resistance in the colonies, namely their decentralized political landscape and the dense subtropical brush forests that harbored them, with no form of transport but human carriers. Nestled in this impenetrable environment of their homeland, surprise raids and middle-range attacks from the concealment of the shrubs proved to be more effective than large-scale, open face-to-face battles (O'Mansky and Demarest 2007). After European contact, the Maya natives used these same strategies quite successfully to confront their aggressors from afar.

## Acknowledgments

We wish to thank the following projects and colleagues for providing material, information, assistance, and valuable comments: Arturo Romano Pacheco (National Institute of Anthropology and History) and the Proyecto Arqueológico Toniná (Centro de Estudios Mesoamericanos y Centroamericanos); Arnoldo Cruz González (National Institute of Anthropology and History) of the Proyecto Arqueológico Palenque; Luz Evelia Campaña (National Institute of Anthropology and History) of the Proyecto Arqueológico Becán; Enrique Nalda and Adriana Velázquez (National Institute of Anthropology and History) of the Proyecto Arqueológico Sur de Quintana Roo; Leticia Vargas (National Institute of Anthropology and History) of the Proyecto Arqueológico Ek Balam; Proyecto Arqueológico Oxtankah (National Institute of Anthropology and History); Juan Pedro Laporte (Archaeological and Ethnological Institute, Guatemala) of the Proyecto Atlas Arqueológico de Guatemala; William Folan (Autonomous University of Campeche) of the Proyecto Arqueológico Calakmul, Ramón Carrasco (National Institute of Anthropology and History) of the Proyecto Arqueológico Calakmul; and Francisco Ortíz Pedraza and José Antonio Pompa y Padilla of the Dirección de Antropología Física/National Institute of Anthropology and History.

# References Cited

Cucina, A., and V. Tiesler
2007    Nutrition, Lifestyle, and Social Status of Skeletal Remains from Nonfunerary and "Problematical" Contexts. In *New Perspectives on Human Sacrifice and Ritual Body Treatments in Ancient Maya Society,* edited by V. Tiesler and A. Cucina, pp. 251–262. Springer, New York.

Foster, L. V.
2002    *Handbook to Life in the Ancient Maya World.* Oxford University Press, Oxford.

Freidel, D. A.
1986    Maya Warfare: An Example of Peer Polity Interaction. In *Peer Polity Interaction and Socio-political Change,* edited by C. Renfrew and J. F. Cherry, pp. 93–108. Cambridge University Press, New York.

Krejci, E., and P. Culbert
1995    Preclassic and Classic Burials and Caches in the Maya Lowlands. In *The Emergence of Lowland Maya Civilization,* edited by N. Grube, pp. 103–116. Acta Mesoamericana no. 14. Anton Saurwein, Möchmühl, Germany.

Martin, S., and N. Grube
2008    *Chronicle of the Maya Kings and Queens.* 2nd ed. Thames and Hudson, New York.

O'Mansky, M., and A. A. Demarest
2007    Status Rivalry and Warfare in the Development and Collapse of Classic Maya Civilization. In *Latin American Indigenous Warfare and Ritual Violence,* edited by R. J. Chacon and R. G. Mendoza, pp. 11–33. University of Arizona Press, Tucson.

Pagliaro, J. B., J. M. Garber, and T. W. Stanton
2003    Evaluating the Archaeological Signatures of Maya Ritual Conflict. In *Ancient Mesoamerican Warfare,* edited by M. K. Brown and T. W. Stanton, pp. 75–90. Altamira, Walnut Creek.

Pérez-Flores, A.
2006    Marcas de violencia en poblaciones prehispánicas mayas: una visión bioarqueológica. B.A. thesis, Universidad Autónoma de Yucatán.

Tiesler, V.
2006    Life and Death of the Ruler: Recent Bioarchaeological Findings. In *Janaab' Pakal of Palenque: Reconstructing the Life and Death of a Maya Ruler,* edited by V. Tiesler and A. Cucina, pp. 21–47. University of Arizona, Tucson.

2007    Funerary and Nonfunerary? New References in Identifying Ancient Maya Sacrificial and Postsacrifical Behaviors from Human Assemblages. In *New Perspectives on Human Sacrifice and Ritual Body Treatments in Ancient Maya Society,* edited by V. Tiesler and A. Cucina, pp. 14–45. Springer, New York.

Torres-Rouff, C., and M. A. C. Junqueira
2006    Interpersonal Violence in Prehistoric San Pedro de Atacama, Chile: Behavioral Implications of Environmental Stress. *American Journal of Physical Anthropology* 130: 60–70.

Tozzer, A. M. (editor)

1941 *Landa's Relación de las Cosas de Yucatan: A Translation.* Papers of the Peabody Museum of Archaeology and Ethnology no. 14. Peabody Museum of Archaeology and Ethnology, Cambridge, Mass.

Tung, T. A.

2007 Trauma and Violence in the Wari Empire of the Peruvian Andes: Warfare, Raids, and Ritual Fights. *American Journal of Physical Anthropology* 133: 941–956.

Velásquez-García, E.

2005 The Captives of Dzibanché. *The PARI Journal* 6(2): 1–4.

Webster, D. L.

2002 *The Fall of the Ancient Maya: Solving the Mystery of the Maya Collapse.* Thames and Hudson, London.

# 9

## Violence against Women

### Differential Treatment of Local and Foreign Females in the Heartland of the Wari Empire, Peru

TIFFINY A. TUNG

## Introduction

Bioarchaeological studies that employ a population-level approach to violence-related trauma are essential for gaining insights into the larger social and political contexts of ancient communities. This bird's-eye view may permit a clearer understanding of social norms regarding the role of violence both in everyday life and in seemingly extraordinary circumstances, such as warfare or ritual. This view of society, however, should be combined with a nuanced, close-up view of the battered and beaten individuals to clarify how broad social ideals directly impacted the lives of certain individuals.

Bioarchaeology is ideally suited to both macro (population) and micro (individual) levels of analysis, because our data lenses, which focus on the skeletons of individuals, can easily move between the two perspectives. If we view skeletons as the bony diaries of people's lives, we can reconstruct individual morbidity profiles (and in the case presented here, the exposure of individuals to violence) and situate them within the larger social arena. These kinds of life histories have been done with great success in bioarchaeology, providing us with detailed views of life experiences of individuals from ancient populations (Hawkey 1998; Martin et al. 2008; Mayes and Barber 2008; Wilson et al. 2007).

In this chapter, I attempt to present that kind of bifocal view, presenting data on population-level cranial trauma and a detailed discussion of bodily injury and mortuary treatment of two females interred at the Wari site of Conchopata in the central highland Peruvian Andes. In this way, I aim to investigate how Wari society and the individual were mutually constituted in terms of norms about violence and female identity and notions of community membership.

## The Wari Empire

In the seventh century AD, the Wari Empire expanded and incorporated various lands and people, ranging from pockets of coastal areas to large sections of productive mid-valley agricultural lands and smaller regions in the high-altitude mountain zones. This era, known as the Middle Horizon in Andean chronology (AD 600–1000), was characterized by the distribution of Wari architectural and iconographic styles across the Andean landscape. For example, Wari administrative sites and Wari-style architecture are seen as far south as the Moquegua Valley in southern Peru, where the site of Cerro Baúl is located, and in northern highland Peru, where the sites of Honcopampa and Viracochapampa (and other smaller Huari sites) are situated (Fig. 9.1). To the southeast, in the Cusco region, Wari sites such as Pikillacta and Cotocotuyoc exhibit Wari-style architectural forms and artifacts (McEwan 2005). Together, these various sites point to conquest, collaboration, and/or incorporation of groups that lived far from the heartland of the Wari Empire. Wari textiles and ceramics (Castillo 2000; Conlee 2010; de la Vera Cruz Chávez 1996; Nash 2010; Owen 2007) and the occasional Wari-style trophy head (Koontz 2011; Tung 2008) also demonstrate the influence of the Wari across much of the Peruvian Andes. The variability in Wari-influenced material culture—ranging from ritual D-shaped structures and orthogonal architecture to Wari polychrome ceramics and textiles—reveals the various levels of interaction of local populations with the imperial core.

## The Role of Militarism and Trophy Heads in Wari Expansion

The development of the Wari Empire and the growing interaction with other cultural groups likely occurred through military expansion, religious indoctrination (Lumbreras 1974; Menzel 1964), and superior

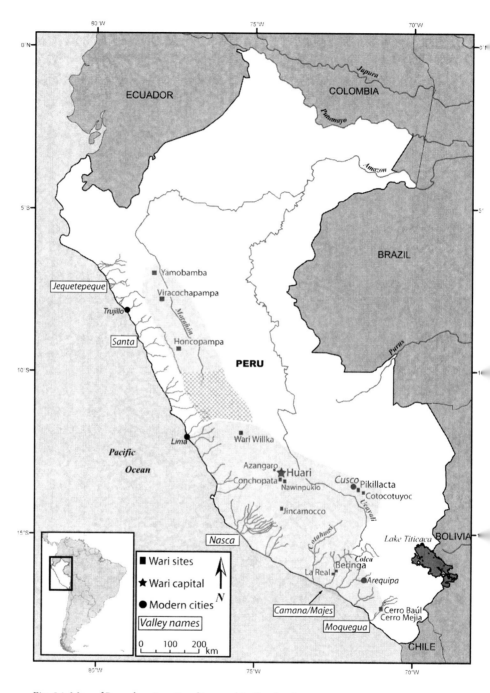

Fig. 9.1. Map of Peru showing sites discussed in the chapter.

practices in agricultural engineering (e.g., water canals and agricultural terraces) that enabled Wari agents to harness new lands and make them productive (Williams 2002). Archaeological and bioarchaeological research in the Wari heartland suggests that military might was widely used to subjugate other groups and expand territory. Militaristic iconography is common on ceramics from the Wari heartland sites of Conchopata and Huari (the capital) (Isbell and Cook 2002; Ochatoma and Cabrera 2002; Ochatoma, Tung, and Cabrera 2008), and weapons such as doughnut stones and a possible bow have been uncovered at Conchopata (Isbell and Cook 2002). In addition, human trophy heads—mostly from adult men but also including a few young children—have been excavated from two ritual structures at Conchopata. Strontium isotope analysis of those trophy heads shows that the majority are from nonlocal individuals, likely foreign enemies, which suggests that Wari military agents traveled to distant locales and took captives back to Conchopata (Tung and Knudson 2008, 2011). Those findings suggest that men and children were targeted for abduction and that they were selected for sacrifice and transformation into trophy heads. Thus, it appears that age and sex were powerful markers of identity that structured how captives (and perhaps others) were to be treated in Wari society.

If violence, militarism, and abductions were part of the Wari repertoire for expanding and maintaining imperial authority, then these strategies warrant further exploration, especially in terms of how these activities structured the lives of Conchopata community members and those who may have been forcibly brought into the community. How common was violence-related trauma at this Wari heartland site, and were there other "foreigners" at Conchopata besides those who were transformed into trophy heads? If so, what was the morbidity profile and lived experience of those outsiders within the Conchopata community?

To address those questions, I report on two reliable osteological indicators for violence: the frequency of cranial trauma and patterns of such trauma among adults. I then briefly present strontium isotope and ancient mtDNA data from Conchopata as a way to identify potential outsiders (other than the trophy heads) and report on osteological findings that reveal insights about how outsiders, particularly women, may have been perceived and treated in Wari society. Bioarchaeological methods of analysis and techniques for distinguishing between accidental and intentional trauma have been presented elsewhere (Tung 2007, 2012) and have been discussed by other authors (Kimmerle and Baraybar 2008; Lovell 1997; Martin and Frayer 1997; Walker 2001).

## A Population View of Violence at Conchopata

The sample includes 44 adult crania that were more than half complete, 10 of which (23 percent) exhibit antemortem head wounds (these numbers exclude adult trophy heads, which I reported in Tung 2008). There are no cases of perimortem cranial trauma, which suggests that no one in the burial sample died shortly after receiving a lethal blow to the head. There is, however, one case in which an elderly female died before her head wounds had completely healed (discussed below).

Males and females exhibit similar levels of cranial trauma: 24 percent of females (6 of 25) and 29 percent of males (4 of 14) (Fisher's exact, $p = 0.519$) show evidence of head wounds (Table 9.1). This suggests that men and women at Conchopata were similarly exposed to violence, at least in terms of frequency of head wounds. None of the five unsexed adults display healed cranial trauma, and none of the 39 children ($< 15$ years old) buried in tombs at Conchopata exhibit any kind of head wound. Child trophy heads are excluded from this calculation; they are clearly a distinct subgroup and those data have been published elsewhere (Tung and Knudson 2010).

Previous studies have shown that older individuals are exposed to more years of risk for violence, so as a group, they are likely to show relatively more head trauma than younger age groups and may exhibit more head wounds per person (Glencross and Sawchuk 2003). A counterargument to this might be that because certain age groups are more likely to engage in violence—and perhaps eventually die from one of those interactions—younger males in particular might exhibit more head wounds (both healed and unhealed) than those who lived fairly peaceably into old age. This pattern can be seen in modern mortality tables, where there is a "bulge" in deaths among late adolescent males and young adult men. The risky behavior and sometimes violent interactions for this demographic group contribute to its relatively high proportion of deaths (Paine 1997).

At Conchopata, cranial trauma differences by age group follows the cumulative effect of age on exposure to trauma Glencross and Sawchuk (2003) have outlined. That is, there is no skull trauma among children and

Table 9.1. Summary of antemortem cranial trauma data at Conchopata

| Juveniles (< 15 yrs) | | Males | | Females | | Unsexed Adults | | Adult Totals | |
|---|---|---|---|---|---|---|---|---|---|
| N/Total | % | N/Total | % | N/Total | % | N/Total | % | N/Total | % |
| 0/39 | 0 | 4/14 | 29 | 6/25 | 24 | 0/5 | 0 | 10/44 | 23 |

a lower frequency of trauma among young adults (14 percent) than among middle-aged adults (29 percent) and older adults (44 percent).

## Injury Recidivism, or Repetitive Hits

Of the 10 injured adults in the sample, half exhibit more than one head wound: three females and one male had two cranial fractures and one male had three head wounds. These multiple head injuries suggest that some may have been in more than one violent incident during their lifetime. It is also possible that the attacker leveled several blows to the head during one violent event. It is difficult to distinguish between the two scenarios when all the wounds are well healed. Only when one wound is well healed and the other is perimortem or partially healed can bioarchaeologists conclude that two separate violent acts occurred.

Among the five Conchopata adults that show more than one wound, one—an elderly female—exhibits signs of injury recidivism. She had a healed wound on the parietal boss and a partially healed wound on the superior of the cranium. She also exhibits postcranial fractures and is likely not natal to the Conchopata community, as discussed below.

## Location of Cranial Wounds

The 10 injured adults exhibit 16 fractures; 69 percent (or 11 of 16) of those wounds are on the posterior of the cranium (on the parietal boss and the occipital bone), 19 percent (or 4 of 16) are on the superior of the head, and about 12 percent (or 2 of 16) are on the anterior (Tung 2012). Given that the majority of wounds are on the posterior, it would appear that this portion of the head was nearly systematically targeted or that the victims were in similar social contexts that frequently exposed the back of the head to trauma. This might include fleeing during raids (Webb 1995) or ducking the head to avoid an oncoming blow (Tung 2012).

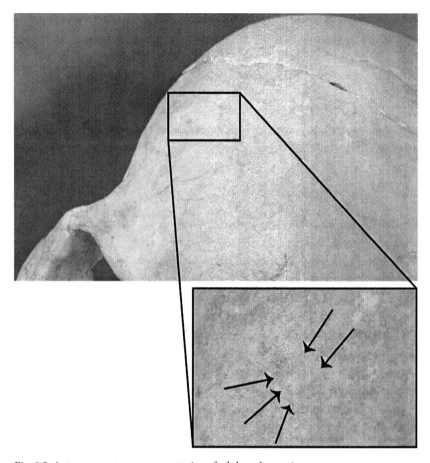

Fig. 9.2. Antemortem trauma on anterior of adult male cranium.

The distribution in head wound location is slightly different between the sexes. The great majority of wounds on females are observed on the posterior (7 of 9, or 78 percent), and not a single wound is on the anterior. In contrast, the location of cranial fractures on men is more evenly dispersed; 57 percent are on the posterior, 29 percent are on the anterior, and 14 percent are on the top of the skull (Fig. 9.2). These patterns suggest that the social contexts in which violence emerged were distinct for men and women. It appears that women were never in face-to-face conflicts that led to anterior craniofacial trauma, whereas the men were.

## Life History of a Battered Female at Conchopata

Among the six women with cranial trauma, one female (aged 47 to 53 years) warrants further discussion because of her repeated injuries. This micro-level view, which situates her within the larger Conchopata community and examines how she is similar to and different from other women, may provide nuanced perspectives about how women—and this woman in particular—were perceived in this Wari community.

Three observations mark her as different from the other women at the site. First, her mortuary treatment was unique. She was buried alone with only a ceramic fragment under her head, a type of funerary treatment that differs from that of the other Conchopata women, who are typically buried with several other individuals and with large quantities of grave goods, such as ceramic bowls, figurines, bottles, copper pins (*tupus*), greenstone (which is similar to turquoise), and Spondylus shells (Tung and Cook 2006). Second, she is the only individual to exhibit the annular form of cranial modification (elongated skull from front to back) (Fig. 9.3). Most others at Conchopata exhibit no cranial modification, and those that do have the fronto-occipital style of modification. Given that cranial modification must be imposed in infancy, it is likely that her parents (or other kin with decision-making power about how her identity

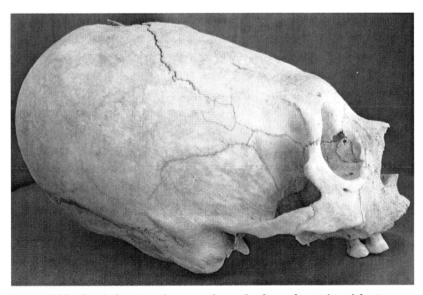

Fig. 9.3. Older female from Conchopata with annular form of cranial modification.

would be corporally expressed) were not local to Conchopata. Third, a previous study of ancient mtDNA of a Conchopata subsample demonstrated that she was the only one of a sample of 14 individuals who belonged to haplogroup D (haplogroup A = 4; haplogroup B = 7; haplogroup C = 2; haplogroup D = 1) (Kemp, Tung, and Summar 2009).

While those three data points suggest that she was not native to Conchopata, the strontium isotope ratio in her upper canine enamel and in her metatarsal bone indicate that she consumed a local diet similar to others at Conchopata from at least age three ($^{87}$Sr/$^{86}$Sr = 0.7058 for both) (Tung and Knudson 2011). The maxillary canine was sampled, and its enamel formation begins at about age three, so it appears that by early childhood this female was already living in or around Conchopata or another region with a similar strontium isotope ratio. Thus, she could have been born in the local area but to parents who were outsiders and marked her as such through a unique form of cranial modification. It is also possible that her parents voluntarily brought her to Conchopata when she was an infant or that she was abducted and eventually adopted into the local community. In either case, an outsider status seems to be marked in her bones (cranial modification) and in her eventual simple treatment in death. How, then, was she treated in life?

The skeletal trauma data suggested that she was not treated well. She exhibits a small circular healed wound (6 × 3.61mm) on the left parietal boss and a large partially healed fracture near the osteometric point of bregma (Fig. 9.4). The fracture near bregma shows a mix of smooth bone and porosity at the margins, suggesting that there was an associated infection. She also exhibits antemortem tooth loss of anterior dentition: both mandibular central incisors and the maxillary right incisors are missing. It is not typical for anterior teeth to exfoliate before the others, and their untimely loss may be related to a facial trauma that today is colloquially known as having one's front teeth knocked out. Granted, it is not clear whether the antemortem tooth loss is related to trauma (and thus it was not counted in the trauma percentages presented above), but in light of her other injuries, it is highly probable that it was. Given that there are two (maybe three) head/facial wounds in various states of healing, it appears that she was a victim of violence in at least two separate events. First, she suffered a nonfatal blow to the posterior of her head (and maybe a hit to her face that dislodged her teeth), and second, she received a severe

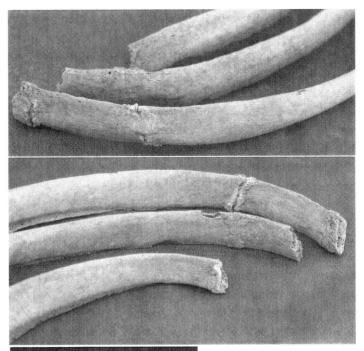

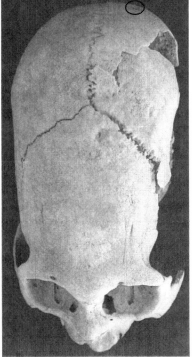

Fig. 9.4. *Top:* Skeletal fractures on the ribs (anterior and posterior views). *Bottom:* Healed wound on left parietal boss, partially healed wound on superior of cranium, and undiagnosed circular lesion/taphonomic change on the frontal bone.

trauma to the superior of her skull that had healed only partially before her death.

This older female also exhibits fractures on six left ribs that primarily affected the sternal portion of ribs four through seven (Fig. 9.4), though the second and third ribs were slightly affected as well. The rib fractures are only partially healed; there is an incomplete union between normal bone and the bony callous, which suggests that the rib fractures occurred shortly before her death, perhaps around the time she received the injury on the superior part of her skull. She has other injuries that are unrelated to violence but suggest a life of physical labor. One of her metacarpals had either a fracture or severe (but well healed) dislocation, and she exhibits compression fractures in lumbar vertebrae three through five.

This female also exhibits a small circular discolored area of bone on the center of the frontal bone, superior to glabella. It is lighter in color and is less dense than the surrounding bone. It may have been caused by an object placed on the center of her forehead in the burial that was later removed by prehistoric inhabitants (archaeologists found no metal disks or other objects that could have caused the discoloration) or it may be a pathological lesion that still needs to be diagnosed.

## Comparing the Older, Foreign Female to the Local Females

The wound on the posterior of the older female's skull is not unlike wounds on the skulls of other injured females at the site. Indeed, all women with at least one head wound exhibit it on the posterior of the skull. This hints at more general social norms regarding the ways that abuse might be inflicted on women at Conchopata, whether during raids, domestic abuse, or corporal punishment enacted in a judicial context. This is similar to what Walker (1997) observed among abused wives in nineteenth-century England, where the highly patterned distribution of wounds (primarily on the face) suggested agreed-upon methods of "disciplining" wives. Although the precise social context in which female violence was enacted at Conchopata is unknown, a general statement about the larger context can be posited: it appears that women were typically in a defensive position when they received the injury.

This older female was treated in other ways that were quite different from how women in general were treated at Conchopata. In addition to her rare cranial modification and unique burial treatment (described above), she had a partially healed wound on the superior part of her skull, which suggests that the injury may have contributed to her death, and her anterior teeth may have been dislodged from a blow to the face. No other women exhibit such brutal and repetitive injuries. In this regard, social norms regarding the "appropriate" way to enact violence against a woman were violated, and she was apparently abused to a much greater and more severe degree than were other women at Conchopata, perhaps due to her outsider status. Bizarre as this might seem to our modern, western sensibilities, a variety of cultural groups (and classes within those groups) view violence against women as an appropriate way to ensure a disciplined, well-functioning family and society (Chambers 1999; Van Vleet 2002; Walker 1997).

In short, the mortuary, osteological, genetic, and strontium isotope data from this elderly female suggest that she was not local to the area or that her mother (haplogroup derives from the maternal line) was not local. Her parents (or other family members) imposed the uncommon form of cranial modification on her when she was an infant, forever marking her as an "outsider." This outsider status combined with her female identity may have structured how she was perceived and treated by other community members at Conchopata. Being a woman and an outsider apparently placed her in a socially precarious position, making her more susceptible than others at Conchopata to maltreatment and attack during life and less likely to receive "proper" burial rites in death.

## Life History of a Sacrificed Adolescent Female

The older female with numerous violence-related traumas was not the only nonlocal woman at Conchopata. There was also an adolescent female, and although her cranium was too poorly preserved to observe for trauma, she warrants discussion because she reveals much about how young nonlocal females were treated at Conchopata. She was buried in front of the ritual D-shaped structure (known as EA72), where 10 human trophy heads were also deposited (Tung 2008). Importantly, this teenage girl exhibits a strontium isotope ratio unlike anyone else at the site ($^{87}Sr/^{86}Sr = 0.71058$). This value is much higher than the local average ($^{87}Sr/^{86}Sr = 0.70584\pm0.00074$), indicating that she was a nonlocal individual (Tung and Knudson 2011). Analysis of her mandibular canine indicates that she could have arrived at Conchopata anytime after age five (enamel formation of the mandibular canine completes around age five); this means that she could have arrived there at age six or seven or even a few days before her death at age 17–22 years.

Additional evidence of her nonlocal status is her unusual burial treatment. She was not interred under a house floor with several other kin and a variety of grave goods, as was the usual funerary custom (Isbell 2004; Tung and Cook 2006). Instead, she was buried alone directly in front of the D-shaped ritual building. She was buried with four small copper pins (*tupus*) that still had textile fragments adhering to them, suggesting that they were used to pin her clothing together (Anita Cook, personal communication 2010). She displayed mild periostitis on her left tibial midshaft and her left ulna. It is unknown if the periostitis was bilateral because the other tibia fragments and ulna were too poorly preserved. Thus, it is unclear if localized trauma or a mild systemic infection affected the shin and lower arm. Her cranium and cervical vertebrae were not well enough preserved to observe for trauma, so it is not known if violence-related trauma to the head or neck was the mechanism of death. Although she could have died from natural causes, her unique burial location and early death in adolescence require that other explanations be explored.

Compelling iconographic, skeletal, and strontium isotope data indicate that Wari warriors traveled to distant locales so they could take men and children captive, sacrifice them at a later time, and transform them into trophies (Tung 2008; Tung and Knudson 2011). This adolescent female may have been taken captive, and she was eventually deposited in front of the ritual building where the trophy heads were found. It is likely that she was sacrificed, as were the trophy head victims. Notably, however, this female captive was treated in a very different manner from the men and child captives. The latter group was dismembered and their heads and hands were separated from their bodies and made into trophies. The cut marks on the crania and hand phalanges attest to the butchering of the men's and children's bodies. They were subsequently burned and smashed on the floor of this centrally located ritual building and a sacrificed camelid was placed on top of the pile of human trophy heads (Ochatoma and Cabrera 2002). In the same space, enormous ceramic urns were intentionally smashed as a ritual offering. Importantly, those urns depicted Wari warriors brandishing weapons and wearing trophy heads (Ochatoma and Cabrera 2002), hinting at the way those captives were obtained.

The female captive, in contrast, was not butchered and transformed into trophy parts. Her body was kept intact and was wrapped in a shroud or clothing before she was placed in the prominent location in front of the entrance to the D-shaped ritual structure. I suggest that her nonlocal status and her gender and age marked her as an ideal sacrifice to sanctify the ritual space and the ceremonies that occurred within it. Moreover, her female identity structured how she was to be treated in sacrifice and death, just as age-based markers of identity structured the treatment of captive children, coding them as appropriate for sacrifice and dismemberment and as trophy head objects. Captive males underwent the same processing as the child captives. Finally, it is also important to note that the adolescent woman was likely captured in a village raid, perhaps when children were also captured for trophies. It is unlikely that she (and the other children) were captured on the battlefield, as it is unlikely that warriors would have encountered adolescent females and children in that setting.

Comparing the Adolescent Female to the Group

Currently, the teenage female in front of the D-shaped building is the only one of 14 females sampled to exhibit a nonlocal strontium isotope ratio, an indication that foreign females were rare at the site (though the older female described above may also have been foreign). The adolescent's nonlocal status may have been known among Conchopata inhabitants and may have ultimately contributed to her unusual deposition and (suspected) sacrifice in front of the ritual structure. Local women did not receive mortuary treatments like she did, nor would they have been considered for sacrifice and trophy head rituals. Instead, local women were given fairly elaborate funerary treatments, and they were interred under the floors of family houses with other kin. Apparently, whether a person was an insider or an outsider was a powerful structuring force in how a decedent was treated in mortuary rituals and one that also affected the likelihood of early (nonaccidental) death .

More broadly, it is unlikely that females voluntarily migrated to Conchopata or that Conchopata men abducted women from distant locales to force them into new social roles as servants or wives. Instead, nearly all the women at Conchopata were natal inhabitants, and as a result, they had remarkably similar lifeways and deathways with only minor variations in health status and numbers of grave goods (Tung and Cook 2006). The adolescent female was the most different from the other women at the site in terms of her mortuary placement and treatment, age at death, and nonlocal status, factors that strongly suggest she was a human sacrifice.

## Conclusion

Based on various lines of data, I have argued that the Wari Empire engaged in the capture of men, women, and children, though the final treatment of the captives varied, apparently structured by their age and sex and perhaps by other personal qualities that are not visible to the bioarchaeologist. The demographic and strontium isotope data on the trophy heads indicate that adult men were the preferred targets for capture, dismemberment, and subsequent transformation into trophy heads (Tung 2008). Children were also apparent targets; they constitute nearly a quarter of the trophy head sample. Women from faraway regions were rarely targets of abduction, and their body parts certainly were not selected as war trophies (only one trophy head out of 31 has been identified as a possible female) (Tung 2008).

The sample of burials and trophy heads at Conchopata includes two examples of foreign females. One was badly beaten, likely a result of her lower social standing in the community, a status that was in large part defined by her outsider identity. The second was an adolescent girl that was likely sacrificed and deposited in front of the ritual building that held the human trophy heads. Her selection as a particular kind of sacrificial victim—her body kept intact and placed in a sacred location—may have been informed by her unusual foreign status and the fact that she was female. Indeed, it is possible that she was abducted solely for the purpose of ritual sacrifice, a practice that was carried out by the later Inka Empire, which commonly sacrificed young children and adolescent girls (Bray et al. 2005; Reinhard 2005; Wilson et al. 2007).

These findings show that although female abduction was rare at Conchopata, when it did occur nonlocal females could either be incorporated into the community for life or sacrificed in an elaborate ceremony. The older foreign female was apparently integrated into Wari society but at a low level in the social hierarchy. The younger female was probably sacrificed, but it is notable that she was not dismembered and made into a trophy head like the foreign men and children. Together, these data suggest that notions of community membership and gender identity were powerful factors in structuring how one was treated in life and death. And among those who were marked as outsiders, age and sex were important in determining treatment in life, the method of sacrifice, and subsequent treatment of the body in death.

## References Cited

Bray, T. L., L. Minc, M. C. Ceruti, J. A. Chávez, R. Perea, and J. Reinhard
2005    A Compositional Analysis of Pottery Vessels Associated with the Inca Ritual of Capacocha. *Journal of Anthropological Archaeology* 24(1): 82–100.

Castillo, L. J.
2000    La Presencia de Wari en San José de Moro. In *Boletín de Arqueología PUCP, No. 4*, edited by P. Kaulicke and W. H. Isbell, pp. 143–79. Pontificia Universidad Católica del Perú, Lima.

Chambers, S. C.
1999    "To the Company of a Man Like My Husband, No Law Can Compel Me": The Limits of Sanctions Against Wife Beating in Arequipa, Peru, 1780–1850. *Journal of Women's History* 11(1): 31–52.

Conlee, C. A.
2010    Nasca and Wari: Local Opportunism and Colonial Ties during the Middle Horizon. In *Beyond Wari Walls: Regional Perspectives on Middle Horizon Peru*, edited by J. J. Jennings, pp. 96–112. University of New Mexico Press, Albuquerque.

de la Vera Cruz Chávez, P.
1996    El Papel de la Sub Region Norte de los Valles Occidentales en la Articulacion entre Los Andes Centrales y Los Andes Centro Sur. In *Integracion Surandina Cinco Siglos Despues*, edited by X. Albó, J. Arratia, L. Hidalgo, A. Nuñez, A. Llagostera, M. Remy, and B. Revesz, pp. 135–157. Centro de Estudios Regionales Andinos Bartolomé de Las Cases, Universidad Católica del Norte, Arica.

Glencross, B., and L. Sawchuk
2003    The Person-Years Construct: Ageing and the Prevalence of Health Related Phenomena from Skeletal Samples. *International Journal of Osteoarchaeology* 13: 369–374.

Hawkey, D. E.
1998    Disability, Compassion, and the Skeletal Record: Using Musculoskeletal Stress Markers (MSM) to Construct an Osteobiography from Early New Mexico. *International Journal of Osteoarchaeology* 8: 326–340.

Isbell, W. H.
2004    Mortuary Preferences: A Wari Culture Case Study from Middle Horizon, Peru. *Latin American Antiquity* 15(1): 3–32.

Isbell, W. H., and A. G. Cook
2002    A New Perspective on Conchopata and the Andean Middle Horizon. In *Andean Archaeology II: Art, Landscape, and Society*, edited by H. Silverman and W. H. Isbell, pp. 249–305. Kluwer Academic Press, New York.

Kemp, B. M., T. A. Tung, and M. Summar
2009    Genetic Continuity after the Collapse of the Wari Empire: Mitochondrial DNA Profiles from Wari and Post-Wari Populations in the Ancient Andes. *American Journal of Physical Anthropology* 140(1): 80–91.

Kimmerle, E. H., and J. P. Baraybar (editors)
2008    *Skeletal Trauma: Identification of Injuries Resulting from Human Remains Abuse and Armed Conflict.* CRC Press, Boca Raton.

Koontz, C. B.
2011    Pre-Wari and Wari Health, Trauma, and Tradition in the Majes and Siguas Valleys. Paper presented at the Center for Latin American Studies Graduate Student Conference, Vanderbilt University.

Lovell, N. C.
1997    Trauma Analysis in Paleopathology. *Yearbook of Physical Anthropology* 40: 139–170.

Lumbreras, L. G.
1974    *The Peoples and Cultures of Ancient Peru.* Smithsonian Institution Press, Washington, D.C.

Martin, D. L., N. J. Akins, B. Crenshaw, and P. K. Stone
2008    Inscribed in the Body, Written on the Bones: The Consequences of Social Violence at La Plata. In *Social Violence in the Prehispanic American Southwest,* edited by D. L. Nichols and P. L. Crown, pp. 98–122. University of Arizona Press, Tucson.

Martin, D. L., and D. W. Frayer (editors)
1997    *Troubled Times: Violence and Warfare in the Past.* Gordon and Breach, Amsterdam.

Mayes, A. T., and S. B. Barber
2008    Osteobiography of a High-Status Burial from the Lower Río Verde Valley of Oaxaca, Mexico. *International Journal of Osteoarchaeology* 18(6): 573–588.

McEwan, G. F.
2005    *Pikillacta: The Wari Empire in Cuzco.* University of Iowa Press, Iowa City.

Menzel, D.
1964    Style and Time in the Middle Horizon. *Nawpa Pacha* 2: 1–105.

Nash, D. J.
2010    Fine Dining and Fabulous Atmosphere: Feasting Facilities and Political Interaction in the Wari Realm. In *Inside Ancient Kitchens: New Directions in the Study of Daily Meals and Feasts,* edited by E. Klarich, pp. 83–110. University Press of Colorado, Boulder.

Ochatoma, J. A., and M. R. Cabrera
2002    Religious Ideology and Military Organization in the Iconography of a D-shaped Ceremonial Precinct at Conchopata. In *Andean Archaeology II: Art, Landscape, and Society,* edited by H. Silverman and W. H. Isbell, pp. 225–247. Kluwer Academic Press, New York.

Ochatoma, J. A., T. A. Tung, and M. Cabrera
2008    The Emergence of a Wari Military Class as Viewed through Art and the Body.

Paper presented at the 73rd annual meeting of the Society for American Archaeology, Vancouver, Canada.

Owen, B.

2007    The Wari Heartland on the Arequipa Coast: Huamanga Ceramics from Beringa, Majes. *Andean Past* 8: 287–373.

Paine, R. R.

1997    Uniformitarian Models in Osteological Paleodemography. In *Integrating Archaeological Demography: Multidisciplinary Approaches to Prehistoric Population*, edited by R. R. Paine. Center for Archaeological Investigations no. 24. Southern Illinois University, Carbondale.

Reinhard, J.

2005    *The Ice Maiden: Inca Mummies, Mountain Gods, and Sacred Sites in the Andes.* National Geographic Society, Washington, D.C.

Tung, T. A.

2007    Trauma and Violence in the Wari Empire of the Peruvian Andes: Warfare, Raids, and Ritual Fights. *American Journal of Physical Anthropology* 133: 941–956.

2008    Dismembering Bodies for Display: A Bioarchaeological Study of Trophy Heads from the Wari Site of Conchopata, Peru. *American Journal of Physical Anthropology* 136(3): 294–308.

2012    *Violence, Ritual, and the Wari Empire: A Social Bioarchaeology of Imperialism in the Ancient Andes.* University Press of Florida, Gainesville.

Tung, T. A., and A. G. Cook

2006    Intermediate Elite Agency in the Wari Empire: The Bioarchaeological and Mortuary Evidence. In *Intermediate Elites in Pre-Columbian States and Empires*, edited by C. Elson and A. R. Covey, pp. 68–93. University of Arizona Press, Tucson.

Tung, T. A., and K. J. Knudson

2008    Social Identities and Geographical Origins of Wari Trophy Heads from Conchopata, Peru. *Current Anthropology* 49(5): 915–925.

2010    Childhood Lost: Abductions, Sacrifice, and Trophy Heads of Children in the Wari Empire of the Ancient Andes. *Latin American Antiquity* 21(1): 44–66.

2011    Identifying Locals, Migrants, and Captives in the Wari Heartland: A Bioarchaeological and Biogeochemical Study of Human Remains from Conchopata, Peru. *Journal of Anthropological Archaeology* 30(3): 247–261.

Van Vleet, K. E.

2002    The Intimacies of Power: Rethinking Violence and Affinity in the Bolivian Andes. *American Ethnologist* 29(3): 567–601.

Walker, P. L.

1997    Wife Beating, Boxing, and Broken Noses: Skeletal Evidence for the Cultural Patterning of Violence. In *Troubled Times: Violence and Warfare in the Past,* edited by D. L. Martin and D. W. Frayer, pp. 145–180. Gordon and Breach, Amsterdam.

2001    A Bioarchaeological Perspective on the History of Violence. *Annual Review of Anthropology* 30: 573–596.

Webb, S.

1995    *Palaeopathology of Aboriginal Australians: Health and Disease Across a Hunter-Gatherer Continent.* Cambridge University Press, New York.

Williams, R. P.

2002    Rethinking Disaster-Induced Collapse in the Demise of the Andean Highland States: Wari and Tiwanaku. *World Archaeology* 33(3): 361–374.

Wilson, A. S., T. Taylor, M. C. Ceruti, J. A. Chavez, J. Reinhard, V. Grimes, W. Meier-Augenstein, L. Cartmell, B. Stern, M. P. Richards, M. Worobey, I. Barnes, and M. T. Gilbert

2007    Stable Isotope and DNA Evidence for Ritual Sequences in Inca Child Sacrifice. *Proceedings of the National Academy of Sciences of the United States of America* 104(42): 16456–16461.

PART IV

RITUALIZED VIOLENCE

# 10

## Meaning and the Bioarchaeology of Captivity, Sacrifice, and Cannibalism

### A Case Study from the Mississippian Period at Larson, Illinois

MALLORIE A. HATCH

## Introduction

Bioarchaeological studies of violent conflict have formed a substantial foundation for reconstructions of past behavior. Diverse forms of interpersonal violence, including warfare and gender violence, have been inferred from human skeletal remains with increasing frequency in the past 15 years. More research, however, is necessary to understand the particular social contexts and meanings, including captivity and violent sacrifice, that created the signatures observed in the human body. As forms of interpersonal violence, captivity and violent sacrifice may leave signatures in the human body, and the meanings communicated by violence may be interpreted from human skeletal remains and their associated archaeological contexts. These interpretations are also through examination of ethnohistories. In eastern North America, ethnohistorical accounts of Native American warfare abound with descriptions of captivity, sacrifice, and cannibalism and their meanings. While ethnohistorical discussions indicate a discrete suite of behaviors that should result in the identification of captivity and sacrifice in human skeletal remains, in practice, captivity and sacrifice often leave signatures similar to secondary mortuary processing and cannibalism. In order to illustrate how bioarchaeologists may evaluate captivity and sacrifice in the archaeological record, a case study from the Mississippian (ca. AD 1000–1450) period Larson site in the central Illinois River valley is presented.

## Violence as Meaning

As captivity and sacrifice commonly occurred in concert with episodes of violence, understanding how violence creates many messages communicated by the acts of captivity and sacrifice provides an important baseline. Violence is always performed as meaningful action that communicates a message between perpetrators, victims, and witnesses (Blok 2000; Bosson 2006; Riches 1986). The message intended by the perpetrators may become entangled in the cultural conceptions of victims and witnesses and may be further complicated by each actor's intense emotions and experiences. The most potent meaning of violence, therefore, comes from the tripartite oppositions between perpetrators, victims, and witnesses (Riches 1986).

Viewing all violent actions as meaningful highlights the messages communicated by violence (Blok 2000; Tilly 2003). For violence to be effective, it must successfully disseminate this meaning. As Blok (2000, 28) argues:

> The effective use of physical force very much depends on its symbolic form. Like all performances, it turns on how it is carried out: it depends on the message, on what people want to say, to communicate. Hence the ritualization of violence. Although violence may be primarily directed at the attainment of specific ends, such as wounding or killing an opponent, it is impossible to understand these violent operations in terms of these easily recognizable goals alone. There are more effective ways to obtain these results.

As a communicative medium, violence transforms the physical human bodies it targets into a message. In this way, those who are the objects of violence are transformed into contested symbols (Verdery 1999). In turn, the resulting bodies of the deceased may represent an especially potent materialization of meaning for both the victims and the perpetrators. Interpreting the materialization of these meanings, however, is complicated by mortuary rituals that occur between death and final deposition of remains (e.g., O'Shea 1981). The archaeological record disguises and alters the meaning and practice communicated by violence.

Despite such a limitation, bioarchaeological analysis should seek to reconstruct and understand the sequences of practices and meanings associated with violent conflict, captivity, and sacrifice. Cannibalism, which is often confused with other violent practices, should also be reconstructed to understand how its patterns may differ. In precontact North America, examination of ethnohistorical accounts of Native American war may be a source for hypotheses that help us understand the culturally specific nature of violent practice. Reports of Eastern Native American warfare abound with descriptions of captive-taking and sacrifice. Yet, as witnesses of violence, European chroniclers largely understood this practice through their own cultural lenses. Their perspectives were often biased by political goals and by preconceived notions of Native American savagery and inferiority. Thus, the meanings intended by the Native American individuals and groups participating in violent conflict may not have been accurately identified or understood. That is why it is necessary to examine such documents critically.

## Captivity, Sacrifice, and Cannibalism as Practice and Meaning

Ethnohistorical reports of captivity, sacrifice, and cannibalism among Eastern and Plains Native Americans commonly discuss these practices as an interrelated series of decisions and the resulting action. Each decision was based in the meaning that was to be communicated, and each decision would have consequences for patterns of traumatic lesions distributed throughout the skeleton. During warfare raids, enemy combatants or noncombatants were often taken captive. Once captives were transported to the captive-taking village, several options for their treatment existed, including adoption, enslavement, and sacrifice. The sequence of actions taken differed depending on the motivations for and the particular circumstances of a conflict. The following discussion, sampled from ethnohistorical documents, describes some of the possible sequences of actions that result in an individual's final interment (Fig. 10.1).

Acquiring captives was often a primary motivation for Eastern Woodlands and Plains Native American warfare (Knowles 1940; Strachey 1849; Thwaites 1899, 1900, 1901; Tooker 1962). Because the raiding party would have to enter deep into enemy territory, women and children were often the preferred captives, as more bravery was required to capture them (Laudonniere 2001; Swanton 1946). Examples abound in *The Jesuit Relations and Allied Documents* of Iroquois treatment of war captives. During the journey after capture to the capturers' villages, these war prisoners were often beaten (e.g., Thwaites 1899, 1900, 1901). These beatings, if severe

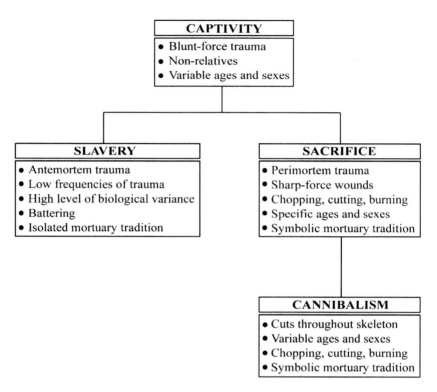

Fig. 10.1. Ethnographic sequences of captivity, slavery, and sacrifice.

enough, would likely cause blunt force fractures to skeletal elements. This period of captivity would manifest as blunt force wounds to the cranium, possibly in combination with fractures throughout the postcranial skeleton (e.g., Martin 1997; Martin, Harrod, and Fields 2010).

Once a war captive was taken, his or her captors could choose whether to allow the captive to remain alive and become adopted into the community or to torture the captive to his or her death to avenge a deceased clan member (Richter 1983; Tooker 1962). Even in cases where a captive was adopted, it is not always clear that he or she was treated as a full-fledged kin member and integrated into the community as a peer (e.g., Edwin 1830; Swanton 2001 [1931]). As slaves, these captives were often traded to other tribes or communities for goods (Hudson 1976). For instance, a white war captive named John Tanner reported receiving daily beatings from his adoptive Shawnee father and the young men of the village. Later, Tanner was traded to an Ojibwa woman for whiskey and other gifts (Edwin 1830). Among the Choctaw, captives were forced to behave like dogs

(Swanton 2001 [1931]). They were given dog-like duties such as guarding the door, growling, cleaning the leftovers on the plates, and gnawing bones. We would expect that such conditions of servitude would pattern bioarchaeologically as battering, which is identified as the presence of numerous traumatic lesions in various states of healing distributed throughout the skeleton (Martin 1997; Martin et al. 2001; Walker 1997; Walker, Cook, and Lambert 1997).

Alternatively, many Eastern and Plains peoples chose to torture and sacrifice war captives to avenge slain clan members (Knowles 1940). Among some Tunica speakers, it was necessary to scalp the victim prior to torture (Charlevoix 1851 [1682–1761]). The ritual of captive sacrifice among the Iroquois was reported to consist of flaying the skin and muscles from the bones of the victim, who was then burned upon a pyre (Thwaites 1901). In the Southeast, victims could be chopped into pieces joint by joint until they expired (Carroll 1836). Victims of these tortures, especially warriors, were expected to remain brave and to resist crying out (Knowles 1940). Warrior victims would scream out a list of their warfare-related heroics. The audience reportedly had no pity for the victims and often would work itself into a fervor. The torturer, in many cases, was expected to remain composed out of respect for the victim. Bioarchaeological signatures of torture, as discussed above, would result in highly variable patterns. Primarily, torture would be observed as perimortem cuts and chops throughout the skeleton. Burning to skeletal elements might also be present.

Cannibalism, the human consumption of conspecific tissue (White 1992), is described by chroniclers of historic Native American conflict as a practice used during the torture and sacrifice of warfare captives (e.g., Knowles 1940; Megapolensis 1909; Thwaites 1898). While many European reports of Native American cannibalism describe the practice only as an illustration of the savagery of Native Americans (e.g., Thwaites 1901), Knowles (1940) reports that cannibalism was often committed to honor the bravery of the victim. A beating heart and the victim's blood were described as the body parts most desirable for consumption, as these tissues were thought to transfer an individual's bravery to the consumer of the flesh (Adair 1775; Knowles 1940; Thwaites 1901). Cannibalism as described in these reports, however, would be difficult to discern in the archaeological record. Few cuts to the skeleton or processing and cooking of skeletal remains were reported.

While the ethnohistorical literature is replete with discussions of captivity, sacrifice, and cannibalism, the behaviors and meanings discussed
in ethnohistories are rarely identifiable in the archaeological record. Furthermore, ethnohistories record little information about the burial locations and mortuary treatments of captive, sacrificed, and cannibalized
individuals. The task of identifying captive, sacrificed, and cannibalized
individuals is further complicated by secondary mortuary disposal, "the
regular, and socially sanctioned removal of the relics of some or all deceased persons from a place of temporary storage to a permanent resting
place" (Metcalf and Huntington 1991, 97). During these secondary mortuary rites, the deceased may be defleshed, producing cut marks and other
forms of modification to the skeleton that must be distinguished from
conflict and cannibalized contexts (Olsen and Shipman 1994; Turner and
Turner 1999).

## Bioarchaeological Methods for Discerning Conflict, Secondary Burial, and Cannibalism

Differentiating between types of conflict (e.g., captivity, slavery, or torture), secondary burial, and cannibalism requires careful examination of
bone modification patterns in the context of the depositional and social
context. Turner and Turner (1999), White (1992), and Olsen and Shipman
(1994) provide particularly stringent criteria for discriminating between
conflict, secondary burial, and cannibalism. The location, length, orientation, and frequency of cut marks provide some of the most useful evidence
for distinguishing between interpersonal violence and secondary burial.
Burning, percussion pits, pot-polishing, vertebral absence, perimortem
fracturing, and peeling and crushing of long-bone epiphyses are important additional criteria for documenting the presence of cannibalism.

### Conflict

Conflict in precontact North America is most readily identified by the
presence of traumatic lesions related to scalping and trophy-taking and
the presence of embedded projectiles. Scalping lesions manifest as long,
primarily horizontal cuts circling the crown of the head (Allen, Merbs,
and Birkby 1985; Hamperl 1967; Hamperl and Laughlin 1959; Neuman
1940). They are most commonly located on the superior frontal squama,

parietals, and occipital. However, scalping wounds are also frequently found in a more inferior location on the skull. In fact, cut marks may be located on the temporals as far down as the suprameatal crest. Cut marks to the mandible and postcrania are infrequent yet may be observed as the result of limb or mandible trophy-taking (Milner 1999). Projectiles or knives embedded in bone are also indications of conflict (Jurmain 1991; Lambert 2002; Milner 1999; Smith 2003).

## Secondary Burial

Secondary burial is best interpreted by the presence of numerous small cuts indicative of defleshing and disarticulation (Olsen and Shipman 1994). A high frequency of cuts, sometimes numbering in the hundreds per element, are located throughout the skull and postcrania. Defleshing marks prominently pattern near the origins and insertions of muscles. They may, however, be located on any surface of the element where soft tissue was removed. Heavy concentrations of cut marks may be prevalent on the mandibular ramus, evidence of attempts to sever the insertions of the muscles of mastication. Cut marks concentrated near the articular surface of bone tend to show evidence of disarticulation found in secondary burial. While elements disarticulated during trophy taking are usually removed and not recovered, elements disarticulated during secondary burial should be recovered with the remainder of the burial.

## Cannibalism

Identification of cannibalism in the archaeological record requires documentation of a number of variables related to bone modification. Most commonly, cannibalism is identified by the presence of human bone modified in manners similar to human processing of animal bone; cannibalized assemblages should be highly fragmented (e.g., Binford 1981; Turner and Turner 1999; White 1992). The number of cut marks on cannibalized remains falls between the limited number identified in situations of violent conflict and the hundreds created during secondary burial processing. These cuts are distributed throughout the cranium, the mandible, and the postcrania. As cannibalism often occurs in the context of warfare, the long circular cuts indicative of scalping may also be present (Turner and Turner 1999).

Percussion pits, which are associated with hammer-and-anvil abrasion during butchering, are also expected to be present in cannibalized assemblages. Spiral and greenstick fractures may indicate that bones were broken while green and may indicate marrow extraction (Turner and Turner 1999; White 1992). The presence of peeled and crushed bone near long-bone epiphyses is further evidence of marrow extraction. Bone surfaces that are abraded and polished are also indicative of cannibalism; the surfaces of such bones are altered by contact with the inner surface of a cooking bowl in a process known as pot polish (White 1992). In cannibalism contexts, only a limited number of vertebrae may be recovered, possibly due to differential transport of preferred body parts for consumption (Turner and Turner 1999). Finally, the cooking of human skeletal remains or their disposal in a hearth may result in the presence of burned bone in a cannibalized assemblage. While White (1992) adopted stringent criteria for identifying cannibalism in Southwest assemblages, these criteria may not be applicable cross-culturally (DeGusta 2000; Stodder 2008). The cultural variation in cannibalized assemblages necessitates that one have an understanding of local and regional cultural contexts and mortuary practices over time before one can label an assemblage as having been cannibalized.

The difficulty in differentiating between warfare-related trauma, secondary mortuary processing, and cannibalism is exemplified by modified bone contexts at the Aztalan site in Wisconsin. Aztalan, a Late Woodland/Mississippian site occupied between AD 1100 and 1300, includes a number of contexts of scattered and modified human bone recovered from habitation debris and refuse pits (e.g., Barrett 1933; Somers 1920 [1892]). Early analysis of these contexts interpreted the bone modification patterns as definitive evidence of cannibalism (Barrett 1933; Holcomb 1952; Somers 1920 [1892]). However, more recent analysis has questioned that interpretation. Goldstein and Sullivan (1986) have emphasized that the taphonomic patterns observed at Aztalan, which include cut marks, burned green bone, spiral fractures, and crushed epiphyseal ends, could have been caused by secondary mortuary processing. In contrast, Rudolph (2009) has interpreted the patterns of bone modification at Aztalan as evidence of intergroup conflict. Nevertheless, as Goldstein and Sullivan (1986) argue, secondary mortuary processing should be considered irrespective of whether a particular death took place in a context of conflict.

Yet identifying interpersonal violence during both life and death is necessary to assess remains for the presence of captivity and sacrifice in the archaeological record. To lay the groundwork for investigating pre-contact Native American captivity and sacrifice, researchers must first distinguish whether an individual was a victim of interpersonal violence. Assessments may then turn to demographic patterns and treatment at death to further differentiate captivity and sacrifice from other forms of interpersonal violence (e.g., Martin et al. 2001; Martin, Harrod, and Fields 2010). The following case study from Larson, Illinois, during the Mississippian period (ca. AD 1000–1450) is presented to assess the viability of identifying evidence of captivity and sacrifice in the archaeological record. This analysis implements the first step in assessments of captivity and sacrifice by distinguishing between the signatures of conflict from secondary burial and cannibalism.

## Case Study: Captivity and Sacrifice at the Mississippian Larson Site, Illinois

The Mississippian period (ca. AD 1000–1450) of the U.S. midcontinent and Southeast is portrayed as a period of intensified conflict (e.g., Brown and Dye 2007; Dye and King 2007; Milner 1999), especially in comparison to the preceding Woodland period (e.g., Carr and Case 2006; Johnston 2002). Evidence of violent conflict has been identified in skeletal remains throughout the period (Berryman 1981; Bridges 1996; Bridges, Jacobi, and Powell 2000; Steadman 2008) and is depicted in iconographic representations of warriors and captives in portable art (e.g., Brown 1996; Brown and Dye 2007; Dye 2004; Emerson 2007). The proliferation of warfare-related portable art in what is referred to as the Southeastern Ceremonial Complex (SECC) coincides with the increased construction of palisades around sites through the Mississippian period (Milner 1998). The practice of captivity and sacrifice during the Mississippian is inferred not only from scenes that depict these practices in the SECC but also from mortuary contexts. At Mound 72 in Cahokia, Illinois, Fowler and colleagues (1999) have documented the practice of captivity and sacrifice from the remains of a number of low-status females.

North of Cahokia, the central Illinois River valley of west-central Illinois (Fig. 10.2) extends for approximately 210 kilometers along the Illinois River from the contemporary village of Hennepin southward to Meredosia (Ham 1994). Conflict during the Mississippian period in this region

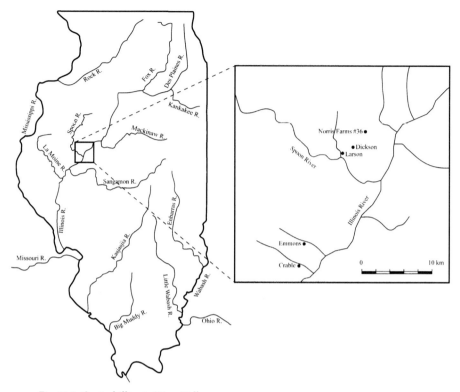

Fig. 10.2. Central Illinois River Valley.

seems to have changed in intensity across phases (Steadman 2008), but conflict had become endemic by the ca. AD 1300 intrusion of the Oneota into the valley (Milner 1995; Milner, Anderson, and Smith 1991; Milner and Smith 1990). Burial of war captives during the Eveland phase (ca. AD 1000–1150) has been inferred from the presence at Dickson Mounds of four headless, handless males with pots placed above the bodies in place of the heads (Conrad 1993; Conrad 2000; Ham 1980). No skeletal trauma was recorded on these remains. At the Kingston Lake site, the remains of headless adult individuals commingled with the remains of a juvenile displaying cut marks across the cranium has been interpreted as evidence of ritual sacrifice and captivity (Cobb and Harn 2002; Conrad 2000; Poehls 1944).

By the Orendorf phase (ca. AD 1150–1250), the intensity of violent conflict had escalated in the central Illinois River valley. At the Orendorf site, two of the five sequentially built settlements were constructed with surrounding palisades (Santure 1981). High-intensity violence was inferred from a study of skeletal trauma at Orendorf. Nine percent of 268 individuals analyzed display conflict-related trauma (Steadman 2008). During the subsequent Larson phase (ca. AD 1250–1300) of the central Illinois River valley, the number of palisaded towns within the region increased, as did population density (Ham 1994; Steadman 2008). Skeletal trauma from the Larson phase, however, has not been comprehensively analyzed. In fact, only isolated reports of individuals with embedded arrow points in skeletal elements and cut marks to the cranium are available from the central Illinois River valley during this phase (Carter, Harn, and Tiné 1998, n.d.; Morse 1969; Neuman 1940; Wilson 2010).

The case study presented here concerns skeletal remains recovered from the Larson site, the type site for the Larson phase. Located on top of a bluff overlooking the Spoon and Illinois Rivers, the Larson site is one of the largest nucleated village settlements in the central Illinois River valley. A pyramidal mound measuring 60 by 60 meters and its associated plaza complex indicate that the Larson site was an important ceremonial and administrative center in the central Illinois valley, and it was one of the largest sites identified in the regional settlement system. Harn (1994) describes the Larson site as a town with an associated village area that extended for eight hectares. Larson's bluff-top location provided a defensive position that was strengthened by the presence of a palisade enclosing the mound and plaza complex. Portions of the site were razed in what were possibly multiple episodes (Harn 1994).

The Larson Salvage Project excavated and recovered 12 burials from the palisade line and village settlement area in 1966 and 1970. No associated artifacts were recovered with any of the interments. Burials 1 through 11 were single inhumations, while Burial 12 is a commingled multiple burial. Skeletal trauma in Burials 1 through 11 is primarily in the form of healed antemortem lesions. Three out of these eleven individuals (27.3 percent) display evidence of interpersonal violence, manifesting as trauma to the face, head, and ribs (Hatch and Cobb n.d.). The commingled remains in Burial 12 were interred in a circular refuse pit (Carter, Harn, and Tiné n.d.). No grave goods were interred with Burial 12. The burial is highly fragmentary, and the majority of fractures on the remains occurred postmortem and show some evidence of burning. A minimum number of ten discrete individuals was estimated in a previous analysis by Carter and colleagues (n.d.). Fragments were rejoined, where possible, and elements were assigned to their corresponding discrete individuals (Table 10.1).

Table 10.1. Sex and age estimates of discrete individuals identified in Burial 12

| Individual | Sex | Age |
|---|---|---|
| A | Possible male | Adult |
| B | Possible female | Young adult |
| C | Indeterminate | Adult |
| D | Indeterminate | Adult |
| E | Indeterminate | Juvenile |
| F | Indeterminate | Juvenile |
| G | Indeterminate | Juvenile |
| H | Indeterminate | Juvenile |
| I | Indeterminate | Juvenile |
| J | Indeterminate | Neonate/infant |

While they are very partially represented, four adults and six juveniles were differentiated. Of the four adults, one is a possible male, one a possible female, and the sex of two could not be estimated (Hatch and Cobb n.d.).

Larson Burial 12 is a particularly anomalous context in the central Illinois River valley. The majority of interments recovered from this region are extended or flexed primary inhumations (Harn 1980). While secondary burial was a common practice in the Mississippian (e.g., Brown 1996; Goldstein and Sullivan 1986), such burials are less abundantly recovered in the region. Burned bone or cremations are even more infrequently documented (Harn 1980; Jeremy Wilson, personal communication, 2009). The uncommon burial context and the presence of skeletal markers of interpersonal conflict have led Carter and colleagues (1998, n.d.) to hypothesize cannibalism as a possible cause of the Burial 12 assemblage. I reanalyzed Burial 12 at Larson to evaluate bone modification practices that discriminate between conflict, secondary mortuary processing, and cannibalism. I used the bioarchaeological methods discussed in the previous section to differentiate between these processes. After I evaluated bone modification practices, I assessed whether these patterns could be caused by captivity and sacrifice.

## Results

The ten commingled individuals interred in Burial 12 at Larson exhibit a complex suite of bone modification. Cut marks, spiral fractures, green fractures, and element burning are observed. No evidence of bone peeling

Table 10.2. Types and frequencies of bone modifications in Burial 12

| | Frequency of Modification | | | |
|---|---|---|---|---|
| | Discrete Individuals (N = 10) | | Unassigned Fragments (N = 695) | |
| Modification Type | N | % | N | % |
| Cut marks | 4 | 40 | 10 | 1.4 |
| Spiral fractures | 0 | 0 | 27 | 3.9 |
| Other perimortem fractures | 1 | 1 | 1 | .001 |
| Burning | 1 | 1 | 34 | 4.9 |

or crushing, percussion scars, pot polish, or banded burning was found. In addition, 87 vertebral fragments (12.7 percent of all fragments recovered) are present, representing a larger percentage of vertebral elements recovered than would be expected in a complete burial. The presence of these vertebrae indicates that they were not preferentially removed from the individuals. Table 10.2 summarizes the patterns of bone modification documented in this study.

Cut Marks

Four of the ten individuals identified in Larson Burial 12 display cut marks to the cranium. Individual A has 16 cut marks and one chopping wound to the cranium. The diffuse pattern of marks circling the skull is suggestive of scalping (Fig. 10.3). As only a fragmentary cranial vault was identified for this individual, it is unknown if cuts are present on the mandible or postcrania. Individual B, represented by a partially complete right segment of the cranial vault and right mandible, exhibits one small cut mark (Fig. 10.4). This insult, measuring approximately 11 mm, is oriented horizontally on the superior aspect of the frontal bone. Additionally, ten cut marks are present on the lateral aspect of the superior mandibular ramus, just inferior to the mandibular condyle of Individual B.

Twelve cut marks and five chop marks are located on the cranium of Individual C. Fourteen of these wounds are positioned just inferior to the temporal lines of the right and left parietal bones. This dense concentration of marks is suggestive of defleshing of the temporalis muscle. The left mandibular ascending ramus displays 29 cut marks. A segment of Individual C's left ilium displays five cut marks on its lateral aspect. Burial D displays 62 small, variably oriented cut marks distributed across

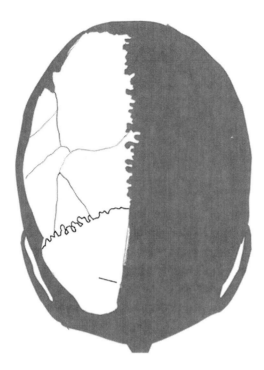

Fig. 10.3. Cut marks to the cranium of Individual A.

Fig. 10.4. Cut marks to the cranium of Individual B.

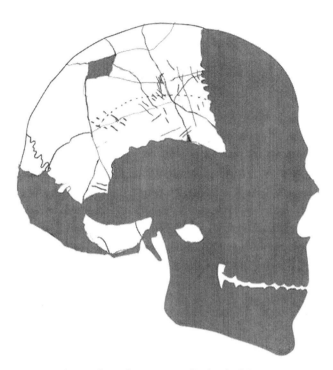

Fig. 10.5. Cut marks to the cranium of Individual D.

the right and left parietal bones (Fig. 10.5). Unfortunately, only the right and left parietal bones and a small portion of the mastoid process of the right temporal bone represent this individual, so patterns of wounds to the mandible and postcranium were not observable.

Ten of the 695 fragments (1.4 percent) not assigned to a discrete individual exhibit cut marks. Cuts were identified on four fragments of unsided parietal, two left temporal bones, a right scapula, an unidentified fragment of a long bone, and two unidentifiable fragments. A total of 60 cut marks were identified on these elements.

### Perimortem Fracture

A perimortem fracture is present on the right mandible of Individual B. The gonial process was fractured from the mandibular ascending ramus and corpus. The fractured gonial angle was not recovered. Spiral fractures are present on 27 of the 695 commingled fragments of Burial 12 (3.9 percent). All these spiral fractures are located on a long-bone shaft with one exception, a metatarsal. A perimortem sawtooth fracture, indicative of a green break, is also present on a fragment of a rib shaft.

## Burning

While present, burning is observed infrequently in Burial 12. Burial B exhibits diffuse scorching throughout the cranium. The scorching is limited to the external vault and is black and light brown in color. Evidence of scorching is also observed on 17 bone fragments, primarily from unidentifiable long bones, although a pubis, an ilium, and a rib fragment also display scorching. Another 17 bone fragments are calcined or have become charcoal, evidence of burning at higher temperatures (Buikstra and Swegle 1989; Shipman, Foster, and Shoeninger 1984). These cranial and long-bone fragments display burning across their broken margins, indicating that burning occurred after the bones were fractured.

## Discussion

Due to the fragmentary nature of the commingled remains from Burial 12, it is difficult to make confident interpretations of the behaviors that created this context. In fact, the preponderance of the bone modification patterns offer conflicting evidence of conflict and mortuary processing. The number, orientation, and distribution of cut marks present on the crania of Individuals A and B are suggestive of scalping. While cut marks are present on Individual B's mandibular ascending ramus, the presence of a perimortem fracture at the gonial angle may be evidence that an attempt to take the mandible as a trophy was made.

In contrast, the concentration of cut marks near the origin sites of the right and left temporalis muscles in conjunction with cuts to the ascending ramus of the mandible of Burial C are suggestive of defleshing. Again, as the temporalis is one of the muscles of mastication that joins the mandible to the cranium, such cut marks may be indicative of attempts to remove the mandible as a warfare trophy. In addition, the high frequency of cuts to the right and left parietal bones of Individual D may be a residue of defleshing for secondary burial. As a mandible was not identified for this individual, it is unclear whether the presence of cut marks may indicate that the mandible was successfully disarticulated and taken as a trophy.

Patterns of cut marks to ten commingled fragments of bone in Burial 12 do not offer clear enough evidence to differentiate between conflict, secondary burial, and cannibalism. However, the low relative frequency (1.4 percent) of fragments with cut marks recovered in Burial 12 is more suggestive of a conflict-related cause.

Possible evidence of cannibalism found in this analysis is weak and limited to the presence of 27 fragments of bone displaying spiral fractures, one greenstick fracture to a rib shaft, scorching to the cranium of Individual B, and 34 burned human bone fragments. Spiral fractures are a particularly weak indicator of cannibalism, as they are commonly created when bones are trampled by large mammals (e.g., Haynes 1983; Lyman 1984). Similarly, the burned bone in Burial 12 may have been caused during the razing of the Larson site rather than by cannibalism. Because no detailed information is available for the vertical provenience of the burned bone fragments (Dawn Cobb, personal communication, 2008), how these bones came to be burned cannot be definitively determined. The assertion that cannibalism was practiced here is further refuted by the absence of peeled or crushed long-bone epiphyses and pot polish, along with the presence of numerous vertebral fragments. Furthermore, unlike Carter and colleagues (1998, n.d.), I did not identify percussion pits on the fragments in Burial 12.

## Conclusion

Taken as a whole, it is most likely that Burial 12 is a residue of intergroup conflict. Scalping and trophy-taking is suggested by the skulls of Individuals A–D. However, it is more difficult to interpret the burned fragments. It is possible that these individuals were superficially buried in the refuse pit and the heat generated during the razing of the Larson site burned the most superficial bone fragments. The hypothesis that the remains were interred superficially may also account for the presence of spiral fractures. Trampling is a more likely explanation for these fractures than an anthropogenic cause because most of the fragmentation observed in Burial 12 occurred postmortem. Nevertheless, the patterns of bone modification documented in this analysis could have been created from a number of different contexts and behaviors. Larson community members may have been killed in an ambush by another group. Alternatively, warfare captives or Larson community members may have been sacrificed in a violent ritual, and secondary disposal practices, rather than postdepositional processes, may have created the fracture and burning patterns observed in the remains. A third possibility is that secondary mortuary rites created the patterns of defleshing, burning, and fragmentation observed in the remains. The unusual depositional context of Burial 12 and the lack of associated grave goods at Larson further complicate any interpretation.

In order to better discern whether or not the commingled human bone assemblage in Burial 12 are the remains of war captives or sacrifices, further research is necessary. Biological distance analysis should be employed to differentiate unrelated warfare captives from fully integrated community members (Fowler, Rose, Vander Leest, and Ahler 1999; Martin and Akins 2001). If the individuals from Burial 12 exhibit high levels of biological affinity with other individuals buried at Larson and Dickson Mounds, it is more likely that they were individuals from the Larson site or from nearby communities killed during violent conflict. However, if the individuals in Burial 12 display high levels of phenotypic variability when compared to other burials from Larson or Dickson Mounds, it is likely that these individuals were war captives who were killed.

While this analysis has been unable to distinguish between captivity and sacrifice at Larson or even to discriminate unequivocally between violent conflict and secondary burial, it has demonstrated the need for researchers to focus on identifying these behaviors in the archaeological record. Violence, as meaningful action, is by its nature communicative. Understanding what is being communicated by the violent contexts viewed in the archaeological record is a complex task. The first step is to interpret the skeletal and mortuary patterns that resulted from violent actions. Violence studies should seek to differentiate between interpersonal violence, mortuary processing, and cannibalism. Analysis may then proceed to assess whether the individuals examined were treated in life as slaves or as sacrifices. Understanding the contexts in which captivity and sacrifice occurred is necessary if we are to interpret the meaning communicated by violence and, ultimately, to reconstruct a rich history of the past.

## Acknowledgments

This work was supported by a research grant from the Arizona State University Graduate and Professional Student Association. Many thanks to Dawn Cobb and the Illinois State Museum for facilitating study of the burials from Larson. For help with figures, thanks are due to Ashley Evans Busch, Jacob Smith, and Brad Feuerstein.

## References Cited

Adair, J.
1775    *The History of the American Indians.* Edward and Charles Dilly, London.
Allen, W. H., C. F. Merbs, and W. H. Birkby
1985    Evidence for Prehistoric Scalping at Nuvakwewtaqa (Chavez Pass) and Grass-hopper Ruin, Arizona. In *Health and Disease in the Prehistoric Southwest,* edited by C. F. Merbs and R. J. Miller, pp. 23–42. Anthropological Research Papers no. 34. Arizona State University, Tempe.
Barrett, S. A.
1933    *Ancient Aztalan.* Bulletin of the Public Museum of the City of Milwaukee no. 13. Public Museum of Milwaukee, Milwaukee.
Berryman, H. E.
1981    The Averbuch Skeletal Series: A Study of Biological and Social Stress at a Late Mississippian Period Site from Middle Tennessee. Ph.D. dissertation, University of Tennessee.
Binford, L. R.
1981    *Bones: Ancient Men and Modern Myths.* Academic Press, New York.
Blok, A.
2000    The Enigma of Senseless Violence. In *Meanings of Violence: A Cross-Cultural Perspective,* edited by G. Aijmer and J. Abbink, pp. 23–28. Berg Publishers, New York.
Bosson, C.
2006    War as Practice, Power, and Processor: A Framework for the Analysis of War and Social Structure Change. In *Warfare and Society: Archaeological and Ethnographic Perspectives,* edited by T. Otto, H. Thrane, and H. Vandkilde, pp. 89–111. Aarhus University Press, Oakville.
Bridges, P. S.
1996    Warfare and Mortality at Koger's Island, Alabama. *International Journal of Osteoarchaeology* 6: 66–75.
Bridges, P. S., K. P. Jacobi, and M. L. Powell
2000    Warfare-Related Trauma in the Late Prehistory of Alabama. In *Bioarchaeological Studies in the Age of Agriculture: A View from the Southeast,* edited by P. M. Lambert, pp. 35–62. University of Alabama Press, Tuscaloosa.

Brown, J. A.

1996    *The Spiro Ceremonial Center: The Archaeology of Arkansas Valley Caddoan Culture in Eastern Oklahoma.* Memoirs of the Museum of Anthropology no. 29. Museum of Anthropology, University of Michigan, Ann Arbor.

Brown, J. A., and D. H. Dye

2007    Severed Heads and Sacred Scalplocks: Mississippian Iconographic Trophies. In *The Taking and Displaying of Human Body Parts as Trophies by Amerindians,* edited by R. J. Chacon and D. H. Dye, pp. 278–298. Springer, New York.

Buikstra, J. E., and M. Swegle

1989    Bone Modification Due to Burning: Experimental Evidence. In *Bone Modification,* edited by R. Bonnichsen and M. H. Sorg, pp. 247–258. Center for the Study of the First Americans, Institute for Quaternary Studies, University of Maine, Orono.

Carr, C., and D. T. Case

2006    *Gathering Hopewell: Society, Ritual, and Ritual Interaction.* Springer, New York.

Carroll, B. R.

1836    *Historical Collections of South Carolina: Embracing Many Rare and Valuable Pamphlets and Other Documents Relating to the History of that State from Its First Discovery to Its Independence in the Year 1776.* 2 vols. Harper and Brothers, New York.

Carter, M. L., D. E. Harn, and A. L. Tiné

1998    Osteological Evidence for Prehistoric Violence at the Larson Site (11F3), Fulton County, Illinois. Paper presented at the 5th Annual Meeting of the Midwest Bioarchaeological and Forensic Anthropology Association, Iowa City, Iowa.

n.d.    Analysis of Human Skeletal Remains from the Larson Site. Manuscript on file, Illinois State Museum.

Charlevoix, P. F. X. d.

1851 [1682–1761]    *Historical Journal of Father Pierre François Xavier de Charlevoix, in Letters Addressed to the Duchess of Lesdiquières.* Appleton and Co., New York.

Cobb, D. E., and A. D. Harn

2002    Bioarchaeological Analysis of Special Purpose Graves from Kingston Lake, Dickson Mounds, and Cahokia: New Perspectives on Programmed Death in Illinois. *Illinois Archaeology* 14: 41–71.

Conrad, G. W.

1993    Two Elaborate Mississippian Graves from the Kingston Lake Site, Peoria County, Illinois. *Illinois Archaeology* 5: 297–314.

Conrad, L. A.

2000    The Middle Mississippian Cultures of the Central Illinois Valley. In *Cahokia and the Hinterlands: Middle Mississippian Cultures of the Midwest,* edited by T. E. Emerson and R. B. Lewis, pp. 119–156. University of Illinois Press, Urbana.

DeGusta, D.

2000    Fijian Cannibalism and Mortuary Ritual: Bioarchaeological Evidence from Vunda. *International Journal of Osteoarchaeology* 10: 76–92.

Dye, D. H.
2004    Art, Ritual, and Chiefly Warfare in the Mississippian World. In *Hero, Hawk, and Open Hand: American Indian Art of the Ancient Midwest and South,* edited by R. F. Townsend, pp. 191–205. Yale University Press, New Haven, Conn.

Dye, D. H., and A. King
2007    Desecrating the Sacred Temples: Chiefly Conflict and Violence in the American Southeast. In *North American Indigenous Warfare and Ritual Violence,* edited by R. J. Chacon and R. G. Mendoza, pp. 160–181. University of Arizona Press, Tucson.

Edwin, J. (editor)
1830    *A Narrative of the Captivity and Adventures of John Tanner (U.S. Interpreter at the Saut de Ste. Marie) during Thirty Years Residence among the Indians of the Interior of North America.* G. and C. and H. Carvill, New York.

Emerson, T. E.
2007    Cahokia and the Evidence for Late Pre-Columbian War in the North American Midcontinent. In *North American Indigenous Warfare and Ritual Violence,* edited by R. J. Chacon and R. G. Mendoza, pp. 129–148. University of Arizona Press, Tucson.

Fowler, M. L., J. C. Rose, B. Vander Leest, and S. R. Ahler (editors)
1999    *The Mound 72 Area: Dedicated and Sacred Space in Early Cahokia.* Reports of Investigations no. 54. Illinois State Museum, Springfield.

Goldstein, L., and N. C. Sullivan
1986    People as Food, Bone as Ritual: Rethinking Old Data. Paper presented at the 51st Annual Meeting of the Society for American Archaeology, New Orleans.

Ham, A. D.
1980    *The Prehistory of Dickson Mounds: The Dickson Excavation.* Reports of Investigations no. 35. Illinois State Museum, Springfield.

1994    *Variation in Mississippian Settlement Patterns: The Larson Settlement System in the Central Illinois River Valley.* Reports of Investigations no. 50. Illinois State Museum, Springfield.

Hamperl, H.
1967    The Osteological Consequences of Scalping. In *Diseases in Antiquity,* edited by D. R. Brothwell and A. T. Sandison, pp. 630–634. Charles C. Thomas, Springfield.

Hamperl, H., and W. S. Laughlin
1959    Osteological Consequences of Scalping. *Human Biology* 31: 80–89.

Harn, A. D.
1980    *The Prehistory of Dickson Mounds: The Dickson Excavations.* Reports of Investigations no. 35. Illinois State Museum, Springfield.

1994    *Variation in Mississippian Settlement Patterns: The Larson Settlement System in the Central Illinois River Valley.* Reports of Investigations no. 50. Illinois State Museum, Springfield.

Hatch, M. A., and D. E. Cobb
n.d. Physical Violence and Trauma at the Larson Site, Illinois.

Haynes, G.
1983 Frequencies of Spiral and Greenbone Fractures on Ungulate Limb Bones in Modern Surface Assemblages. *American Antiquity* 48: 102–114.

Holcomb, G. R.
1952 An Analysis of Human Remains from Aztalan. M.S. thesis, University of Wisconsin–Madison.

Hudson, C. M.
1976 *The Southeastern Indians.* Charles Hudson, Knoxville.

Johnston, C. A.
2002 Culturally Modified Human Remains from the Hopewell Mound Group. Ph.D. dissertation, Ohio State University.

Jurmain, R.
1991 Paleoepidemiology of Trauma in a Prehistoric Central California Population. In *Human Paleopathology: Current Synthesis and Future Option,* edited by D. J. Ortner and A. C. Aufderheide, pp. 241–248. Smithsonian Institution Press, Washington, D.C.

Knowles, N.
1940 The Torture of Captives by the Indians of Eastern North America. *Proceedings of the American Philosophical Society* 82: 151–225.

Lambert, P. M.
2002 The Archaeology of War: A North American Perspective. *Journal of Archaeological Research* 10(3): 207–241.

Laudonniere, R. de
2001 *Three Voyages.* Translated by C. E. Bennett. University of Alabama Press, Tuscaloosa.

Lyman, R. L.
1984 Broken Bones, Bone Expediency Tools, and Bone Pseudotools: Lessons from the Blast Zone around Mount St. Helens, Washington. *American Antiquity* 49: 315–333.

Martin, D. L.
1997 Violence against Women in the La Plata River Valley (A.D. 1000–1300). In *Troubled Times: Violence and Warfare in the Past,* edited by D. L. Martin and D. W. Frayer, pp. 45–75. Gordon and Breach, Amsterdam.

Martin, D. L., and N. J. Akins
2001 Unequal Treatment in Life as in Death: Trauma and Mortuary Behavior at La Plata (AD 1000–1300). In *Ancient Burial Practices in the American Southwest,* edited by D. R. Mitchell and J. L. Brunson-Hadley, pp. 223–248. University of New Mexico Press, Albuquerque.

Martin, D. L., N. J. Akins, A. H. Goodman, and A. C. Swedlund
2001 *Totah: Time and the Rivers Flowing: Excavations in the La Plata Valley.* Vol. 5 of *Harmony and Discord: Bioarchaeology of the La Plata Valley.* Office of Archaeological Studies, Museum of New Mexico, Santa Fe.

Martin, D. L., R. P. Harrod, and M. Fields
2010    Beaten Down and Worked to the Bone: Bioarchaeological Investigations of Women and Violence in the Ancient Southwest. *Landscapes of Violence* 1(1): Article 3. Available at http: //scholarworks.umass.edu/lov/vol1/iss1/.

Megapolensis, J., Jr.
1909    A Short Account of the Mohawk Indians, 1644. In *Narratives of New Netherland, 1609–1644,* edited by J. F. Jameson, pp. 163–180. Charles Scribner's Sons, New York.

Metcalf, P., and R. Huntington
1991    *Celebrations of Death: The Anthropology of Mortuary Ritual.* Cambridge University Press, Cambridge.

Milner, G. R.
1995    An Osteological Perspective on Prehistoric Warfare. In *Regional Approaches to Mortuary Analysis,* edited by L. A. Beck, pp. 221–244. Plenum Press, New York.
1998    Archaeological Evidence for Prehistoric and Early Historic Intergroup Conflict in Eastern North America. In *Deciphering Anasazi Violence: With Regional Comparisons to Mesoamerican and Woodland Cultures,* edited by P. Y. Bullock, pp. 69–91. HRM Books, Santa Fe.
1999    Warfare in the Prehistoric and Early Historic Eastern North America. *Journal of Archaeological Research* 7: 105–151.

Milner, G. R., E. Anderson, and V. G. Smith
1991    Warfare in Late Prehistoric West-Central Illinois. *American Antiquity* 56(4): 581–603.

Milner, G. R., and V. G. Smith
1990    Oneota Human Skeletal Remains. In *Archaeological Investigations at the Morton Village and Norris Farms 36 Cemetery,* edited by S. K. Santure, A. D. Harn, and D. Esarey, pp. 111–148. Reports of Investigations no. 45. Illinois State Museum, Springfield.

Morse, D.
1969    *Ancient Disease in the Midwest.* Reports of Investigations no. 15. Illinois State Museum, Springfield.

Neuman, G. K.
1940    Evidence for the Antiquity of Scalping from Central Illinois. *American Antiquity* 5: 287–289.

O'Shea, J.
1981    Social Configurations and the Archaeological Study of Mortuary Practices: A Case Study. In *The Archaeology of Death,* edited by R. Chapman, I. Kinnes, and K. Randsborg, pp. 39–52. Cambridge University Press, Cambridge.

Olsen, S. L., and P. Shipman
1994    Cut Marks and Perimortem Treatment of Skeletal Remains on the Northern Plains. In *Skeletal Biology in the Great Plains: Migration, Warfare, Health, and Subsistence,* edited by D. W. Owsley and R. L. Jantz, pp. 377–387. Smithsonian Institution Press, Washington, D.C.

Poehls, R. L.

1944    Kingston Lake Site Burials. *Journal of the Illinois State Archaeological Society* 1: 36–38.

Riches, D.

1986    The Phenomenon of Violence. In *The Anthropology of Violence,* edited by D. Riches, pp. 1–27. Blackwell, New York.

Richter, D. K.

1983    War and Culture: The Iroquois Experience. *William and Mary Quarterly* 40: 528–559.

Rudolph, K. Z.

2009    A Taphonomic Analysis of Human Skeletal Material from Aztalan: Cannibalism, Hostility, and Mortuary Variability. M.S. thesis, University of Wisconsin–Milwaukee.

Santure, S. K.

1981    The Changing Community Plan Settlement C. In *The Orendorf Site Preliminary Working Papers,* edited by D. Esarey and L. A. Conrad, pp. 5–80. Archaeological Research Laboratory, Western Illinois University, Macomb.

Shipman, P., G. Foster, and M. Shoeninger

1984    Burnt Bone and Teeth: An Experimental Study of Color, Morphology, Crystal Structure, and Shrinkage. *Journal of Academic Sciences* 11: 307–325.

Smith, M. O.

2003    Beyond Palisades: The Nature and Frequency of Late Prehistoric Deliberate Violent Trauma in the Chickamauga Reservoir of East Tennessee. *American Journal of Physical Anthropology* 121(4): 303–318.

Somers, A. N.

1920 [1892]    Prehistoric Cannibalism in America. *Wisconsin Archaeologist* 19: 20–24. Reprinted from *Popular Science Monthly* 42(10).

Steadman, D. W.

2008    Warfare-Related Trauma at Orendorf, a Middle Mississippian Site in West-Central Illinois. *American Journal of Physical Anthropology* 136(1): 51–64.

Stodder, A. L. W.

2008    Taphonomy and the Nature of Archaeological Assemblages. In *Biological Anthropology of the Human Skeleton,* 2nd ed., edited by M. A. Katzenberg and S. R. Saunders, pp. 71–116. John Wiley and Sons, Hoboken.

Strachey, W.

1849    *The Historie of Travaile into Virginia Britannia: Expressing the Cosmographie and Commodities of the Country, Together with the Manners and Customs of the People.* Hakluyt Society, London.

Swanton, J. R.

1946    Indians of the Southeastern United States. In Bureau of American Ethnology Bulletin no. 137. Government Printing Office, Washington, D.C.

2001 [1931]    *Source Material for the Social and Ceremonial Life of the Choctaw Indians.,* University of Alabama Press, Tuscaloosa. Originally published as Bureau of American Ethnology Bulletin no. 113.

Thwaites, R. G. (editor)

1898   *Jesuit Relations and Allied Documents: Travels and Explorations of the Jesuit Missionaries in New France, 1610–1791.* Vols. 4, 10, 13, 22. Burrows Brothers, Cleveland.

1899   *Jesuit Relations and Allied Documents: Travels and Explorations of the Jesuit Missionaries in New France, 1610–1791.* Vol. 49. Burrows Brothers, Cleveland.

1900   *Jesuit Relations and Allied Documents: Travels and Explorations of the Jesuit Missionaries in New France, 1610–1791.* Vol. 62. Burrows Brothers, Cleveland.

1901   *Jesuit Relations and Allied Documents: Travels and Explorations of the Jesuit Missionaries in New France, 1610–1791.* Vol. 71. Burrows Brothers, Cleveland.

Tilly, C.

2003   *The Politics of Collective Violence.* Cambridge University Press, Cambridge.

Tooker, E.

1962   An Ethnography of the Huron Indians, 1615–1649. In *Bulletin, No. 190, Bureau of American Ethnology.* Smithsonian Institution Press, Washington, D.C.

Turner, C. G., II, and J. A. Turner

1999   *Man Corn: Cannibalism and Violence in the Prehistoric American Southwest.* University of Utah Press, Salt Lake City.

Verdery, K.

1999   *The Political Lives of Dead Bodies: Reburial and Postsocialist Change.* Columbia University Press, New York.

Walker, P. L.

1997   Wife Beating, Boxing, and Broken Noses: Skeletal Evidence for the Cultural Patterning of Violence. In *Troubled Times: Violence and Warfare in the Past,* edited by D. L. Martin and D. W. Frayer, pp. 145–180. Gordon and Breach, Amsterdam.

Walker, P. L., D. C. Cook, and P. M. Lambert

1997   Skeletal Evidence for Child Abuse: A Physical Anthropological Perspective. *Journal of Forensic Sciences* 42(2): 196–207.

White, T. D.

1992   *Prehistoric Cannibalism at Mancos 5MTUMR-2346.* Princeton University Press, Princeton, N.J.

Wilson, J. J.

2010   Modeling Life through Death in Late Prehistoric West-Central Illinois: An Assessment of Paleodemographic and Paleoepidemiological Variability. Ph.D. dissertation, Binghamton University, State University of New York.

# 11

## Performances of Imposed Status

### Captivity at Cahokia

KATHRYN M. KOZIOL

## Introduction

Captive experiences vary greatly based on the culture, gender, and age of captives and the interpersonal relationships sought by both captor and captive in specific contexts. Recent and historic captivity events point to large differences in how captors treat/have treated captives. Relationships between captives and other non-elites from the captors' own societies are undoubtedly different in hierarchically arranged societies. For instance, in some cases, captives were included in a society, while in other groups captives were physically removed from the society or killed.

Furthermore, we know that the length of captivity ranged greatly throughout the historic periods. Culture and interpersonal dynamics were key factors that determined how long a person would be held captive (Cole 2000; Demos 1994; Driver 1969; Gallay 2002). Some periods of captivity lasted only a few hours, while others lasted for the rest of the captive's life. These differences were evident during the early period of European interactions with various indigenous populations in North America. There is no reason to assume that such differences did not exist in the ancient past, although a full account of individualized experiences is not obtainable. When individuals are identifiable as outsiders and specifically as captives, it is likely that distinctions exist in the burial contexts that bioarchaeologists can point out.

Situated in the southern portion of the Cahokia site in Illinois, Mound 72 offers a rich mortuary context of over 260 burials excavated from the Middle Mississippian Period. These burials were placed in the mound during multiple construction phases, discussed at length elsewhere (Byers 2006; Dancey 2005; Rose 1999). In past analysis, most of the burials within Mound 72 have been overlooked because of the focus on the shell-bird burial group. These burials include four mass female graves, a charnel house group, several groups of male sacrifices, the mass burial of a mixed-sex group of 39 individuals (in the lower level of Feature 229), the burials of individuals and groups who died of natural causes, and groups of later "intrusive" burials.

Of the 260 burials excavated at Mound 72, 175 are of individuals who were killed and interred in multiple distinct features in the mound (Features 105, 106, 101, 205, 214, 229, and 237). Buried in four pit-style graves, 118 of the killed individuals are females who are biologically distinct from other individuals buried in Mound 72. Previous studies have described these killed females as ritualized sacrificial inclusions, but the fact that they were biologically distinctive from the rest of the Cahokian population could also support the interpretation that they were captives, which is the primary focus of this chapter. Here, I have considered the individuals who were placed in social roles that were undesirable and that led to their death as captives. Willingly killed individuals, like those associated with Feature 101, will be discussed as "retainers" because they (and possibly their surviving relatives) seem to have received benefits from their participation.

I explore the Cahokian mortuary behaviors from the perspective of performance-based cultural theories, and thus I view the mortuary behavior that produced the Mound 72 context as creating new relationships and realities for the living population (Noyes and Abrahams 1999; Piot 1999; Schieffelin 1985). This perspective has driven me to consider the identities and relationships that Cahokians were expressing in relation to the individuals who were buried, some of which may be identifiable at the group level through distinctions in mode of death and burial arrangement, a result of cultural performances that reinforced roles and created their cultural reality. In the case of captives, I view these identities as ones that were imposed upon the deceased by the Cahokians who arranged them. A few details of these identities and realities may be inferred through viewing the Mound 72 burials as a mythic tableau (Brown 2003, 2005) or may be visible on the general group level (i.e., as a shared captive status with various potential identities). In the case of the burials at Mound 72, applying this modern mortuary perspective allows the interpretation to move beyond simple economic assessments of burials and further develops the discussion of how we should identify and discuss violent behaviors enacted on captives. The Mound 72 mortuary context provides evidence of captivity, warfare, selective killing, and the performances of cosmological myths.

It is still not possible to clearly identify specific forms of violence from evidence on human remains. Specifically, questions exist about what kind of events led to the intentional deaths of at least 175 individuals at Cahokia. Researchers also do not know where the 118 female captives who were brought to and killed at Cahokia were born. Furthermore, it is unclear how all the Mound 72 interments (the individuals who were killed and those who were not) relate to larger enactments of cosmological and social relations. This is an example of how individuals buried in Mound 72 experienced differences in modes of death and burial. These females who had been captured by the Cahokians were interred in distinct pit-style burials throughout the mound that were separate from the burials of individuals who were not killed. They were also separate from the violently killed individuals in the lower levels of Feature 229.

Bioarchaeological studies of the physical remains of some individuals in Mound 72 have been extremely useful in demonstrating differences between the populations present at Cahokia., Researchers have seen differences in diet based on group membership as well as variable rates of infectious lesions among groups interred in Mound 72 (Ambrose, Buikstra, and Krueger 2003; Hedman 2006; Milner 1991, 2007; Milner and Buikstra 2006; Powell 2000; Powell and Cook 2005; Rose 1999; Yerkes 2005). These studies provide much-needed data that have been used to understand how different communities at Cahokia and outside Cahokia interacted on a biological level. It is clear that there were biological differences (i.e., in age, sex, and hereditary traits) among groups buried in Mound 72. The differential burial patterns at this site also show evidence of visible social differences among individuals related to age and gender. Perhaps these differences are related to a collective myth that included outsiders in collective social reconstructions. Distinctions between Cahokians and non-Cahokians were recognizable to the population that was doing the burying. These distinctions are clear enough to encourage continued research about these burials.

Captives often are not included in the political or economic structures of the captive society and should not be categorized among the low-status members of that society. The status of the captive is contingently negotiated based on interactions between specific captives and their captors that can lead to the inclusion or exclusion of the captives from the captor's society. The experiences of two captives taken by the Comanche in 1836, Rachel Plummer and Cynthia Ann Parker, demonstrate this point. The great difference in the experiences of these two individuals is likely related to the age at which each was captured (Cole 2000, 62, 104). Cynthia, who was eight years old when she was taken captive, assimilated so well into the Comanche community that she later fought against her removal and reintegration into the white world. In contrast, Rachel was a grown woman who was pregnant when she and her son James were taken. After Rachel gave birth, her infant was killed by a group of Comanche. The written account of her captivity emphasized the abuses she endured and her desire to flee (Cole 2000, 63; Plummer 1973 [1839]). Differences in captives' emotional experiences could have been influenced by the age and sex of the captive, the goals of the captors, and the individual captive's personal reactions to his or her captors (Cole 2000; Demos 1994; Driver 1969; Gallay 2002). These variables determined variations in length of captivity and interactions between captors and captives.

Socioeconomic and political status is most often interpreted from burial inclusions/treatments that are seen as reflections of status in life (Binford 1971; Goldstein 1980; Saxe 1970). However, for captives the issue of these types of status does not apply in the same way. Status is determined among members of the same social group. Because captives often come from outside a social group, they do not fit within the scale of status the captor group has established. It is likely that most captives never gained access to insider status, not even the lowest status within the captor society. By seeing "captive" as a unique and separate status that is different from "low status," we are able to better understand the positionality of captives.

Cahokians (re)created their social relationships through mortuary performances (Noyes and Abrahams 1999; Piot 1999; Schieffelin 1985). It is assumed that captors imposed a captive identity on those they dominated as they situated captives in the Cahokian-centered cosmological context.

Thus, through the burial of captives we may gain insight into how Cahokians situated themselves and others in their world. That being said, we can recognize that the Cahokian world view incorporates both natural and supernatural themes, and mortuary interpretations should also include both.

## Methods and Materials

The materials used in this analysis were excavated from Mound 72 at Cahokia during the 1967–1971 University of Wisconsin–Milwaukee field sessions under the direction of Melvin L. Fowler. Though many of the remains were poorly preserved, Jerome Rose analyzed those that were recoverable. The sex of these individuals was assessed using a modification of Acsadi and Nemeskeri's 1970 metric technique by incorporating information from Bass (1987), Brothwell (1972), and Krogman and Iscan (1986). Dental development, dental attrition, and epiphyseal closures were used to assess the ages of individuals (Bass 1987; Brothwell 1972; Cohen 1974; Schour and Massler 1944). Using the osteological and mortuary theories available for analysis in 1974, Rose combined these data in a detailed report that was later included in the Illinois State Museum Report series (Rose 1999).

For this study, I evaluated the original burial forms, excavation notes, and unpublished photographs. These were graciously shared by Jerome Rose and Ann Early. My analysis incorporates a reevaluation of the theoretical advances in mortuary research and in anthropological understanding of population construction.

### Paleopathological Evidence of Population Distance

There are large variations among the mass graves contained in Mound 72. The most visible violent actions were done against individuals in the lower level of Feature 229. In this morbid tableau, these individuals were violently killed and dumped into this pit before some of the earlier victims had even died (Fowler et al. 1999; Rose 1999). The biodistance analysis compiled by Jerome Rose (1999) and Janice Cohen (1974) demonstrated that these individuals were fellow Cahokians who at least sometimes reproduced with other Cahokians who were buried in ways that marked them as members of higher-status groups.

Compared to the other burials in Mound 72, the group burial in the lower level of Feature 229 appears chaotic and messy, largely distinctive from the burials of the four killed female groups and the male foursome in Feature 106. This might indicate that the group buried in the lower level of Feature 229 breached cultural rules and were punished by receiving less care in their mortuary arrangement. Alternatively, this could be an example of a specific community of Cahokians that was made into captives and excluded from the burial practices afforded to other Cahokians because of their community membership rather than because of any particular behavior. In other words, their biological connections to the potentially higher-status groups at Cahokia does not appear to have improved their status or to have reduced their social distance from these biological relatives. In fact, for unknown reasons, this group in the lower level of Feature 229 was killed more violently than the externally acquired females appear to have been. It is important to note that none of the captive individuals from Mound 72 displayed evidence of prolonged torture, which would be expected if their deaths gained status for living relatives (Williamson 2007).

Other bioarchaeological analysis of the Mound 72 data set supports population distance models. For example, studies of dentition and diet support ideas that the females in the four mass graves were captives who were imported into Cahokia. Janice Cohen's report (1974) concludes that many if not all of these female victims were from an unknown but clearly separate population. This contrasts with the individuals in the mixed male and female burials in the lower level of Feature 229. Dental data links these individuals to the same population as the individuals who were shrouded and buried on cedar litters in the "litter burials" in the upper levels of this feature; if they were captives, then they were from a distinct community at Cahokia. However, the dental traits of the exclusively female groups of killed individuals determine that they were not genetically related to the individuals buried in either level of Feature 229 (Cohen 1974; Rose 1999, 81–82). Previous researchers have said only that these females were not part of the reproductive pool of the "elites" buried at Mound 72 but have not offered theories about where exactly they came from. Were they members of a community at Cahokia that lacked sexual access to the individuals who have been interpreted as elites? Or, as Rose (1999, 82) suggests, were they taken from an outside population as tribute or trophies? The dental distinctions support the idea that these female groups were taken from a population outside of Cahokia, as do the dietary data. Together these data demonstrate that different populations were represented in the Mound 72 burials, but these should not be read simply as ethnic boundaries, as some bioarchaeologists have done when dietary and biological distances are encountered (Kakaliouras 2010; Ousley, Jantz, and Freid 2009; Sparks and Jantz 2003). Though the diets of the exclusively female group seem different than others in Mound 72 (Ambrose, Buikstra, and Krueger 2003; Hedman 2006; Yerkes 2005), these differences often relate multiple factors, including ethnic preferences and restrictions based on age and gender.

Ethnicities are not fixed biological phenomena. They are flexible social categories that are used to define in-group members and to distinguish outsiders. Of course, distinctions exist in phenotypic population markers (i.e., facial features, complexion, etc.) that we can recognize in living populations and sometimes reconstruct in bioarchaeological studies, but these should not be conflated with socially defined categories, including the category of ethnicity. Ethnic groups share customs and beliefs but are not always endogamous. Instead, bioarchaeological researchers interested in ethnicity should look for symbolic differences that are further supported by dietary distinctions and should recognize that biological differences between populations cannot be assumed to be a direct proxy for ethnicity. Symbolic and dietary data can be compared to differences in dental or cranial biodistance, but they cannot and should not be read as independent markers of ethnicity (Armelagos and Van Gerven 2003). In other words, physical markers that demonstrate biological distance between populations that may or may not have been equivalent to important social categories.

Ambrose, Buikstra, and Krueger's 2003 analysis demonstrated dietary differences in maize consumption among individuals interred in the mound. It is possible that these differences represent a distinct foodway (Brown and Mussell 1985). Indirectly, the dietary research based on maize and protein consumption at Cahokia (Ambrose, Buikstra, and Krueger 2003; Hedman 2006; Yerkes 2005) supports the notion that the killed females were captured from an external population. The dietary findings demonstrate that the captive females ate more maize and less protein than others interred in the mound. Additionally, the Ambrose et al. 2003 study found that the individual in Burial 12—likely the burial of a retainer (individuals killed to accompany others in death) that was included in the shell-bird burial arrangement of Feature 101 (an elite burial that has been repeatedly interpreted as the highest-status burial in Mound 72)—consumed a high-protein, low corn diet that has been interpreted as a special diet that was reserved for elite members of society. This suggests that we should not attempt to make direct links between dietary status and health and social position and that retainers in Mississippian populations may have enjoyed special benefits—in this case, a better diet than most Cahokians.

While Ambrose et al. (2003) argue that dietary differences may have been based on the gender and class of an individual, they may instead be attributed to the foodways of different populations (Brown and Mussell 1985; Yerkes 2005). For instance, when Richard Yerkes 2005 expanded the isotope analysis to include sites in Cahokia's hinterlands, he found that the population at Cahokia ate less maize than their neighbors. The stable isotope studies do not support the notion that Cahokians were forced to increase their maize consumption because of decreasing deer populations on the American Bottom. In fact, the delta $^{13}C$ values for the early Mississippians (AD 1000–1150) at Cahokia are less positive than values obtained from Mississippian burials at sites in Cahokia's hinterland. These bone chemistry data suggest that the residents of Cahokia consumed less maize and ate more meat than the inhabitants of outlying sites (Yerkes 2005, 249).

These findings are further supported by Kirstin Hedman's 2006 research on Late Mississippian period Cahokian diets confirming the indication that there was differential maize consumption by site. Hedman explored the role of biological sex and maize consumption with surprising results, namely that gendered differences in diets at some locations (i.e., the East St. Louis Quarry site) challenge some assumptions about the maize consumption of males and females. Males at the East St. Louis Quarry site ate more maize and animals that consumed $C_4$-enriched protein (such as maize, sugar cane, millet, and sorghum) than did their female counterparts (Hedman 2006, 265). At this point, there is little reason to theorize that the diet of elites was different from that of non-elites at Cahokia. In fact, the dietary differences (Ambrose, Buikstra, and Krueger 2003; Hedman 2006; Yerkes 2005) support the idea that the females who were killed and buried in Mound 72 were from a neighboring (or even distant) population whose members consumed a different diet from those living at Cahokia. The social and biological distance between the killed females included in the Mound 72 burials and members of the local Cahokian population could have further reduced their opportunities to gain status and rank positions that have been identified among native Cahokians. The interpretation that these females are not from the local Cahokian population does not negate or diminish the results from any of the isotope analyses mentioned above. Instead, this moves the discussion toward dietary distinctions that may have emerged between cultural groups that may indicate both ethnic foodways (Brown and Mussell 1985) and differential access to certain foods based on gender at some locales (Ambrose, Buikstra, and Krueger 2003; Hedman 2006). However, diet alone is not enough to establish an ethnic group. Therefore, this assessment includes mode of death, burial arrangement, and dental biodistance.

Despite variations in diet, the captive females at Cahokia were relatively healthy. This is especially evident when we consider the patterns of their pathological lesions. A few of the females were afflicted by health conditions that lead to cribra orbitalia and porotic hyperostosis, but at the time of their deaths there were no severe cases. None of the remains showed signs of treponematosis, a nonvenereal form of syphilis (Rose 1999). This could be a result of lag between infection and changes in the skeleton (Wood et al. 1992), or it may indicate that these females were not experiencing extended periods of exposure to populations that were afflicted by this infectious disease.

The captive females experienced relatively low rates of periostitis, which was becoming increasingly prevalent at some urbanizing locations during the Middle Mississippian Period (Lallo 1973; Powell 2000). Tibial lesions, which are sometimes indicative of infection from treponematosis (Larsen 1997; Milner and Buikstra 2006, 635; Powell 2000; Powell and Cook 2005), were not pronounced in these females (i.e., no saber shins or severe lesions on the crania and extremities were observed). Though treponematosis is not dependent on population size, as some diseases are (i.e., measles), it is highly communicable from person to person and could spread very quickly in more densely populated areas such as Cahokia. The Mound 72 captive females (and the rest of the individuals interred in the mound) had surprisingly low rates of reactive tibiae lesions (including those related to periostitis) compared to other contemporary sites (Lallo 1973). This comparatively low rate of periostitis could indicate that these females were not exposed to the same pathological conditions prevalent in other populations at this time. This could indicate that they were specifically selected because they did not have active or obviously healed lesions on their skin. In fact, Rose (1999) found higher rates of periostitis infections among those interpreted as "middle status" individuals.

In addition to the risk of exposure to infectious diseases such as treponematosis, these females were living during a period when populations may have experienced increases in chronic infections related to rising rates of sedentism and reliance on agriculture, such as infections from parasites (Cohen 1989; Larsen and Sering 2000; Steckel and Rose 2002). These conditions were also underrepresented in these females. When combined, these pathological data suggest social distinctions between these captives and their captors and limited interactions between these two social groups.

Cultural Evidence of Social Distance

The Mound 72 burials further indicate that models that rank levels of physical violence based on concepts of biodistance are a poor proxy for social distance. For instance, acts of violence were more visibly enacted on the four headless, handless males in Feature 106 and on the individuals in the lower level of Feature 229, who were more closely related biologically to their captors than to the killed female groups. This demonstrates that at Cahokia visible violence was not positively correlated with the biodistance of the captive populations from their captors. It is possible that females were harmed in ways that did not leave marks on their skeletal remains. (Humiliation, rape, or injury to the soft tissues do not survive for later interpretation.)

Gender distinctions in patterns of violence are known in historic accounts of captivity from North America (Cole 2000; Demos 1994; Driver 1969) and in modern contexts (Malkki 1995). Given the differences in how the bodies and burials of the captive females were handled at Mound 72 compared to the other captives at that site, gender cannot be ruled out as a structuring principle. Differences between the female, male, and mixed interments could serve as a reminder that when populations create classifications based on gender, ethnic, and other social variables, the social distance (Hinton 1996) that is constructed may not correlate with the biological distance of populations. We may never know whether some captives were treated differently because they were female, because they were not native to Cahokia, or for both reasons. Historic accounts of captive experiences sometimes include obvious revisions. These changes and omissions in captivity narratives are examples of how individuals who were captured distance themselves from specific forms of violent acts that could compromise their ability to be fully reincorporated into their own communities. Specifically, details about sexual assault and acts of female bravery are often excluded or are written from the perspective of a witness (Cole 2000, 51–52).

The cause of death of the female captives is not clear. It is likely that they were poisoned or were poisoned and strangled (Rose 1999). Both practices have been documented in the historic accounts of the Natchez. Descriptions of "black drink" (Hudson 1979) and ideas of cultural competency come to mind. The ritual practice of drinking and subsequent ritualized regurgitation of the yaupon holly (*Illex vomitoria*) is documented in southeastern populations from the early historic period. Archaeological evidence of ritual shell cups found in Hopewell and Mississippian graves extend the evidence of use farther back in time. If the females were given "black drink" that contained lethal ingredients and did not know to regurgitate it, they would have been singled out as different from those who successfully participated in the ritualized consumption and regurgitation of "black drink." This lack of cultural knowledge may have cost them their lives. Although this example is of course speculative, it may explain how so many females died with so little trauma to their remains. Ultimately, what we can say is that these females did not die of natural causes, indicated by their limited age ranges and the shared timing of their deaths. Additionally, they were interred with no observable evidence of long-term abuse, which could indicate a short period of captivity.

The intentional selection of young females in their reproductive years from an outside population to participate in lethal rituals requires us to discuss violent acts that are infrequently discussed when talking about prehistoric violence; namely selective massacres and genocidal behaviors. Continued selection and use of external females for lethal rituals during the AD 1000–1050 range may strengthen the theory that populations were targeted to diminish their reproductive success. The ritual killing of females in contexts outside of typical warfare practices should not preclude discussions of other forms of violence. This is especially true for cases where so many reproductive females from outside populations were clearly selected. Targeting a population's reproductive females would have significant demographic effects on the population(s) from which these females were taken. Warfare or raiding would have been the likely mechanism for gaining access to females from communities outside Cahokia, so whether these sacrificed female captives at Cahokia were part of a ritual killing or an attempt at population eradication, the point is that these behaviors are not necessarily discrete. Violent acts should not be viewed as exclusive categories of experience, as they often overlap in their form and meaning(s).

## Results

### Rethinking the Mound 72 Mortuary Context

The Mound 72 story goes beyond representations of elite hierarchy and enactments of hero-figures. It also includes bioarchaeological clues that hint at social relationships. For instance, we can guess at the relative length of captivity of the females taken into Cahokia. For the females brought into Cahokia, captivity was a seemingly short experience, given their young age range as well as their apparent exclusion from living out their natural lives at Cahokia. The mortuary performances that resulted in the Mound 72 arrangement illuminate some of the social distinctions the Cahokians made between themselves and the female captives from outside the community that reinforced the Cahokian understanding of their cultural reality (Noyes and Abrahams 1999; Schieffelin 1985). These distinctions are especially visible in the mode of death of the female captives and in the purposeful positioning of their bodies after death. Cahokians distinguished captive burials based on gender, age, and biodistance from others buried in Mound 72. In doing so, the Cahokians re-created their social realities.

### Economic Models and Captive Identity

The focus on the shell-bird burials in the mortuary reconstructions of Mound 72 is a result of popular theories that link socioeconomic status with grave goods and other interpretations of burial performance. Problematically, these can reduce the interpretation of the majority of individuals buried in Mound 72 to a performance of sociopolitical power (Porubcan 2000). That is, these theories suggest that captives were killed to reify the status positions and sociopolitical power of the elite, but they do not ask why particular individuals were chosen as captives or why they were buried in ways that differentiated the captives from other members of the Cahokian population. Other distinctions are then glossed over and muted and are even seen as unimportant for future research. We need to remember that even if the victims were interpreted by Cahokians as equivalent to the material status of grave goods, this status was created by their captivity and deaths and it was through these mechanisms that they gained these materialized personas (Binford 1971; Saxe 1970).

Interpretations that center on economics do not offer the best models for understanding the relationships created by and between the individuals burying the dead. This is especially true within the Mound 72 context because of the presence of foreign captives. At least three perspectives of the females' captive status would have existed: how the Cahokians viewed the captives, how the captives imagined their own captivity, and how the captives would have been imagined by members of their own population. There is no way to infer how captives were positioned in their own society, but we can assume that it was different from the Cahokian perspective. Captive status may place these individuals into a unique category in the society of their captors, but that status may have been more like the reconstructed identities of modern displaced individuals such as refugees (Malkki 1995) than like a "low status" or even non-elite category within a captor society.

It is problematic to assume that all populations interacted with their captives identically or that all captives are treated the same by the same captors. In fact, historical and ethnohistorical accounts depict great diversity in treatment of captives (Cole 2000; Demos 1994; Driver 1969). The female captives at Cahokia were likely taken during a raid or warfare event and then kept in unknown conditions for an unknown period of time. Later they were killed and interred in various sand-lined pits throughout Mound 72. Their stories are likely vastly different from those of the mixed male/female captives in the lower level of Feature 229. In addition, the captives killed at Mound 72 were vastly different from the "retainer" sacrifices associated with the shell-bird burials in Feature 101.

The retainers were perhaps willing participants in a ritual that brought honor to their families, similar to the social mechanism recorded by Le Page du Pratz among the eighteenth-century Natchez (Rose 1999; Swanton 1911). This interpretation is suggested because the retainers were not biologically distinctive from the shell-bird individuals. Therefore, it is suggested that their biological similarity to elite individuals enabled these individuals to participate in kinship-based honor rituals in which the foreign females could not participate. This participation in prestige-gaining strategies may have directly benefited the retainers through the improved diet mentioned above (Ambrose, Buikstra, and Krueger 2003). An alternative explanation is that retainers were selected from both elite and non-elite sectors of society to participate in these rituals. Perhaps their biodistance allowed the individuals who are interpreted as retainers to gain access to status that captives, regardless of their origin, were denied.

## Captivity in the Southeast during the Early Historic Period

Throughout the historic period in the New World, there are many recorded instances of captives taken during raids and warfare. These accounts included stories of Europeans who were taken captive, but they also include descriptions of indigenous captives being taken from other native populations. For example, Thomas Nairne wrote about the Yamasee raids in Florida during the period 1699–1706, when indigenous groups sought to capture and enslave members of other indigenous populations (Gallay 2002, 65, 127–128). In some cases, the raiders kept those they captured, while in others, they sold their captives to Europeans as slaves. In some communities, Europeans could acquire indigenous slaves only if they had been enslaved during "just wars," were criminals, or had inherited their slave status (Gallay 2002). Thus, for the Europeans in these communities, raids and indigenous warfare provided the justification for enslaving some indigenous persons.

Frequently, captives in these accounts were females and children, and these captives were sometimes eligible for adoption by members of the captor population. If the captors were traveling long distances, they would sometimes kill individuals who could not make the journey easily or would otherwise slow the group down while it was retreating to the safety of its village (Cole 2000; Demos 1994; Driver 1969). Individuals who were brought from distant locations needed to be healthy and able to keep up with the movement of the raiding party. Adoption ceremonies occurred in the presence of the entire captor group so that members who had not participated in the raid had the option of adopting captives. Often implicit in these accounts is the idea that when a captive (particularly if the captive was female or a child) arrived at the captors' village, they would be incorporated into the population as either adoptive members or slaves. This would not be without exception, as there are many cases of revenge captivity and killings that occurred at the captors' village, but the idea of revenge captivity does not fit well with the Mound 72 data. There is no evidence that Cahokians suffered an attack prior to the start of the construction of Mound 72 that could lead to the explanation that the females were captured and killed as part of a vengeance cycle.

Distinctions in mode of death and burial were created to differentiate Cahokian females from non-Cahokian females, who were clearly seen as expendable to the Cahokians who killed them. This is not the same situation as the Natchez or Taensa sacrifices, where relatives were sacrificed to accompany spouses and/or great leaders, or infants were immolated to appease angry deities (Gallay 2002, 118–122; Swanton 1911). If these females at Cahokia were killed to appease a deity or a human leader who demanded human sacrifices, there is little reason to assume that they gained any status for themselves or their families because of their outsider status. Furthermore, there is no reason to assume that they shared the beliefs of their captors.

## Discussion

### The Differential Burials of Captives: Performances of Social Distance

Social and biological distancing are evident in the burials of the groups killed at Cahokia. The distances were enacted primarily by the Cahokians, who killed and arranged their captives to fit into their mythic tableau (Brown 2003, 2005). This is where the mortuary program at Mound 72 begins to get exceptionally interesting. Ultimately, through identifying the specific groups of individuals and understanding what they were selected for by the Cahokians, perhaps we can better understand more details about specific themes and messages embedded in this mound.

The ethnohistorical data that discuss Eastern Woodlands and Plains groups describe differences in the roles captor societies assigned to captives. These roles included using captives as servants or slaves, using the physical bodies of captives as vessels for displaced souls, killing captives to meet the demands of deities, and taking captives to replace but not to embody the souls of lost members of a kin group (Gallay 2002; Hall

1997). However, no evidence exists that would support interpretations of servitude or adoption into the Cahokian population.

Short captivity is suggested for the killed females interred in mass graves at Mound 72 for several reasons. First, all of the females were young and relatively healthy. In fact, this is why Jerome Rose (1999) discussed the possibility that they were chosen based on their perceived beauty. Individuals who were visibly ill or marred (at least on the osteological level) were not included with these female groups. There were no indications that the tibial lesions that were present in this data set was a result of the prevalence of infectious disease such as treponematosis, a disease that was occurring with increasing frequency in the growing communities of the Middle Mississippian Period(Powell 2000). This is very interesting, as treponemal infections were present at nearby sites (Milner 1991; Milner, Anderson and Smith 1991; Steadman 2008), and given Cahokia's large population, treponemal infections would likely have been present. Perhaps those who were not healthy were left behind or perished during the journey to Cahokia.

The assessment that these females were fairly healthy counters the conventional interpretation that captive females were unhealthy (Ambrose, Buikstra, and Krueger 2003; Pauketat 2009). Though these females apparently ate more maize than other individuals buried in the mound and as a result were more likely to develop dental caries, assigning a low health status based on this evidence may not accurately portray their overall well-being. In addition, the fact that they ate more maize than others at Cahokia does not necessarily demonstrate that Cahokians made distinctions between the diets of elites and non-elites but could be explained as a dietary difference based on gender, age, or ethnicity. Since the imported females did not fit into the categories of social hierarchy, status, and ranks that were evident at Cahokia, it is likely that they were treated differently based on a combination of both their outsider status and their gender identity. Furthermore, the assumption that nutritional differences automatically benefit the elites in a ranked society is problematic, because unhealthy foods may be valued as elite goods.

It is curious, but not entirely strange, that there were no visible indications of violence on the remains of any of the female captives who were interred without males. This does not preclude the possibility that their bodies were subjected to physical violence; whatever violence they may have endured did not produce skeletal lesions. What we do know is that these females were brought into Cahokia and killed shortly thereafter. This is partially evidenced by the absence of healed pathological lesions that could be suggestive of longer-term captivity (Cole 2000; Demos 1994; Wilkinson 1997). It is also supported by the fact that the age range of this group is small and the fact that the diet of these women was distinct from that of the rest of the Cahokian population. Basically, their captivity did not last long enough for there to be homogenizing changes in their body chemistry. This of course assumes that at Cahokia, they would have eaten the same food as the rest of the population since food resources in the area were abundant. The inclusion of these captive females in this important mortuary context opens interesting topics for discussion that include social distancing, ethnicity, and our ability to detect differential gendered violence in the prehistoric record.

Differential Captivity

The reasons why individuals are taken captive may influence how the body is treated and used in the mortuary context. These reasons cannot be fully reconstructed without written or oral evidence, but bioarchaeological evidence of bodily trauma or of the selection of specific groups of individuals contains clues that suggest differences in actions performed on various groups of captive bodies. These differences indicate how Cahokians physically situated and used the bodies of their captives to create and enact social realities that went beyond the mythic context. For instance, the neat burial arrangement of the females in layered rows separated by woven mats and the absence of evidence of physical stress (infection or abuse) may indicate that the physical appearance of the women's bodies was an important criterion for inclusion in this mortuary performance. Alternatively, this assemblage may indicate that only the healthy survived the journey to Cahokia. Furthermore, the neat arrangement of the bodies of the female captives marks a clear distinction between the method of execution of these women and the methods used to kill the mixed-sex group buried in the lower level of Feature 229. The latter group was killed at the gravesite, and some were still alive as they fell into the burial pit. These individuals were not neatly arranged; their bodies fell into a shared grave. This followed a rather systematic bludgeoning on the back of their skulls with a large blunt object. The force exerted by the executioner(s) resulted in the decapitation of three individuals and the partial decapitation of a fourth. These individuals were not killed so the captors could have trophy limbs (Owsley and Berryman 1975; Smith 1997), and they were not selected based on their gender. The accidental nature of the beheading was indicated by the fact that the heads were thrown into the pit with the burials instead of being used in a display associated with trophies.

The lower level of Feature 229 also contrasts greatly with the burials in the upper level. The upper-level burials are separated from those in the lower level by wooden planks and are buried in a neat row of litters. Cohen's (1974) dental analysis demonstrated that these two groups were biologically similar to each other, although they were socially distinct Cahokians. The visibly violent deaths and messy arrangement of the group buried in the lower level of Feature 229 continues to pose a challenge to interpretations that link the groups of killed individuals in Mound 72 with the earlier mound feature that contained shell-bird imagery (Feature 101). Instead, the striking juxtaposition of the upper and lower levels of this feature likely represents a performance of the structured cosmos (sky-earth world and dome imagery). It is important to note that there are no other archaeologically known burial groups from the Mississippian Period that closely resemble this late (AD 1100–1150) feature in Mound 72. Only by looking at the upper and lower levels of Feature 229 separately can we recognize similarities to other burials. For instance, the upper portion is similar to a burial described in the 1931 report on the Powell Mound excavations at Cahokia (Ahler and DePuydt 1987, 4) and the later Caddoan litter burials at Spiro (Brown 1971, 1981). The dual layering in Feature 229 is reminiscent of the layering in the four pits with the foreign female captives, which included layers that were separated by matting. The separation was much more distinctive in Feature 229, which used wooden planks as opposed to matting. Several attributes of the lower level of Feature 229 distinguish it from other captive burials in Mound 72, such as the small biodistance between the captives in the lower level and the individuals interred in the upper level, the visibly violent deaths of these local captives, and the separation in time of these killings and other killings at Mound 72.

The final group of potential captives included in this discussion was also distinguished from the imported captive females. This group of four headless, handless males in Feature 106 may represent a human platform associated with various cosmologically important ritual events (Hall

2000). These four males were visibly mutilated, but ethnohistorical accounts of some indigenous honor-gaining rituals suggest that this act should not be automatically assumed to be an act of denigration (Fowler et al. 1999, 187). An honor-gaining context seems appropriate because the mutilation was performed postmortem and because the sharp cutting close to the base of the skulls demonstrates that care was taken to remove the heads of the males included in this burial (Rose 1999). Unlike the accidentally removed skulls in Feature 229, it is likely that the skulls of these four males were used in other contexts, such as in dedication ceremonies. This practice of using skulls and limbs in dedications is seen in other Mississippian Period contexts, including the skull found in the Jondro Mound (Fowler et al. 1999, 178) and the hands found in an infant burial at the Norris Farms No. 36 cemetery (Santure, Harn, and Esarey 1990, 105). The careful cutting and the absence of limbs in Feature 106 support the idea that the missing limbs were used for other purposes. Since the biodistances of the Mound 72 population were calculated based on dental traits, the genetic relatedness of these four males is not known. The possibility that they were captives is strong; if they were, their burial arrangements suggest an interesting scenario in which captives were not necessarily dishonored, even though they were killed.

The symbolic positioning and bodily treatment of the four headless, handless males correspond to powerful cosmological ideas relating to Green Corn ceremonies, and somewhat surprisingly, this group does not represent a unique form of burial in the Mississippian world (Fowler et al. 1999, 187–189; Hall 2000; Harn 1980). The regional and cosmological significance of this burial is discussed in detail in Robert Hall's "Sacrificed Foursomes and Green Corn Ceremonialism" (2000), where this feature is compared with a similar burial unearthed at the Dickson Mound site. Hall explores the cosmological myths that relate to this symbolic arrangement and found that such arrangements were widespread in both Southeastern and Mesoamerican populations. Though this mythic mortuary performance distinguishes these four males from other captives in Mound 72, all the captives buried in this mound were used in various performances of Cahokian identity during its multiple burial and construction phases.

## Conclusion

Great strides have been made in our understanding of prehistoric violence and captivity and the research methods used to interpret these events. Now we can take our interpretations further. We can explore issues of imposed status and identity, incorporating new perspectives of status that are free from the assumption that captives were simply assimilated into lower-status echelons of captor societies.

The complex data set from Mound 72 at Cahokia demonstrates the importance of joint subfield research. The various forms of violence that were enacted on the bodies of individuals and groups interred in a single mound context were made visible through collaborative research that employed bioarchaeological and biocultural methods (Goldstein 2006). Attempts to define these behaviors as discrete forms of violence can obscure the meaning of this context. Instead, we should recognize how performances of violence are related to how captors situated themselves and others in the world, constructing these relationships by imposing their own realities onto those they dominated. Ultimately, deconstructing this context reveals that the captive experience varied greatly at Cahokia.

## Acknowledgments

This research was carried out as part of my dissertation project at the University of Arkansas, under the direction of Dr. Jerome Rose. I thank Dr. Rose for sharing his data and expertise with me for this analysis.

## References Cited

Acsadi, G., and J. Nemeskeri
1970    *History of Human Lifespan and Mortality.* Akademai Kiado, Budapest.
Ahler, S. R., and P. J. DePuydt
1987    *A Report on the 1931 Powell Mound Excavations, Madison County Illinois.* Reports of Investigations no. 43. Illinois State Museum, Springfield.
Ambrose, S. H., J. E. Buikstra, and H. W. Krueger
2003    Status and Gender Differences in Diet at Mound 72, Cahokia, Revealed by Isotopic Analysis of Bone. *Journal of Anthropological Archaeology* 22(3): 217–226.
Armelagos, G. J., and D. P. Van Gerven
2003    A Century of Skeletal Biology and Paleopathology: Contrasts, Contradictions, and Conflicts. *American Anthropologist* 105(1): 53–64.

Bass, W. M.

1987    *Human Osteology: A Laboratory and Field Manual.* 3rd ed. Missouri Archaeological Society, Columbia.

Binford, L. R.

1971    Mortuary Practices: Their Study and Their Potential. In *Approaches to the Social Dimensions of Mortuary Practices,* edited by J. A. Brown. Society for American Archaeology, Washington, D.C.

Brothwell, D. R.

1972    *Digging Up Bones.* 2nd ed. British Museum (Natural History), London.

Brown, J. A.

1971    The Dimensions of Status in the Burials at Spiro. In *Approaches to the Social Dimensions of Mortuary Practices,* edited by J. A. Brown, pp. 92–112. Society for American Archaeology, Washington, D.C.

1981    The Search for Rank in Prehistoric Burials. In *The Archaeology of Death,* edited by R. Chapman, I. Kinnes, and K. Randsborg, pp. 25–37. Cambridge University Press, Cambridge.

2003    The Cahokia Mound 72-Sub1 Burials as Collective Representation. *Wisconsin Archeologist* 84 (1–2): 83–99.

2005    Ancient Spiro Cosmology. Colloquia presentation at the University at Arkansas, Fayetteville, March 28.

Brown, L. K., and K. Mussell

1985    *Ethnic and Regional Foodways in the United States: The Performance of Group Identity.* University of Tennessee Press, Knoxville.

Byers, A. Martin

2006    *Cahokia: A World Renewal Cult Heterarchy.* University Press of Florida, Gainesville.

Cohen, J.

1974    Population Differences in Dental Morphology View in Terms of High and Low Heritability. *American Journal of Physical Anthropology* 41: 473.

Cohen, M. N.

1989    *Health and the Rise of Civilization.* Yale University Press, New Haven, Conn.

Cole, K. S.

2000    "For Here Forlorn and Lost I Tread": The Gender Differences between Captivity Narratives of Men and Women from 1528 to 1886. M.A. thesis, Youngstown State University.

Dancey, W. S.

2005    The Enigmatic Hopewell of the Eastern Woodlands. In *North American Archaeology,* edited by Timothy R. Pauketat and Diana DiPaolo Loren, pp. 108–137. Blackwell Publishing, Malden, Mass.

Demos, J.

1994    *The Unredeemed Captive.* Random House, New York.

Driver, H. E.

1969    *Indians of North America.* 2nd ed. Chicago University Press, Chicago.

Fowler, M. L., J. C. Rose, B. Vander Leest, and S. R. Ahler (editors)
1999    *The Mound 72 Area: Dedicated and Sacred Space in Early Cahokia.* Reports of Investigations no. 54. Illinois State Museum, Springfield.
Gallay, A.
2002    *The Indian Slave Trade: The Rise of the English Empire in the American South, 1670–1717.* Yale University Press, New Haven, Conn.
Goldstein, L.
1980    *Mississippian Mortuary Practices: A Case Study of Two Cemeteries in the Lower Illinois Valley.* Scientific Papers no. 4. Northwestern University Archaeological Program, Evanston.
2006    Mortuary Analysis and Bioarchaeology. In *Bioarchaeology: The Contextual Analysis of Human Remains,* edited by J. E. Buikstra and L. A. Beck, pp. 375–388. Academic Press, Burlington.
Hall, R. L.
1997    *An Archaeology of the Soul: North American Indian Belief and Ritual.* University of Illinois Press, Urbana.
2000    Sacrificed Foursomes and Green Corn Ceremonialism. In *Mounds, Modoc, and Mesoamerica: Papers in Honor of Melvin L. Fowler,* edited by S. R. Ahler, pp. 245–253. Reports of Investigations no. 28. Illinois State Museum, Springfield.
Harn, A. D.
1980    *The Prehistory of Dickson Mounds: The Dickson Excavations.* Reports of Investigations no. 35. Illinois State Museum, Springfield.
Hedman, K. M.
2006    Late Cahokian Subsistence and Health: Stable Isotope and Dental Evidence. *Southeastern Archaeology* 25(2): 258–274.
Hinton, A. L.
1996    Agents of Death: Explaining the Cambodian Genocide in Terms of Psychosocial Dissonance. *American Anthropologist* 98(4): 818–831.
Hudson, C. M.
1979    *Black Drink: A Native American Tea.* University of Georgia Press, Athens.
Kakaliouras, A. M.
2010    Race Is . . . Only as Race Does: Essentialism and Ethnicity in (Bio) Archaeology and Skeletal Biology. *The SAA Archaeological Record* 10(3): 16–20.
Krogman, W. M., and M. Y. Iscan
1986    *The Human Skeleton in Forensic Medicine.* Charles C. Thomas, Springfield.
Lallo, J. W.
1973    The Skeletal Biology of Three Prehistoric American Indian Societies from Dickson Mounds. Ph.D. dissertation, University of Massachusetts, Amherst.
Larsen, C. S.
1997    *Bioarchaeology: Interpreting Behavior from the Human Skeleton.* Cambridge University Press, Cambridge.
Larsen, C. S., and L. E. Sering
2000    Inferring Iron-Deficiency Anemia from Human Skeletal Remains: The Case of

the Georgia Blight. In *Bioarchaeological Studies in the Age of Agriculture: A View from the Southeast,* edited by P. M. Lambert, pp. 116–133. University of Alabama Press, Tuscaloosa.

Malkki, L. H.

1995    *Purity and Exile: Violence, Memory, and National Cosmology among Hutu Refugees in Tanzania.* University of Chicago Press, Chicago.

Milner, G. R.

1991    Health and Cultural Change in the Late Prehistoric American Bottom, Illinois. In *What Mean These Bones? Studies in Southeastern Bioarchaeology,* edited by M. L. Powell, P. S. Bridges, and A. M. W. Mires, pp. 52–69. University of Alabama Press, Tuscaloosa.

2007    Warfare, Population, and Food Production in Prehistoric Eastern North America. In *North American Indigenous Warfare and Ritual Violence,* edited by R. J. Chacon and R. G. Mendoza, pp. 182–201. University of Arizona Press, Tucson.

Milner, G. R., E. Anderson and V. G. Smith

1991    Warfare in Late Prehistoric West-Central Illinois. *American Antiquity* 56(4): 581–603.

Milner, G. R., and J. E. Buikstra

2006    Skeletal Biology: Northeast. In *Handbook of North American Indians, Volume 3, Environment, Origins, and Population,* edited by D. H. Ubelaker, pp. 630–639. Smithsonian Institution Press, Washington, D.C.

Noyes, D., and R. D. Abrahams

1999    From Calendar Custom to National Memory: European Commonplaces. In *Cultural Memory and the Construction of Identity,* edited by D. Ben-Amos and L. Weissberg, pp. 77–98. Wayne State University Press, Detroit.

Ousley, S. D., R. L. Jantz, and D. Freid

2009    Understanding Race and Human Variation: Why Forensic Anthropologists Are Good at Identifying Race. *American Journal of Physical Anthropology* 139(1): 68–76.

Owsley, D. W., and H. E. Berryman

1975    Ethnographic and Archaeological Evidence of Scalping in the Southeastern United States. *Tennessee Archaeologist* 31: 41–60.

Pauketat, T.

2009    *Cahokia: Ancient America's Great City on the Mississippi.* Viking-Penguin, New York.

Piot, C.

1999    *Remotely Global: Village Modernity in West Africa.* University of Chicago Press, Chicago.

Plummer, R.

1973 [1839]    Narrative of the Capture and Subsequent Sufferings of Mrs. Rachel Plummer, Written by Herself. In *Held Captive by Indians: Selected Narratives, 1642–1836,* edited by R. VanDerBeets, pp. 333–366. University of Tennessee Press, Knoxville.

Porubcan, P.

2000    Human and Nonhuman Surplus Display at Mound 72, Cahokia. In *Mounds, Modoc, and Mesoamerica: Papers in Honor of Melvin L. Fowler,* edited by S. R. Ahler, pp. 207–225. Reports of Investigations no. 28. Illinois State Museum, Springfield.

Powell, M. L.

2000    Ancient Diseases, Modern Perspective: Treponematosis and Tuberculosis in the Age of Agriculture. In *Bioarchaeological Studies in the Age of Agriculture: A View from the Southeast,* edited by P. M. Lambert, pp. 6–34. University of Alabama Press, Tuscaloosa.

Powell, M. L., and D. C. Cook

2005    *The Myth of Syphilis: The Natural History of Treponematosis in North America.* University Press of Florida, Gainesville.

Rose, J. C.

1999    Mortuary Data and Analysis. In *The Mound 72 Area: Dedicated and Sacred Space in Early Cahokia,* edited by M. C. Fowler, J. C. Rose, B. Vander Leest, and S. R. Alher, pp. 63–82. Reports of Investigations no. 54. Illinois State Museum, Springfield.

Santure, S. K., A. D. Harn, and D. Esarey (editors)

1990    *Archaeological Investigations at the Morton Village and Norris Farms 36 Cemetery.* Reports of Investigations no. 45. Illinois State Museum, Springfield.

Saxe, A. A.

1970    Social Dimensions of Mortuary Practices. Ph.D. dissertation, University of Michigan.

Schieffelin, E. L.

1985    Performance and the Construction of Reality. *American Ethnologist* 12(4): 707–724.

Schour, I., and M. Massler

1944    *Development of Human Dentition.* 2nd ed. American Dental Association, Chicago.

Smith, M. O.

1997    Osteological Indications of Warfare in the Archaic Period of the Western Tennessee Valley. In *Troubled Times: Violence and Warfare in the Past,* edited by D. L. Martin and D. W. Frayer, pp. 241–266. Gordon and Breach, Amsterdam.

Sparks, C. S., and R. L. Jantz

2003    Changing Times, Changing Faces: Boas's Immigrant Study in a Modern Perspective. *American Anthropologist* 105: 333–337.

Steadman, D. W.

2008    Warfare Related Trauma at Orendorf, a Middle Mississippian Site in West-Central Illinois. *American Journal of Physical Anthropology* 136(1): 51–64.

Steckel, R. H., and J. C. Rose (editors)

2002    *The Backbone of History: Health and Nutrition in the Western Hemisphere.* Cambridge University Press, Cambridge.

Swanton, J. R.
1911    Indian Tribes of the Lower Mississippi Valley and Adjacent Coast of the Gulf of Mexico. Bureau of American Ethnology Bulletin no. 43. Smithsonian Institution Press, Washington, D.C.

Wilkinson, R. G.
1997    Appendix B: Human Skeletal Remains from La Coyotera. In *Archaeology of the Cañada de Cuicatlán, Oaxaca*, edited by C. S. Spencer and E. M. Redmond, pp. 614–619. Anthropological Papers no. 80. American Museum of Natural History, New York.

Williamson, Ron
2007    "Otinontsiskiaj ondaon" ("The House of Cut-off Heads"): The History and Archaeology of Northern Iroquoian Trophy Taking. In *The Taking and Displaying of Human Body Parts as Trophies by Amerindians*, edited by Richard J. Chacon and David H. Dye, pp. 190–221. Springer, New York.

Wood, J. W., G. R. Milner, H. C. Harpending, K. M. Weiss, M. N. Cohen, L. E. Eisenberg, D. L. Hutchinson, R. Jankauskas, G. Česnys, M. A. Katzenberg, J. R. Lukacs, J. W. McGrath, E. A. Roth, D. H. Ubelaker, and R. G. Wilkinson
1992    The Osteological Paradox: Problems of Inferring Prehistoric Health from Skeletal Samples. *Current Anthropology* 33(4): 343–370.

Yerkes, R. W.
2005    Bone Chemistry, Body Parts, and Growth Marks: Evaluating Ohio Hopewell and Cahokia Mississippian Seasonality, Subsistence, Ritual, and Feasting. *American Antiquity* 70(2): 241–265.

# 12

## Biological Distance Analysis in Contexts of Ritual Violence

WILLIAM N. DUNCAN

## Introduction

In the past decade, there has been a considerable increase in research by physical anthropologists and archaeologists that focuses on ritual violence (Andrushko et al. 2005; Andrushko, Schwitalla, and Walker 2010; Chacon and Dye 2007; Chacon and Mendoza 2007a, 2007b; Eeckhout and Owens 2008; Spence et al. 2004; Sugiyama 2005; Tiesler and Cucina 2007; Tung 2008). One question that has received particular attention is how to identify who was subjected to such treatment, through sacrifice, trophy taking, or other forms of mortuary violence. Researchers have used detailed taphonomic (Tiesler 2007), contextual (Weiss-Krejci 2005), theoretical (Duncan 2005), and methodological analyses (Spence et al. 2004) to this end. One area that has been largely absent from the discussion is biological distance (with notable exceptions; see Coruccini and Shimada 2002; Sutter and Verano 2007). This is surprising because physical anthropologists have long wrestled with whether or not and to what degree cultural boundaries influence biological relatedness and whether such boundaries are made on the basis of race (Brace et al. 1993; Edgar and Hunley 2009), ethnicity (Lai 2001), language (Chen and Sokal 1995; Simmons, Gajdusek, and Nicholson 1967), or other social divisions (Brewer-Carias, Le Blanc, and Neel 1976). Contexts that provide evidence of ritual violence are unique in this discussion because they illustrate cultural boundaries that were intentionally acknowledged and

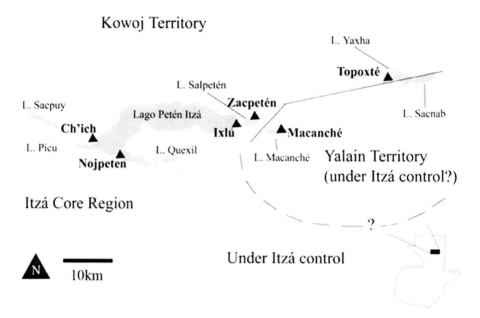

Fig. 12.1. Petén lakes region. Modified from Duncan 2011.

created. Assessing phenotypic variability with reference to these bound-aries can thus provide some answers to questions such as whether those who practiced ritual violence were biologically distinct from those who were subjected to violence or whether victims were selected in whole or part because of kinship. Considering sacrifice in this context is impor-tant because it avoids (or attempts to avoid) the lamentable tendency for studies of ritual violence to be sensationalist without locating the vio-lence within larger anthropological discussions (Knüsel 2010). This study presents a biological distance analysis of sacrificial victims from a Maya skull row to assess evidence of kinship among the victims and in doing so highlights the potential of and limitations of biodistance analysis in contexts of ritual violence.

Prior to contact with Europeans, two social groups dominated the Petén lakes region, the Itzá to the west and the Kowoj to the east (Fig. 12.1). Ethnohistorical (Jones 1998), linguistic (Hofling 2009), and archaeo-logical research (Rice and Rice 2009) around the Petén lakes in north-ern Guatemala over the last 30 years has worked to identify these groups and understand their relationships. This research has shown that the two groups were locked in an ongoing struggle for control of territory around the Petén lakes. Warfare was conducted not by standing armies but by raiding groups fighting over land and resources. One strategy of this warfare was taking captives for sacrifice (Jones 1998). We know that kinship influenced the selection of rulers and military leaders, but no one has ever demonstrated whether victims of sacrifice who were taken through military action were related to each other.

## Ixlú-2023

Archaeological investigation of the Itzá and the Kowoj (as well as their relationships) recovered a series of skull pairs and rows around the lakes region at the sites of Ixlú and Nojpeten and Ixlú and Macanché (respectively) that sheds light on this question (Fig. 12.1). The Ixlú sample is notable because it is the only site where skull rows and pairs were found in the same structure. Ixlú is best known for its Terminal Classic component, but excavations in the 1990s by Prudence and Don Rice identified a number of Postclassic structures, including Structure 2023, a small temple in the main plaza of the site. The building consisted of a platform and two associated altars, the temple itself, and a C-shaped bench placed on top of the temple (Fig. 12.2). Twenty-one skulls were found in Structure 2023; fifteen skulls were placed in rows in the middle of the temple and the remaining six skulls were placed in three pairs on the center line of the structure (Fig. 12.3). All of the skulls faced east. Four dismembered postcrania were placed perpendicular to the skull pairs on the western side of the temple (Fig. 12.4). Previous analysis has shown that the postcrania all belonged to late adolescent to young adult males (15–35 years of age).

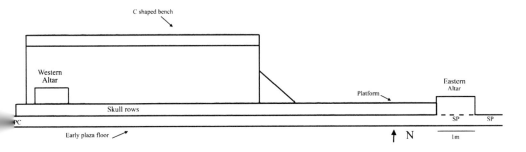

Fig. 12.2. Profile of Structure 2023, Ixlú, Guatemala. Modified from Duncan 2011.

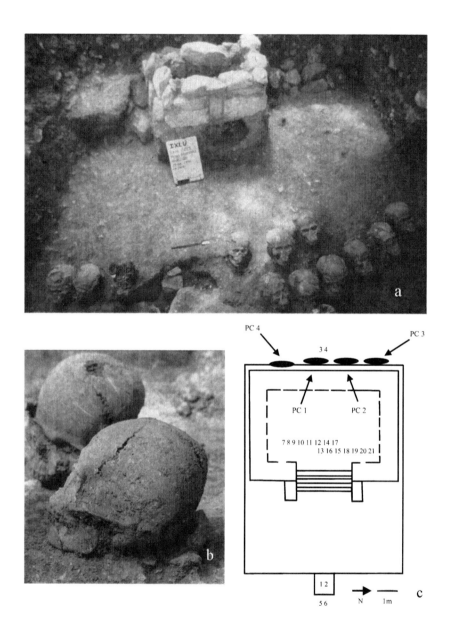

Fig. 12.3. Skull rows (a); Skull pair (b); Plan view of Structure 2023, Ixlú, Guatemala (c). Modified from Duncan 2011.

Fig. 12.4. Postcranium with long bone bundle from Structure 2023, Ixlú, Guatemala. Photo by William Duncan.

The skulls for which age and sex could be assessed and determined were late adolescent (n = 4) and adult (n = 14) males (n = 11) (Duncan 2011). A number of factors suggest that these individuals were most likely captured and sacrificed in events to dedicate two construction phases of the temple. These include the demography of the assemblage, the absence of grave goods, the mortuary treatment of the remains, and the fact that articulated cervical vertebrae are present in 16 of the skulls (Duncan 2011). In the first episode, Skulls 3, 4, 5, and 6 were buried on top of an older plaza floor and under the platform of the temple (Fig. 12.2). The remaining skulls were buried in the platform and were associated with the altars on top of the platform and on the eastern side of the platform in the second event.

## Intracemetery Biodistance Analysis

Biodistance studies have a long history in physical anthropology, using both osteodental metric and nonmetric traits, but most studies have focused on intercemetery or population levels of analysis (see Larsen 1997 for an extensive list of examples). In Mesoamerica biodistance analysis has been applied successfully in central Mexico (Aubry 2008; Christensen 1997, 1998a, 1998b; Walker 2006) and in the Maya area for both archaeological (Austin 1978; Jacobi 2000; Lang 1990; Scherer 2007; Wrobel 2004) and living populations (for trait frequencies, see Escobar, Connelly, and Lopez 1977; and Escobar, Melnick, and Connelly 1976).

Researchers have recently begun to pay attention to smaller-scale analysis that looks at data within sites and cemeteries as well as between individuals in a single context. Like other biodistance analyses, intracemetery analyses are ultimately based on the idea that people who are related are more likely to be phenotypically similar to one another than people who are not related. This idea is based on a considerable body of literature that includes work with animals (e.g., Grüneberg 1950), twin studies (e.g., Biggerstaff 1973), and pedigree studies among living human populations (e.g., Harris and Bailit 1980). Because it is not possible to use craniometrics with the sample from Structure 2023, I used dental morphology. This methodology poses a particular set of questions, namely whether dental morphology exhibits sufficient resolution to differentiate small-scale phenetic distinctions and evolutionary processes (Dudar 2005; Scott and Turner 1997). Comparing dental and genetic data from living populations highlights the potential for future work and the limitations of the current work. Among the Yanomamo, Brewer-Carias et al. (1976) found that relationships calculated on the basis of genetic and dental matrices data were generally in accord with one another, which supported the findings of anthropometric analysis (Spielman 1973). However, Palomino et al. (1977) found lower correlations on an intratribal level than Brewer-Carias and colleagues did. Similarly, Harris (1977) compared distances generated by dental traits and other markers among Solomon Islanders and found that dental morphology reflected subpopulation divisions less accurately than other biological markers. McClelland (2003) found that intrasite biological distances generally supported conclusions suggested by isotopic analysis. Thus there are still outstanding questions to be resolved in order to apply biodistance analysis on an intrapopulation level. At what kinship level does dental morphology lose sensitivity for assessing biological distances? How do we interpret distances based on dental morphology in terms of actual lineal or collateral kinship categories?

Even with these problems, it is clear that intracemetery studies have proven useful for shedding light on questions in a number of archaeological contexts. Stojanowski and Schillaci (2006; also see Buikstra,

Frankenberg, and Konigsberg 1990) provide a recent comprehensive review of the history and current state of intracemetery analysis, noting that most studies fall into one of five categories: postmarital residence (Lane and Sublett 1972; Schillaci and Stojanowski 2003; Spence 1974; Tomczak and Powell 2003); assessments of cemetery structure to identify evidence of kinship on varying levels (Alt, Pichler, and Vach 1995; Alt et al. 1997; Alt and Vach 1991, 1995a, 1995b, 1998; Bondioli, Corruccini, and Macchiarelli 1986; Case 2003; Česnys and Tutkuvienė 2007; Corruccini and Shimada 2002; Dudar, Waye, and Saunders 2003; Howell and Kintigh 1996; Rösing 1986; Sjøvold 1976; Spence 1996; Usher and Allen 2005; Velemínský and Dobisíková 2005); assessments of aggregate phenotypic variability (Stojanowski 2003b, 2005a, 2005b); time-structured variability (Konigsberg 1990; Owsley, Bennett, and Jantz 1982; Owsley and Jantz 1978; Stojanowski 2003a); and age-structured variability (Stojanowski and Schillaci 2006). Researchers have conducted small-scale analyses in central Mexico (Spence 1974) and in the Maya area (Hammond, Pretty, and Saul 1975; Jacobi 2000; Rhoads 2002) to consider whether biological variability is related to mortuary patterns. Although Ugalde Morales and Pompa Padilla (2003) considered developmental defects in one skull rack and Whittington (1999) noted that data on nonmetric cranial traits were collected at Iximché, other analysis of kinship in skull deposits has not been done in Mesoamerica.

## Present Objectives

Authors have used a variety of methods in intracemetery research, but these methods tend to reflect the nature of the sample, specifically whether they are small graves or spatially structured (Stojanowski and Schillaci 2006). Small-sample biodistance analyses typically either use rare traits (Alt, Pichler, and Vach 1995; Alt et al. 1997; Alt and Türp 1998; Alt and Vach 1991, 1992, 1995a, 1995b; Gejvall and Henschen 1968; Sjøvold 1975, 1976) or Q mode analyses of metric data (Adachi et al. 2003; Adachi et al. 2006) to consider biological relationships between individuals (Stojanowski and Schillaci 2006). Analysis of structured cemeteries has typically focused on comparing variability within and between previously defined subgroups and/or among all of the individuals buried in a cemetery. Metric data are analyzed using the mean measure of divergence (Birkby 1982) or discriminant function (Bartel 1979; Gao and Lee 1993) or by calculating Euclidean distances between individuals (Bondioli, Coruccini, and Macchiarelli 1986; Corruccini and Shimada 2002). Nonmetric data are frequently dichotomized and analyzed as a chi square (Rubini 1996; Strouhal and Jungwirth 1979) or by comparing Jaccard coefficients (Spence 1974). This study presents an interesting case because of the size, structure, and state of preservation of the sample and the potential for comparative analysis. Craniometric data were not desirable due to the poor state of preservation of the crania in the sample. In addition, there is no usable contemporaneous "normal" burial set to which one might compare the skulls. However, the deposits are spatially and temporally structured. Calculating chi squares variable by variable to compare mortuary and phenotypic variability after dichotomization was not desirable because that process requires considerable Bonferroni adjustment and because cells with fewer than five are common in this data set. Jaccard coefficients present an alternative to this. A third option is to retain rank-order data to identify patterns in variation that may remain hidden when categorical data are used.

## Materials and Methods

I scored 61 traits from the Arizona State University Dental Anthropology System (ASUDAS) (Turner, Nichol, and Scott 1991) and noted the presence or absence of hyperdontia on 17 individuals in the skull deposits. I included five of the individuals from the skull pairs and 12 from the skull rows. Other rare traits described by Alt and Türp (1998) that do not overlap with the ASU system, such as malocclusion and discrete osteological traits or other rare dental traits, were generally not observable or not present. I determined the maximum score of the trait per individual and calculated a Kendall tau to identify significantly correlated variables.

I subjected the remaining data traits to two types of analysis—calculations of Jaccard coefficients and interindividual Euclidean distances—which I then ranked and considered in a chi-square analysis. The Jaccard coefficient of similarity considers similarity between sets of dichotomous data by comparing the number of similar scores to the total number of potential matches on an individual-by-individual basis. Absence of a trait in both individuals (double zeros) is not scored, unlike simple matching coefficients (Sokal and Sneath 1963). Spence (1974) considers Jaccard coefficients by partitioning them in terms of the Triangular Cumulative Similarity (TCS) and Square Cumulative Similarity (SCS). The former is a measure of within-group similarity, the latter a measure of between-group similarity. So for this sample, if the row and pair TCS scores are higher than the SCS score (which compares the similarity between rows and pairs), then it would suggest greater similarity within groups than between them. This would suggest that phenetic similarity is reflected in mortuary patterning and that the decision to place individuals in either rows or pairs reflects kinship. The same kind of partitioning is calculated for interment events.

Another option is to calculate interindividual Euclidean distances and then rank them to see if the smaller distances are within groups. Missing data for the remaining traits were imputed with the mode score for the respective traits. I performed a principal components analysis (PCA) on the data using PASW 17 (SPSS Inc. 2009) and extracted all of the components. Goodman (1973) has shown that by dividing the component scores for each individual by the square root of the respective eigenvalues, one can scale the scores appropriately, thereby making the new axes equal in length. I then calculated the interindividual Euclidean distances from the scaled scores. These distances were then ranked (because distances are nonparametric) (Bondioli, Corruccini, and Macchiarelli 1986), and partitioned to consider patterns of variation relative to mortuary treatment and episode of deposition. I calculated a chi square to test if the within-group distances were in fact the smallest distances (ibid.). There was a total of 136 interindividual distances. I performed a chi-square test to determine if the 76 within-group distances for rows and pairs were the smallest. Another chi-square test was performed to determine which 42 within-group distances for the first and second episodes of deposition were the smallest. It should be noted that the use of Q mode correlation coefficients has been criticized in some contexts on mathematical grounds (Corruccini 1985; Legendre and Legendre 1998), though it has been employed usefully in other biological distance analyses for pattern recognition rather than for formal parametric testing (Adachi et al. 2003; Adachi et al. 2006; Matsumura and Hudson 2005; Matsumura et al. 2006). Finally, I used clinical data to test significant frequencies of rare traits among the individuals.

## Results

Traits were scored twice on 12 individuals to check for intraobserver error, which was similar to that reported by Nichol and Turner (1986). Traits were scored in only one of two sessions in 6.29 percent of the comparisons and had a discrepancy of one grade or more than one grade between sessions in 11.2 percent and 3.93 percent of the comparisons, respectively. A Kendall tau found significant relationships between cusp number and cusp 6 for the mandibular first molar ($tau = .529$, $p = .029$) and the mandibular second molar ($tau = .619$, $p = .008$) as well as the $M_1$ and $M_2$ protostylids ($tau = .663$, $p = .005$). After deleting traits for these reasons and reasons mentioned above, seven traits remained: the number of roots for the maxillary third premolar ($P^3$), the metacone and cusp 5 of the maxillary second molar ($M^2$), the cusp number and protostylid of the mandibular first molar ($M_1$), and cusp number of the mandibular second molars ($M_2$) and supernumerary teeth. Break points for dichotomization were similar to those used by Scherer (2004).

There is considerable similarity among the TCS scores (Table 12.1), with the exception of the crania in pairs and the crania that were deposited first, which likely is due to small sample size. The SCS scores are slightly smaller than the overall TCS scores. This may reflect greater within-group homogeneity, but it is more likely that having fewer comparisons resulted in more similarity. Spence (1974) notes that this is a common problem with Jaccard coefficients. Thus, analysis of the traits in a dichotomous

Table 12.1. Triangular cumulative similarity (TCS) and square cumulative similarity (SCS) scores from the skull rows and pairs from Structure 2023, Ixlú, Guatemala

| | TCS | | | SCS | |
|---|---|---|---|---|---|
| | N/Total | % | | N/Total | % |
| All skulls | 119/389 | 30.6 | Pairs versus rows | 41/153 | 26.8 |
| Pairs | 3/18 | 16.7 | 1st deposition compared to | | |
| Rows | 116/371 | 31.3 | 2nd deposition[1] | 43/165 | 26.1 |
| 1st deposition | 1/5 | 20.0 | | | |
| 2nd deposition | 118/384 | 30.7 | | | |

1. This SCS compares scores for individuals in the first episode of deposition to the individuals in the second episode. The numerator reflects the number of times two individuals had the same score. The denominator reflects the total number of comparisons.

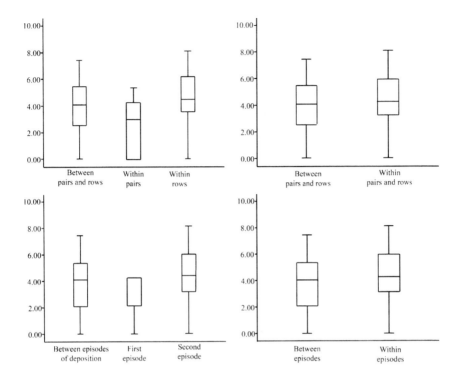

Fig. 12.5. Partitioned Euclidean distances from skull burials in Structure 2023, Ixlú, Guatemala.

fashion provides no clear evidence of increased phenotypic similarity among individuals who received similar mortuary treatment or who were interred at a similar time.

Euclidean distances, which were partitioned as described above (Fig. 12.5), show no evidence that within-group distances were smaller than between-group distances. The small box and whisker plot for the within-group variation for the first episode of deposition reflects the small sample size. When the distances are ranked and tested in chi squares to determine if the within-group distances are the smallest for both mortuary treatment and time of interment, none of the tests are significant at a .05 level (pairs and rows Yates's correction $x^2 = 0.08$, df = 1, Yates's p-value = 0.777; episodes of deposition Yates's correction $x^2 = 0.006$, df = 1, Yates's p-value = 0.938).

Three crania (1, 7, and 16) exhibited supernumerary mandibular premolars, and individuals 1 and 7 exhibited them bilaterally (Fig. 12.6). Individual 1 exhibited supernumerary teeth between the $P_4$ and $M_1$. Both supernumerary teeth were lingual to the tooth row. The left was tuberculate, while the right was conical. Individual 7 exhibited a left supernumerary tooth lingual to $P_3$ that displaced the latter buccally. The extra tooth was molariform, exhibited 5 cusps, and had a distinct talonid. The right supernumerary tooth was tuberculate, had a single primary cusp and a distal accessory cusp, and was found between $P_3$ and $P_4$. Skull 16 exhibited a supernumerary tooth between $P_3$ and $P_4$ on the right side. It was tuberculate with a larger buccal cusp and two accessory lingual cusps. All of the teeth were assessed visually (see Duncan 2009 for more description).

There is no current reason to think that Mesoamerican populations, specifically Maya populations, have elevated frequencies of hyperdontia. In a review of the literature, I found estimates of hyperdontia that ranged from 0.1 percent to 3.6 percent, and I estimate the odds of finding supernumerary premolars to be no higher than 1 in 625 (Duncan 2009). The calculation of the likelihood that three individuals would exhibit this trait (even without accounting for bilaterality) is statistically significant (0.02 percent) (Duncan 2009).

## Discussion and Conclusion

Skulls have long been a source of fascination in Mesoamerica. Europeans reported skull racks with over 130,000 skulls (Durán 1971) and roads that were paved with the skulls of enemies in Mesoamerica (Mendoza 2007). Skulls are frequently referred to in indigenous literature (Miller 1999, 2007), in indigenous iconography (Moser 1973; Vail and Hernández 2007), and in indigenous languages and metaphors (Carlsen and Prechtel 1991). Skulls were burned (Alonso et al. 2002; Kelley 1978; Pijoan Aguadé 1981), plastered (Robicsek 1991), painted (Eckholm 1942; Lister 1955), and carved (Harrison-Buck, McAnany, and Storey 2007; Robicsek 1991). They were used to honor ancestors and targeted to violate enemies. To this end trophy skulls were displayed in a variety of ways, including burying them in rows, burying them collectively in a single deposit (Barrett and Scherer 2005; Massey 1989), burying individual skulls adjacent to one another in separate pits (Whittington 2003) and in vessels (Drucker 1943), and displaying them on racks and as mobiles (Hers 1989; Kelley 1978; Martin,

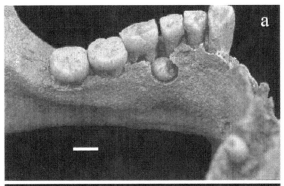

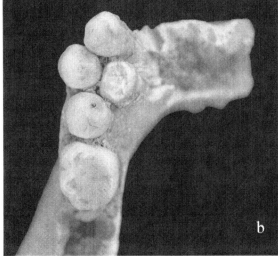

Fig. 12.6. Supernumerary teeth from Individuals 1 (a), and 7 (b), from Structure 2023, Ixlú, Guatemala. Modified from Duncan 2009, 2011; scale 5mm.

Nelson, and Pérez 2004; Pickering 1985; Pijoan Aguadé and Lory 1997; Sanchez Saldaña 1972; Wilkinson 1997). In addition, the head was the seat of animating essences associated with personhood among the Maya (*baah*; Houston, Stuart, and Taube 2006, 60–68) and of individual destiny among the Aztecs (López Austin 1988, 204). Despite the omnipresence of skulls in Mesoamerican indigenous cultures, there has been little consideration of biodistance among skull deposits in the region.

This study has implications for our understanding of who was being sacrificed prior to contact in Postclassic Petén and for our understanding of skull deposits in Mesoamerica in general. As noted above, the individuals in the skull rows and skull pairs were most likely sacrificial victims who had been captured as a part of the internecine raiding that helped define the relationships between the Itzá and the Kowoj. The presence of hyperdontia in three crania indicates that at least those individuals were related to one another and suggests that at least they were most likely part of a lineage or other corporate group who were captured during battle or raiding. Future studies of skull deposits in Mesoamerica should consider biodistance analysis to determine if other victims of ritual violence were selected on the basis of kinship.

The Ixlú skull deposits also highlight both the strength and weakness of intracemetery biological distance analysis. Clearly finding three individuals with nonsyndromic supernumerary teeth is not a random phenomenon, and it is reasonable to interpret the results as reflecting membership in a corporate group because we know the Maya had such social groups. However, beyond that, there is currently no way to connect presence of a rare trait among three individuals or intrasite biological distance patterns to any specific emically recognized kinship categories. This, of course, will continue to be a problem across cultures because there are no universal cultural kinship categories. However, future work may be able to build on recent efforts (Adachi et al. 2003; Adachi et al. 2006; Matsumura and Hudson 2005; Matsumura, Hudson, Koshida, and Minakawa 2006) to connect correlations of biological features to kinship categories within specific cultural contexts.

A second issue that future studies may resolve is the absence of standard methodology when confronted with small sample sizes (see Petersen 2000). In this study, dichotomized and rank-order data yielded similar results, but future studies will assess how often and under what circumstances retaining rank-order data is useful when considering kinship in small cemetery contexts.

Finally, and perhaps most important, this study highlights the fact that we cannot know if the absence of significant biological patterns within the whole sample is actually due to a lack of patterning among the crania or if the variation of the dental traits in question simply lack sufficient sensitivity to identify hidden, meaningful patterns within the sample . Dental traits' sensitivity for discerning intrapopulation patterns is likely population specific, and thus this will continue to be an issue for intracemetery analyses in the immediate future. That said, as researchers (e.g., Kavanagh, Evans, and Jernvall 2007; Smith et al. 2009; Townsend et al. 2009) make progress toward greater understanding of the connections between genetics, development, and dental morphology, we may be able to identify other ways to analyze traditional dental traits or other phenotypic characteristics that reflect genetic relationships within populations with greater sensitivity.

## Acknowledgments

I would like to thank the editors for inviting me to participate in this volume and Drs. Robert S. Corruccini, Christopher Stojanowski, and Prudence Rice for their long-term (and continuing) support for this project. All of the members of Proyecto Maya Colonial and the faculty and students of CUDEP in Guatemala, notably Lics. Romulo Sánchez Polo, Ivo Romero, and Mara Reyes, made valuable contributions to this project, for which I am truly grateful. This project would not have been possible without cooperation from members of IDAEH in Guatemala, in particular Lics. Boris Aguilar and Sheila Flores. Carmen Arendt and Felix Duncan provided much-valued listening, feedback, and support while I was writing this manuscript. Funding was provided in part by NSF Doctoral Dissertation Improvement Grant BCS 0125311 and a travel grant from St. John Fisher College. Although the efforts of the aforementioned people improved this manuscript considerably, any remaining errors are solely mine.

## References Cited

Adachi, N., Y. Dodo, N. Ohshima, N. Doi, M. Yoneda, and H. Matsumara
2003    Morphologic and Genetic Evidence for the Kinship of Juvenile Skeletal Specimens from a 2,000-Year-Old Double Burial of the Usu-Moshiri Site, Hokkaido, Japan. *Anthropological Science* 111: 347–363.
Adachi, N., T. Suzuki, K. Sakaue, W. Takigawa, N. Ohshima, and Y. Dodo
2006    Kinship Analysis of the Jomon Skeletons Unearthed from a Double Burial at the Usu-Moshiri Site, Hokkaido, Japan. *Anthropological Science* 114: 29–34.
Alonso, S. L., Z. L. Rodríguez, and C. S. Sánchez
2002    *Costumbres Funerarias y Sacrificio Humano en Cholula Prehispánica*. Instituto de Investigaciones Antropológicas, Universidad Nacional Autónoma de México, México, D.F.
Alt, K. W., S. Pichler, and W. Vach
1995    Familial Relationships of Inhabitants of a Late-Roman Villa Rustica. In *Forensic Odontology and Anthropology*, edited by B. Jacob and W. Bonte, pp. 263–67. Vol. 7 of *Advances in Forensic Sciences*. Köster, Berlin.
Alt, K. W., S. Pichler, W. Vach, B. Klima, E. Vliek, and J. Sedlmeier
1997    Twenty-Five-Thousand-Year-Old Triple Burial from Dolní Věstonice: An Ice-Age Family? *American Journal of Physical Anthropology* 102: 123–131.

Alt, K. W., and J. C. Türp

1998    Hereditary Dental Anomalies. In *Dental Anthropology: Fundamentals, Limits, and Prospects,* edited by K. W. Alt, Friedrich W. Rösing, and Maria Teschler-Nicola , pp. 95–128. Springer, New York.

Alt, K. W., and W. Vach

1991    The Reconstruction of "Genetic Kinship" in Prehistoric Burial Complexes: Problems and Statistics. In *Classification, Data Analysis, and Knowledge Organization,* edited by H. H. Bock and P. Ihm, pp. 299–310. Springer Verlag, New York.

1992    Non-Spatial Analysis of "Genetic Kinship" in Skeletal Remains. In *Analysis and Modeling Data and Knowledge,* edited by M. Schader, pp. 247–256. Springer Verlag, Berlin.

1995a   Detection of Kinship Structures in Skeletal Remains. In *Forensic Odontology and Anthropology,* edited by B. Jacob and W. Bonte, pp. 27–34.Vol. 7 of *Advances in Forensic Sciences.* Köster, Berlin.

1995b   Odontologic Kinship Analysis in Skeletal Remains: Concepts, Methods, and Results. *Forensic Science International* 74: 99–113.

1998    Kinship Studies in Skeletal Remains—Concepts and Examples. In *Dental Anthropology: Fundamentals, Limits, and Prospects,* edited by K. W. Alt, Friedrich W. Rösing, and Maria Teschler-Nicola, pp. 537–554. Springer, New York.

Andrushko, V. A., K. A. S. Latham, D. L. Grady, A. G. Pastron, and P. L. Walker

2005    Bioarchaeological Evidence for Trophy-Taking in Prehistoric Central California. *American Journal of Physical Anthropology* 127(4): 375–384.

Andrushko, V. A., A. W. Schwitalla, and P. L. Walker

2010    Trophy-Taking and Dismemberment as Warfare Strategies in Prehistoric Central California. *American Journal of Physical Anthropology* 141(1): 83–96.

Aubry, B. S.

2008    Dental Biodistance Analysis and Evidence for Interregional Interaction in Pre-Contact Mesoamerican. *American Journal of Physical Anthropology* Supplemental 46: 61–62.

Austin, D.

1978    The Biological Affinity of the Ancient Populations of Altar de Sacrificios and Seibal. *Estudios de Cultura Maya* 11: 57–73.

Barrett, J. W., and A. K. Scherer

2005    Stones, Bones, and Crowded Plazas: Evidence for Terminal Classic Maya Warfare at Colha, Belize. *Ancient Mesoamerica* 16: 101–118.

Bartel, B.

1979    A Discriminant Analysis of Harappan Civilization Human Populations. *Journal of Archaeological Science* 6: 49–61.

Biggerstaff, R.

1973    Heritability of the Carabelli Cusp in Twins. *Journal of Dental Research* 52: 40–44.

Birkby, W. H.

1982    Biosocial Interpretations from Cranial Non-Metric Traits of Grasshopper Pueblo Skeletal Remains. In *Multidisciplinary Research at Grasshopper Pueblo Arizona,* edited by W. A. Longacre, S. J. Holbrook, and M. W. Graves, pp. 36–41. Anthropological Papers of the University of Arizona no. 40. University of Arizona Press, Tucson.

Bondioli, L., R. S. Corruccini, and R. Macchiarelli

1986    Familial Segregation in the Iron Age Community of Alfedena, Abruzzo, Italy Based on Osteodental Trait Analysis. *American Journal of Physical Anthropology* 71: 393–400.

Brace, C. L., D. P. Tracer, L. A. Yaroch, J. E. Robb, K. Brandt, and R. Nelson

1993    Clines and Clusters Versus "Race": A Test in Ancient Egypt and the Case of a Death on the Nile. *American Journal of Physical Anthropology* 36: 1–31.

Brewer-Carias, C., S. Le Blanc, and J. V. Neel

1976    Genetic Structure of a Tribal Population, the Yanomama Indians: XIII. Dental Microdifferentiation. *American Journal of Physical Anthropology* 44: 5–14.

Buikstra, J., S. R. Frankenberg, and L. W. Konigsberg

1990    Skeletal Biological Distance Studies in American Physical Anthropology: Recent Trends. *American Journal of Physical Anthropology* 82: 1–7.

Carlsen, R., and M. Prechtel

1991    The Flowering of the Dead: An Interpretation of Highland Maya Culture. *Man,* n.s. 26(1): 23–42.

Case, D. T.

2003    Who's Related to Whom? Skeletal Kinship Analysis in Medieval Danish Cemeteries. Ph.D. dissertation, Arizona State University.

Česnys, G., and J. Tutkuvienė

2007    Topographical Approach to Kinship Assessment within Population According to Discrete Cranial Traits: The 5th–6th cc. Plinkaigalis Cemetery. *Acta Medica Lituanica* 14(1): 7–16.

Chacon, R. J., and D. H. Dye (editors)

2007    *The Taking and Displaying of Human Body Parts as Trophies by Amerindians.* Springer Science and Business Media, New York.

Chacon, R. J., and R. G. Mendoza (editors)

2007a    *Latin American Indigenous Warfare and Ritual Violence.* University of Arizona Press, Tucson.

2007b    *North American Indigenous Warfare and Ritual Violence.* University of Arizona Press, Tucson.

Chen, J., and R. R. Sokal

1995    Worldwide Analysis of Genetic and Linguistic Relationships of Human Populations. *Human Biology* 67(4): 595–612.

Christensen, A. F.

1997    Cranial Non-Metric Variation in North and Central Mexico. *Anthropologischer Anzeiger* 55: 15–32.

1998a    Colonization and Microevolution in Formative Oaxaca, Mexico. *World Archaeology* 30: 262–285.

1998b    Skeletal Evidence for Familial Interments in the Valley of Oaxaca, Mexico. *Journal of Human Evolution* 34: 333–360.

Corruccini, R. S.

1985    Incorrect Size Correction. *American Journal of Physical Anthropology* 66: 91–92.

Corruccini, R. S., and I. Shimada

2002    Dental Relatedness Corresponding to Mortuary Patterning at Huaca Loro, Peru. *American Journal of Physical Anthropology* 117: 113–121.

Drucker, P.

1943    *Ceramic Stratigraphy at Cerro de las Mesas, Veracruz, Mexico.* Bureau of American Ethnology Bulletin no. 141. Government Printing Office, Washington, D.C.

Dudar, J. C.

2005    Comment on Sutter and Cortez. *Current Anthropology* 46: 536–537.

Dudar, J. C., J. S. Waye, and S. R. Saunders

2003    Determination of a Kinship System Using Ancient DNA, Mortuary Practice, and Historic Records in an Upper Canadian Pioneer Cemetery. *International Journal of Osteoarchaeology* 13: 232–246.

Duncan, W. N.

2005    The Bioarchaeology of Ritual Violence in Postclassic El Petén, Guatemala (AD 950–1524). Ph.D. dissertation, Southern Illinois University.

2009    Supernumerary Teeth from Two Mesoamerican Archaeological Contexts. *Dental Anthropology* 22: 39–46.

2011    Bioarchaeological Analysis of Sacrificial Victims from a Postclassic Maya Temple from Ixlú, El Petén, Guatemala. *Latin American Antiquity* 22(4) 549–572.

Durán, D.

1971    *Book of the Gods and Rites of the Ancient Calendar.* Translated by D. Heyden and F. Horcasitas. University of Oklahoma Press, Norman.

Eckholm, G. A.

1942    *Excavations at Guasave, Sinaloa, Mexico.* Anthropological Papers no. 38. American Museum of Natural History, New York.

Edgar, H. J. H., and K. Hunley

2009    Race Reconciled? How Biological Anthropologists View Human Variation. *American Journal of Physical Anthropology* 139: 1–4.

Eeckhout, P., and L. S. Owens

2008    Human Sacrifice at Pachacamac. *Latin American Antiquity* 19: 375–398.

Escobar, V., P. M. Connelly, and C. Lopez

1977    The Dentition of the Queckchi Indians: Anthropological Aspects. *American Journal of Physical Anthropology* 47: 443–452.

Escobar, V., M. Melnick, and P. M. Connelly

1976    The Inheritance of Bilateral Rotation of Maxillary Central Incisors. *American Journal of Physical Anthropology* 45: 109–116.

Gao, Q., and Y. K. Lee
1993    A Biological Perspective on Yangshao Kinship. *Journal of Anthropological Archaeology* 12: 266–298.

Gejvall, N. G., and F. Henschen
1968    Two Late Roman Skeletons with Malformation and Close Family Relationship from Ancient Corinth. *Opuscula Athenia* 8: 179–193.

Goodman, M.
1973    Genetic Distances: Measuring Dissimilarity among Populations. *Yearbook of Physical Anthropology* 17: 1–38.

Grüneberg, H.
1950    Genetical Studies on the Skeleton of the Mouse. *Journal of Genetics* 50: 112–141.

Hammond, N., K. Pretty, and F. P. Saul
1975    A Classic Maya Family Tomb. *World Archaeology* 7: 57–78.

Harris, E. F.
1977    Anthropologic and Genetic Aspects of the Dental Morphology of Solomon Islanders, Melanesia. Ph.D. dissertation, Arizona State University.

Harris, E. F., and H. L. Bailit
1980    The Metaconule: A Morphologic and Familial Analysis of a Molar Cusp in Humans. *American Journal of Physical Anthropology* 53: 349–358.

Harrison-Buck, E., P. A. McAnany, and R. Storey
2007    Empowered and Disempowered during the Late to Terminal Classic Transition: Maya Burial and Termination Rituals in the Sibun Valley, Belize. In *New Perspectives on Human Sacrifice and Ritual Body Treatments in Ancient Maya Society*, edited by V. Tiesler and A. Cucina, pp. 74–101. Springer, New York.

Hers, M. A.
1989    *Los Toltecas en Tierras Chichimecas*. Universidad Nacional Autónoma de México, México, D.F.

Hofling, A.
2009    The Linguistic Context of the Kowoj. In *Identity, Migration, and Geopolitics: The Kowoj in Late Postclassic Petén, Guatemala*, edited by P. M. Rice and D. S. Rice, pp. 70–80. University of Colorado Press, Boulder.

Houston, Stephen, David Stuart, and Karl Taube
2006    *The Memory of Bones: Body, Being, and Experience among the Classic Maya*. University of Texas Press, Austin.

Howell, T. L., and K. W. Kintigh
1996    Archaeological Identification of Kin Groups using Mortuary and Biological Data: An Example from the American Southwest. *American Antiquity* 61: 537–554.

Jacobi, K.
2000    *Last Rites for the Tipu Maya: Genetic Structuring in a Colonial Cemetery*. University of Alabama Press, Tuscaloosa.

Jones, G.
1998    *The Conquest of the Last Maya Kingdom*. Stanford University Press, Stanford, Calif.

Kavanagh, K. D., A. R. Evans, and J. Jernvall
2007    Predicting Evolutionary Patterns of Mammalian Teeth from Development. *Nature* 449: 427–449.

Kelley, E. A.
1978    The Temple of the Skulls at Alta Vista, Chalchihuites. In *Across the Chichimec Sea: Papers in Honor of J. Charles Kelley,* edited by C. L. Riley and B. C. Hedrick, pp. 102–126. Southern Illinois University Press, Carbondale.

Knüsel, C. J.
2010    Courteous Knights, Holy Blissful Martyrs, and Cruel Avengers: A Consideration of the Changing Social Milieu of Medieval Warfare from the Perspective of Human Remains. *American Journal of Physical Anthropology* 141(S50): 146.

Konigsberg, L. W.
1990    Analysis of Prehistoric Biological Variation under a Model of Isolation by Geographic and Temporal Distance. *Human Biology* 62: 49–70.

Lai, S.
2001    Opinion: HLA-DRB Alleles Polymorphism in Four Ethnic Populations in Northwestern China. *Clinica Chimica Acta* 313: 3–7.

Lane, R., and A. J. Sublett
1972    Osteology of Social Organization: Residence Pattern. *American Antiquity* 37: 186–201.

Lang, C. A.
1990    The Dental Morphology of the Ancient Maya from Lamanai and Tipu, Belize: A Study of Population Movement. M.A. thesis, Trent University.

Larsen, C. S.
1997    *Bioarchaeology: Interpreting Behavior from the Human Skeleton.* Cambridge University Press, Cambridge.

Legendre, P., and L. Legendre
1998    *Numerical Ecology.* 2nd ed. Elsevier Science, Amsterdam.

Lister, R. H.
1955    *The Present Status of the Archaeology of Western Mexico: A Distributional Study.* University of Colorado Studies Series in Anthropology no. 5. University of Colorado Press, Boulder.

López Austin, Alfonso
1988    *The Human Body and Ideology: Concepts of the Ancient Nahuas.* University of Utah Press, Salt Lake City.

Martin, D. L., B. A. Nelson, and V. R. Pérez
2004    Patrones de Modificacion en Huesos Humanos de La Quemada, Zacatecas: Hallazgos Preliminares. In *Perspectiva Taphonómica,* edited by C. M. Pijoan Aguadé and X. L. Cruchaga, pp. 155–172. Serie Antropología Fisica. Instituto Nacional de Antropología e Historia, México, D.F.

Massey, V. K.
1989    *The Human Skeletal Remains from a Terminal Classic Skull Pit at Colha, Belize.* Papers of the Colha Project, Vol. 3. Texas A&M University, College Station.

Matsumura, H., and M. J. Hudson
2005    Dental Perspectives on the Population History of Southeast Asia. *American Journal of Physical Anthropology* 127: 182–209.
Matsumura, H., M. J. Hudson, K. Koshida, and Y. Minakawa
2006    Embodying Okhotsk Ethnicity: Human Skeletal Remains from the Aonae Dune Site, Okushiri Island, Hokkaido. *Asian Perspectives* 45: 1–23.
McClelland, J. A.
2003    Refining the Resolution of Biological Distance Studies Based on the Analysis of Dental Morphology: Detecting Subpopulations at Grasshopper Pueblo. Ph.D. dissertation, University of Arizona.
Mendoza, R. G.
2007    The Divine Gourd Tree: Tzompantli Skull Racks, Decapitation Rituals, and Human Trophies in Ancient Mesoamerica. In *The Taking and Displaying of Human Body Parts as Trophies by Amerindians,* edited by R. J. Chacon and D. H. Dye, pp. 400–443. Springer, New York.
Miller, V.
1999    The Skull Rack in Mesoamerica. In *Mesoamerican Architecture as a Cultural Symbol,* edited by J. Kowalski, pp. 341–360. Oxford University Press, New York.
2007    Skeletons, Skulls, and Bones in the Art of Chichen Itzá. In *New Perspectives on Human Sacrifice and Ritual Body Treatments in Ancient Maya Society,* edited by V. Tiesler and A. Cucina, pp. 165–189. Springer, New York.
Moser, C. M.
1973    *Human Decapitation in Ancient Mesoamerica.* Studies in Pre-Columbian Art and Archaeology no. 11. Dumbarton Oaks, Washington, D.C.
Nichol, C. R., and C. G. Turner II
1986    Intra- and Interobserver Concordance in Classifying Dental Morphology. *American Journal of Physical Anthropology* 69: 299–315.
Owsley, D. W., S. M. Bennett, and R. L. Jantz
1982    Intercemetery Morphological Variation in Arikara Crania from the Mobridge Site (39WW1). *American Journal of Physical Anthropology* 58: 179–185.
Owsley, D. W., and R. L. Jantz
1978    Intracemetery Morphological Variation in Arikara Crania from the Sully Site (39SL4), Sully County, South Dakota. *Plains Anthropologist* 23: 139–146.
Palomino, H., R. Chakraborty, and F. Rothhammer
1977    Dental Morphology and Population Diversity. *Human Biology* 49: 61–70.
Petersen, H. C.
2000    On Statistical Methods for Comparison of Intrasample Morphometric Variability: Zalavar Revisited. *American Journal of Physical Anthropology* 113: 79–84.
Pickering, R. B.
1985    Human Osteological Remains from Alta Vista, Zacatecas: An Analysis of the Isolated Bone. In *The Archaeology of West and Northwest Mesoamerica,* edited by M. S. Foster and P. C. Weigand, pp. 289–326. Westview Press, Boulder.

Pijoan Aguadé, C. M.

1981    *Evidencias Rituals en Restos Oseos.* Instituto Nacional de Antropología e Histo-
        ria, México, D.F.

Pijoan Aguadé, C. M., and J. M. Lory

1997    Evidence of Human Sacrifice, Bone Modification and Cannibalism in Ancient
        Mexico. In *Troubled Times: Violence and Warfare in the Past,* edited by D. L.
        Martin and D. W. Frayer, pp. 217–239. Gordon and Breach, Amsterdam.

Rhoads, M.

2002    Population Dynamics at the Southern Periphery of the Ancient Maya World:
        Kinship at Copán. Ph.D. dissertation, University of New Mexico.

Rice, P. M., and D. S. Rice (editors)

2009    *Identity, Migration, and Geopolitics: The Kowoj in Late Postclassic Petén, Guate-
        mala.* University of Colorado Press, Boulder.

Robicsek, F.

1991    Three Decorated Skulls Found in the Maya Area. *Mexcion* 13(4): 65–69.

Rösing, F. W.

1986    Kith or Kin? On the Feasibility of Kinship Reconstruction in Skeletons. In *Sci-
        ence in Egyptology,* edited by A. R. David, pp. 223–237. Manchester University
        Press, Manchester.

Rubini, M.

1996    Biological Homogeneity and Familial Segregation in the Iron Age Population
        of Alfedena (Abruzzo, Italy), Based on Cranial Discrete Traits Analysis. *Inter-
        national Journal of Osteoarchaeology* 6: 454–462.

Sanchez Saldaña, P.

1972    El tzompantli de Tlatelolco. In *Religion en Mesoamerica: XII Mesa Redonda,*
        edited by J. L. King and N. C. Tejero, pp. 387–392. Sociedad Mexicana de An-
        thropología, México, D.F.

Scherer, A. K.

2004    Dental Analysis of Classic Period Population Variability in the Maya Area.
        Ph.D. dissertation, Texas A&M University.

2007    Population Structure of the Classic Period Maya. *American Journal of Physical
        Anthropology* 132: 367–380.

Schillaci, M. A., and C. M. Stojanowski

2003    Postmarital Residence and Biological Variation at Pueblo Bonito. *American
        Journal of Physical Anthropology* 120: 1–15.

Scott, G. R., and C. G. Turner, II

1997    *The Anthropology of Modern Human Teeth: Dental Morphology and Its Variation
        in Recent Human Populations.* Cambridge University Press, Cambridge.

Simmons, R. T., D. C. Gajdusek, and M. K. Nicholson

1967    Blood Group Genetic Variations in Inhabitants of West New Guinea, with a
        Map of the Villages and Linguistic Groups of South West New Guinea. *Ameri-
        can Journal of Physical Anthropology* 27: 277–302.

Sjøvold, T. A.

1975 Allocation of Single or Some Few Individuals to One of Two or More Groups by Means of Non-Metrical Variants in the Skeleton. *Osaa* 2: 41–46.

1976 A Method for Familial Studies Based on Minor Skeletal Variants. *Osaa* 7: 97–107.

Smith, R., H. Zaitoun, T. Coxon, M. Karmo, G. Kaur, G. Townsend, E. F. Harris, and A. Brook

2009 Defining New Dental Phenotypes Using 3-D Image Analysis to Enhance Discrimination and Insights into Biological Processes. *Archives of Oral Biology* 54: S118–S125.

Sokal, R. R., and P. H. Sneath

1963 *Principals of Numerical Taxonomy*. W. H. Freeman, San Francisco.

Spence, M. W.

1974 Residential Practices and the Distribution of Skeletal Traits in Teotihuacán, Mexico. *Man*, n.s. 9: 262–273.

1996 Nonmetric Trait Distribution and the Expression of Familial Relationships in a Nineteenth-Century Cemetery. *Occasional Publications in Northeastern Anthropology* 52: 53–67.

Spence, M. W., C. White, F. J. Longstaffe, and K. Law

2004 Victims of the Victims: Human Trophies Worn by Sacrificed Soldiers from the Feathered Serpent Pyramid, Teotihuacán. *Ancient Mesoamerica* 15: 1–15.

Spielman, R. S.

1973 Differences among Yanomama Indian Villages: Do Patterns of Allele Frequencies, Anthropometrics and Map Locations Correspond? *American Journal of Physical Anthropology* 39: 461–480.

SPSS Inc.

2009 PASW Statistics 17.0. SPSS Inc., Chicago.

Stojanowski, C. M.

2003a Differential Phenotypic Variability among the Apalachee Populations of La Florida: A Diachronic Perspective. *American Journal of Physical Anthropology* 120: 352–363.

2003b Matrix Decomposition Model for Investigating Prehistoric Intracemetery Biological Variation. *American Journal of Physical Anthropology* 122: 216–231.

2005a Apalachee Mortuary Practices: Biological Structure of the San Pedro y San Pablo de Patale Mission Cemetery. *Southeastern Archaeology* 24: 165–179.

2005b Spanish Colonial Effects on Native American Mating Structure and Genetic Variability in Northern and Central Florida: Evidence from Apalachee and Western Timucua. *American Journal of Physical Anthropology* 128: 273–286.

Stojanowski, C. M., and M. A. Schillaci

2006 Phenotypic Approaches for Understanding Patterns of Intracemetery Biological Variation. *American Journal of Physical Anthropology* 131: 49–88.

Strouhal, E., and J. Jungwirth

1979 Paleogenetics of the Late Roman Early Byzantine Cemeteries at Sayala, Egyptian Nubia. *Journal of Human Evolution* 8: 699–703.

Sugiyama, S.
2005    *Human Sacrifice, Militarism, and Rulership: Materialization of State Ideology at the Feathered Serpent Pyramid, Teotihuacán*. Cambridge University Press, New York.

Sutter, R. C., and J. W. Verano
2007    Biodistance Analysis of the Moche Sacrificial Victims from Huaca de la Luna Plaza 3C: Matrix Method Test of Their Origins. *American Journal of Physical Anthropology* 132: 193–206.

Tiesler, V.
2007    Funerary and Nonfunerary? New References in Identifying Ancient Maya Sacrificial and Postsacrificial Behaviors from Human Assemblages. In *New Perspectives on Human Sacrifice and Ritual Body Treatments in Ancient Maya Society*, edited by V. Tiesler and A. Cucina, pp. 14–45. Springer, New York.

Tiesler, V., and A. Cucina (editors)
2007    *New Perspectives on Human Sacrifice and Ritual Body Treatments in Ancient Maya Society*. Springer, New York.

Tomczak, P. D., and J. F. Powell
2003    Postmarital Residence Practices in the Windover Population: Sex-Based Dental Variation as an Indicator of Patrilocality. *American Antiquity* 68: 93–108.

Townsend, G., T. Hughes, M. Luciano, M. Bockman, and A. Brook
2009    Genetic and Environmental Influences on Human Dental Variation: A Critical Evaluation of Studies Involving Twins. *Archives of Oral Biology* 54: S45–S51.

Tung, T. A.
2008    Dismembering Bodies for Display: A Bioarchaeological Study of Trophy Heads from the Wari Site of Conchopata, Peru. *American Journal of Physical Anthropology* 136(3): 294–308.

Turner, C. G., II, C. R. Nichol, and G. R. Scott
1991    Scoring Procedures for Key Morphological Traits of the Permanent Dentition: The Arizona State University Dental Anthropology System. In *Advances in Dental Anthropology*, edited by M. A. Kelley and C. S. Larsen, pp. 13–32. Wiley-Liss, New York.

Ugalde Morales, J. F., and J. A. Pompa Padilla
2003    Anomalías Dentales de Desarrollo Asociadas a la Colección Prehispánica Tzompantli. *Revista de la Asociación Dental Mexicana* 60: 219–24.

Usher, B. M., and K. L. Allen
2005    Identifying Kinship Clusters: SatScan for Genetic Spatial Analysis. *American Journal of Physical Anthropology* Supplemental 40: 210.

Vail, G., and C. Hernández
2007    Human Sacrifice in Late Postclassic Maya Iconography and Texts. In *New Perspectives on Human Sacrifice and Ritual Body Treatments in Ancient Maya Society*, edited by V. Tiesler and A. Cucina, pp. 120–164. Springer, New York.

Velemínský, P., and M. Dobisíková
2005    Morphological Likeness of the Skeletal Remains in a Central European Family

from 17th to 19th Century. *HOMO—Journal of Comparative Human Biology* 56: 173–196.

Walker, C. M.

2006     The Bioarchaeology of Newly Discovered Burial Caves in the Sierra, Tarahumara. Ph.D. dissertation, University of Oregon.

Weiss-Krejci, E.

2005     Victims of Human Sacrifice in Multiple Tombs of the Ancient Maya: A Critical Review. In *Antropología de la Eternidad: La Muerte en la Cultura Maya,* edited by A. C. Ruiz, M. H. Ruz, and M. J. I. Ponce de León, pp. 355–382. Sociedad Española de Studios Mayas Universidad Nacional Autónoma de México, México, D.F.

Whittington, S. L.

1999     *Determination of Late Postclassic Kaqchikel Maya Diet, Disease, and Cause of Death through Analysis of Skeletons from Iximché, Guatemala.* Foundation for the Advancement of Mesoamerican Studies, Inc., Crystal River, Fla.

2003     Descriptions of Human Remains and Burial Structures. In *Archaeology and Ethnohistory of Iximché,* edited by C. R. Nance, S. L. Whittington and B. E. Borg, pp. 205–240. University Press of Florida, Gainesville.

Wilkinson, R. G.

1997     Appendix B: Human Skeletal Remains from La Coyotera. In *Archaeology of the Cañada de Cuicatlán, Oaxaca,* edited by C. S. Spencer and E. M. Redmond, pp. 614–619. Anthropological Papers no. 80. American Museum of Natural History, New York.

Wrobel, G.

2004     Metric and Nonmetric Dental Variation among the Ancient Maya of Northern Belize. Ph.D. dissertation, Indiana University.

# Conclusion

## Implications and Future Directions

RYAN P. HARROD, DEBRA L. MARTIN, AND VENTURA R. PÉREZ

Bioarchaeological studies that focus on violence, as the chapters in this volume demonstrate, contribute unique and nuanced insights to theories about why violence is ubiquitous in human groups. Invigorating the practice of bioarchaeology with a strong set of theoretical frameworks provides a nonreductionist and complex set of interpretations that are culturally specific and historically situated yet universally applicable to aiding in explaining human behavior. One major goal of any analysis of human behavior is to better understand the full range of human behaviors and the cultural logic that motivates and reproduces those behaviors. The benefit of a bioarchaeological approach is that it provides a way to investigate the temporal and spatial patterning of behaviors, which sheds light on their origin and evolution.

While skeletal evidence of human violence is prevalent in the bioarchaeological record, the challenge is how to best document this evidence in a way that avoids an etic perspective that ignores the culture of the people being studied. The fine-grained analysis that the authors in this volume use places trauma data in a particular place at a particular time and provides the beginnings of a more comprehensive view of the histories and experiences of past cultures. In addition to developing a greater understanding of who was doing what to whom and why, bioarchaeological data have revealed how violent acts are part of the cultural landscape. While cultural anthropologists such as Whitehead (2004) and many others have taken this approach for some time, bioarchaeologists have begun to do so only recently (for examples, see chapters in the volume edited by Agarwal and Glencross [2011]). Taken in their cumulative context, events involving traumatic injury provide the raw data for theories about larger processes of social welfare and social control; they also provide a tangible and graphic reminder of how a society is doing. Bioarchaeological data also provide crucial information about the burial context such as where burials are placed, how bodies are treated and prepared, and the health profile and injury status of people prior to death. Careful analysis of all of these factors can shed light on the activities of the perpetrators of violence and the activities of surviving family and community members.

The loss of a sister to captivity, the slaying of a warrior in battle, the death of a grandmother caught in the cross fire, or the abduction of a child into slavery are each examples of episodes that have collective meaning to a larger group, beyond the individual. Each violent event was an experience that required ideological and sometimes ritual interpretation to help survivors make sense of it all.

This collection of studies of violence in the past is a small step toward providing different ways to think about the relationship between violence and lived experience and between lived experience and cultural processes. It is a step toward explaining human behavior, and this understanding can be used today to better understand how to prevent or eradicate violence in human groups. This volume prompts readers not to see violence as a necessary evil or as abhorrent behavior but to imagine how ancient societies used violence to solve problems. The challenge is to figure out what those culturally specific problems were. These chapters show that violence has been used to solve "problems" in many shapes and forms. Retribution for past injustices, maintaining hierarchy within the society, making tribute to the gods, or blaming someone for droughts or epidemics are all ways that humans used violence to attempt to control human, natural, and supernatural forces. The studies in this volume suggest that violence was used extensively in the past to solve problems. One implication that could be drawn is that it will likely be used in the present and future for the same reason: people use violence because they perceive it as a way to solve their problems. Humans are not intrinsically violent, yet the skills honed over millions of years of hunting and producing weapons have made it easy for them to incorporate violence in their behavioral repertoire. If we are to hope to decrease the use of violence, we must first understand its myriad uses and functions within complex cultural systems.

## The Future of Bioarchaeology

Though the focus of this volume is on bioarchaeological approaches to understanding violence, the overall message is that bioarchaeology must ask questions that move beyond the bones to understand who people were and what roles they held in their society. According to Scheper-Hughes and Lock (1987, 7–8), there are three ways to think about the body: first as the individual body, second as the social body, and finally as the body politic or political body. Human remains not only represent the life history of individual people but also reveal complex cultural and political elements of the society in which the people lived.

In *The Body as Material Culture: A Theoretical Osteoarchaeology*, Sofaer (2006) writes that recent developments in social theory provide a way to think of the body as socially constructed. Sofaer suggests that human remains are a particular kind of "archaeological body" and that one can use theories based on gender, class, or any other foci to analyze how a body interfaced with violence within communities in the ancient past. This groundbreaking work provides important insights that open up the study of human remains by using theoretical frameworks that take into consideration how bodies reveal a great deal of information about the culture and individuals they represent, especially in terms of the various levels of identity the persons who occupied the bodies had within their culture.

An anthropological approach to understanding the body is a key to identifying and reconstructing individual, cultural, and political identity. These identities provide tools for re-creating human history that otherwise would remain hidden forever. The analytical power inherent in revealing hidden identities has arguably been most effectively demonstrated in studies of social inequality. Through the analysis of differential patterns of health, nutrition, and exposure to trauma within a population, bioarchaeologists can reveal varying degrees of social stratification and hierarchy within a society.

In systems of social inequality, human bodies provide a record of status differentiation through markers on the bones that provide traces of debts and obligations between members of the society. Edmund Leach's theories about debt, relationship, and power can be productively used to formulate hypotheses about how debt and inequality are manifested on human bodies. Leach's thesis is that "structures of social relationship are not only structures of indebtedness, they are also structures of *power*" (1982, 156). The study of hierarchy and social inequality is only one issue that can be addressed through bioarchaeological research. It is important that future researchers realize that bioarchaeology must address the same questions as any other anthropological study by moving beyond simply looking at the bones. Bioarchaeologists should ask questions about the individual's role in the culture by addressing issues of identity as it is related to gender, ethnicity, class and more, and some researchers are already doing so (Agarwal and Glencross 2011).

## Parting Thoughts

Bioarchaeologists must constantly remind themselves that the data they reconstruct as demographic, pathological, or traumatic at the population level are life history events at the individual level. Births, puberty, sicknesses, crises, tragedies, marriages, and death are biocultural transition points that find expression through beliefs and rituals in all cultures. These events provide points of focus for kin and group identities and are crucial temporal events for each generation. Bioarchaeologists are in a unique position to view acts of violence from a number of perspectives. In particular, the voices that bioarchaeologists give to the victims of violence through analysis of their bones and graves are an important dimension of studying and teaching about violence. Victims become active participants in the ways that bioarchaeologists seek to construct the larger context, as violent encounters must be viewed from the vantage point of the victims and their relationships with the perpetrators. Sometimes bioarchaeologists can even infer who the witnesses of public and performative acts of violence were. The importance of recognizing these three roles is that each plays a part in understanding violence in the past (Krohn-Hansen 1994; Whitehead 2004).

We hope that scholars and teachers will use these case studies to further their own understanding of how violence works. One of the goals of bioarchaeological research is to produce interpretive results that have implications for people living today. Although some of what bioarchaeologists do may be considered esoteric, volumes such as this one may help readers begin to make connections between violence as it was enacted in the past and violence as we see it enacted today. We understand very well how performance and public display were motives for violence for the

Maya and the Mississippian cultures, yet these were precisely what we saw as motives for the gruesome violence in Rwanda and Croatia and even now in the Mexican-U.S. borderlands. We have learned from the ancient world that violence is often meant to be performative and to carry messages far beyond the killing of individuals (Whitehead 2004). The studies in this volume have presented a range of case studies in which the complexity, variability, and ambiguities in the total picture of how violence works were enhanced by using theoretical frameworks that are responsive to the variables underlying violent interactions. More analysis at this level of contextualization and sophistication will continue to reveal new ways to ask questions about violence. This will ultimately enable us to explain aspects of human behavior related to violence.

## References Cited

Agarwal, S. C., and B. A. Glencross (editors)
2011    Social Bioarchaeology. Wiley-Blackwell, Malden.
Krohn-Hansen, C.
1994    The Anthropology of Violent Interaction. Journal of Archaeological Research 50(4): 367–381.
Leach, E. R.
1982    Social Anthropology. Oxford University Press, Oxford.
Scheper-Hughes, N., and M. M. Lock
1987    The Mindful Body: A Prolegomenon to Future Work in Medical Anthropology. Medical Anthropology Quarterly, n.s. 1(1): 6–41.
Sofaer, J. R.
2006    The Body as Material Culture: A Theoretical Osteoarchaeology. Cambridge University Press, Cambridge.
Whitehead, N. L. (editor)
2004    Violence. School of American Research Press, Santa Fe.

# Contributors

Charles R. Cobb is professor of archaeology in the South Carolina Institute of Archaeology and Anthropology at the University of South Carolina.

Andrea Cucina is facultad de ciencias antropológicas at the Universidad Autónoma de Yucatán, Mérida, Mexico.

William N. Duncan is assistant professor in the Department of Sociology and Anthropology at East Tennessee State College in Johnson City.

Ryan P. Harrod is assistant professor of anthropology at the University of Alaska Anchorage.

Mallorie A. Hatch is a doctoral candidate in the School of Human Evolution and Social Change at Arizona State University, Tempe.

Haagen D. Klaus is assistant professor in the Department of Behavioral Sciences at Utah Valley University in Orem.

Kathryn M. Koziol is adjunct instructor in the Department of Anthropology at the University of Arkansas Global Campus in Rogers.

Kristin A. Kuckelman is senior research archaeologist at the Crow Canyon Archaeological Center in Cortez, Colorado.

Pierre Liénard is assistant professor in the Department of Anthropology at the University of Nevada, Las Vegas.

Debra L. Martin is Lincy Professor of Anthropology and chair in the Department of Anthropology at the University of Nevada, Las Vegas.

Robert T. Montgomery is a doctoral student in the Department of Anthropology at the University of Arkansas, Fayetteville.

Ann M. Palkovich is professor of anthropology in the Department of

Sociology and Anthropology at George Mason University in Fairfax, Virginia.

Ventura R. Pérez is assistant professor in the Department of Anthropology at the University of Massachusetts Amherst.

Megan Perry is associate professor in the Department of Anthropology at East Carolina University in Greenville.

Dawnie Wolfe Steadman is professor of anthropology in the Department of Anthropology, University of Tennessee in Knoxville.

Vera Tiesler is facultad de ciencias antropológicas at the Universidad Autónoma de Yucatán, Mérida, Mexico.

Tiffiny A. Tung is associate professor in the Department of Anthropology at Vanderbilt University, Nashville.

Giovanna Vidoli is a doctoral student in the Department of Anthropology, Binghamton University, State University of New York.

Heather Worne is assistant professor in the Department of Anthropology at the University of Kentucky.

# Index

CPSIA information can be obtained at www.ICGtesting.com
Printed in the USA
LVOW09s1207191114

414373LV00006B/236/P